Religious Studies, Theology, and Human Flourishing

THE HUMANITIES AND HUMAN FLOURISHING

Series editor: James O. Pawelski

Other volumes in the series

Philosophy and Human Flourishing
Edited by John J. Stuhr

History and Human Flourishing
Edited by Darrin M. McMahon

Literary Studies and Human Flourishing
Edited by James F. English and Heather Love

Religious Studies, Theology, and Human Flourishing
Edited by Justin Thomas McDaniel and Hector Kilgoe

Theater and Human Flourishing
Edited by Harvey Young

Cinema, Media, and Human Flourishing
Edited by Timothy Corrigan

Music and Human Flourishing
Edited by Anna Harwell Celenza

Visual Arts and Human Flourishing
Edited by Selma Holo

The Humanities and Human Flourishing
Edited by James O. Pawelski

Religious Studies, Theology, and Human Flourishing

Edited by

JUSTIN THOMAS MCDANIEL AND
HECTOR KILGOE

OXFORD
UNIVERSITY PRESS

OXFORD
UNIVERSITY PRESS

Oxford University Press is a department of the University of Oxford. It furthers
the University's objective of excellence in research, scholarship, and education
by publishing worldwide. Oxford is a registered trade mark of Oxford University
Press in the UK and certain other countries.

Published in the United States of America by Oxford University Press
198 Madison Avenue, New York, NY 10016, United States of America.

Library of Congress Cataloging-in-Publication Data
Names: McDaniel, Justin, editor.
Title: Religious studies, theology, and human flourishing /
[edited by] Justin Thomas McDaniel and Hector Kilgoe.
Description: New York, NY : Oxford University Press, [2024] |
Series: The humanities and human flourishing |
Includes bibliographical references and index.
Identifiers: LCCN 2023049366 (print) | LCCN 2023049367 (ebook) |
ISBN 9780197658345 (paperback) | ISBN 9780197658338 (hardback) |
ISBN 9780197658352 (epub) | ISBN 9780197658369
Subjects: LCSH: Religion—Study and teaching. | Well-being—Religious aspects.
Classification: LCC BL41.R47 2024 (print) | LCC BL41 (ebook) |
DDC 200.7—dc23/eng/20231106
LC record available at https://lccn.loc.gov/2023049366
LC ebook record available at https://lccn.loc.gov/2023049367

DOI: 10.1093/oso/9780197658338.001.0001

Paperback printed by Marquis Book Printing, Canada
Hardback printed by Bridgeport National Bindery, Inc., United States of America

Contents

Series Editor's Foreword   vii
Editors and Contributors   xxiii

Introduction Aporias and Affordances: An Introduction to the
Study of Religion, Theology, and Human Flourishing   1
   Justin Thomas McDaniel

PART I. APORIAS: DEFINING AND DEBATING RELIGIOUS STUDIES, THEOLOGY, AND POSITIVE PSYCHOLOGY

1. Sometimes a Little Pessimism Is Good for the Soul: Human
   Flourishing and a Plea for Complexity   21
   Pamela Cooper-White

2. Disenchantment with Disenchantment: Or, Can Christian
   Theology yet Speak?   40
   Ellen T. Charry

3. Discerning the Shape of Flourishing Life: Theology and
   the Humanities   63
   Matthew Croasmun

PART II. AFFORDANCES: NEW WAYS OF TEACHING AND LEARNING RELIGIOUS STUDIES AND THEOLOGY AFTER THE EUDAEMONIC TURN

4. *Sanmati*, the Art of "Generous Orientation": Flourishing amid
   Religious Difference   81
   Leela Prasad

5. Suffering, Joy, and Wonder: Teaching toward the Fullness of
   Life   101
   Mary Clark Moschella

6. The Perfumed Life: Teaching a Humanities of Unsettling   117
   Noah Salomon

7. From the Head to the Heart: Rethinking Approached to
   Teaching Buddhism at a Regional State University in the
   Bible Belt   135
   Jeffrey Samuels

8. Fighting Spirit: Lessons from a Military Experiment in
   Spiritual Training   152
   Steven Weitzman

9. Lab Courses for the Humanities: Monastic Living and
   Existential Despair   165
   Justin Thomas McDaniel

Index   187

Series Editor's Foreword

Imagine being invited to a weekend meeting to discuss connections between the humanities and human flourishing. You talk about ways in which the humanities can help us understand what human flourishing is—and is not. You explore how the humanities can help increase human flourishing. And you consider whether human flourishing is an absolute good or whether it comes with certain limits and even potential dangers. How do you imagine the conversation playing out? What contributions might you make to the discussion?

The volumes in this series were borne out of just such a meeting—or, rather, a series of such meetings, each gathering including a dozen or so scholars in a particular discipline in the humanities (understood to be inclusive of the arts). These disciplines include philosophy, history, literary studies, religious studies and theology, theater, cinema and media, music, and the visual arts. Participants were asked to consider how their work in their discipline intersects with well-being (taken to be roughly synonymous with human flourishing) along with a series of specific questions:

- How does your discipline conceptualize, understand, and define well-being?
- What does your discipline say about the cultivation of well-being? How does it encourage the implementation of well-being?
- In what ways does your discipline support flourishing? Do some approaches within your discipline advance human flourishing more effectively than others do? Are there ways in which certain aspects of your discipline could more effectively promote well-being?
- Does your discipline contribute to well-being in ways that are unique and that are not attempted in other endeavors outside of your discipline?
- Are there ways in which your discipline can obstruct human flourishing?

As might be expected, the conversations in these meetings were rich and wide ranging. Some of them headed in expected directions; others were more surprising. Each of them yielded opportunities to question assumptions and deepen perspectives. The conversations were rooted in disciplinary contexts and questions but yielded many generalizable insights on how to conceptualize human flourishing more clearly, how to cultivate it more effectively, and how to avoid the negative consequences that occur by understanding it in incomplete or overblown ways. I cannot properly describe or even summarize the richness of the discussions here, but I would like to point out a few of the highlights included in each of the resulting volumes.

Philosophy and Human Flourishing, edited by John J. Stuhr, addresses a number of fundamental questions. What is the value of discussing human flourishing in a world that in so many ways is decidedly not flourishing? In what ways is flourishing similar to and different from happiness? What is the role of morality in human flourishing? How does it relate to systemic privilege and oppression? To what degree is flourishing properly the concern of individuals, and to what degree is it a function of communities and societies? What are key factors in the fostering of flourishing? In addressing these questions, philosophers explore concepts such as mattering, homeostasis, pluralism, responsibility, and values, and they consider the roles of individuals, educational institutions, and governments.

History and Human Flourishing, edited by Darrin M. McMahon, centers on the question "What is the value of history for life?" This core question leads to a number of further inquiries. Is history only about the past, or does it have important implications for the present and the future? If the latter, then how can historical inquiry most effectively contribute to well-being? Does such inquiry currently focus in an imbalanced way on ill-being—on prejudices, class struggles, and wars? Such work is doubtless of great importance, not least because it investigates how claims about happiness can serve as propaganda for continued oppression. But would hope for the future be more effectively kindled and concrete steps toward its realization more adeptly guided by increased attention to what has gone well in the past and what we can learn from it or by more focus on how humans have responded positively to adversity?

Literary Studies and Human Flourishing, edited by James F. English and Heather Love, focuses on the transformative power of literature. Scholars examine a range of topics, including the reparative possibilities of a literary encounter, the value of bibliotherapy and of therapeutic redescription, the genre of "uplift," and evolving methods for studying the activities and experiences of readers. A central question of this volume concerns the limits on transformations effected through literature. Several contributors worry that harnessing literary studies to the enterprise of human flourishing might lead readers merely to conform rather than to transform. To what extent might human flourishing serve as a palliative, enabling and encouraging readers to adapt to individual lives that lack moral depth and to social conditions that are rife with injustice and, thus, obstruct the difficult and unsettling work of disruptive transformation that is needed for lasting individual and collective betterment?

Religious Studies, Theology, and Human Flourishing, edited by Justin Thomas McDaniel and Hector Kilgoe, explores ways in which individual and collective well-being can be increased through various religious perspectives and practices, including the Hindu concept of *sanmati* ("goodwill," "wisdom," and "noble-mindedness"), Buddhist meditation, and the cultivation of spiritual joy even while facing adversity. Scholars consider challenging questions concerning the proper contexts for learning *about* religion and for learning *from* religion, the right balance between the acknowledgment of suffering and the fostering of well-being, and the relationship between human flourishing and nonhuman worlds (including both natural and supernatural domains). A concern of some of these scholars is whether human flourishing entails a false universalism, one that seeks to reduce cultural diversities to one particular notion of what is desirable or even acceptable, and whether such a notion could be used to rate the value of different religions or even to ban religious practices (e.g., fasting, celibacy, or other ascetic austerities) that might be deemed misaligned with well-being.

Theater and Human Flourishing, edited by Harvey Young, considers the unique resources of theater and performance for imagining and enhancing well-being. Because theater involves both performers and audience members, it is inherently communal in ways that many humanities disciplines and art forms are not. Theater allows groups of people—often strangers—to come together and experience the world in new ways. More than just an escape from ordinary life or a simple mirroring of reality, theater can provide opportunities for a communal reimagining of the world through explorations of new ways of thinking, feeling, and relating that can be experienced and then enacted in order to bring about a more flourishing future. Scholars examine connections between theater and human flourishing in more and less traditional spheres, looking at ways that performance practices can be used to critique inadequate notions of human flourishing and to increase well-being in a wide variety of contexts, ranging from community theater to organizations serving soldiers with post-traumatic stress disorder, and from oppressed groups to politically divided societies.

Cinema, Media, and Human Flourishing, edited by Timothy Corrigan, looks to film and a whole range of contemporary forms of digital media for what they can teach us about the nature of human flourishing and how it can be cultivated. These forms of communication have vast audiences and thus great power to support or subvert well-being. Contributors to this volume observe that human flourishing often seems to come piecemeal and as a hard-won result of conflict and struggle, and they explore ways in which well-being can be supported by collaborative practices for creating content, by the particular ways that narratives are crafted, by certain genres, and by the various values that are embraced and transmitted. Contributors also consider how these popular forms can support individuals and groups on the margins of society by making more visible and sympathetic their struggles toward flourishing.

Music and Human Flourishing, edited by Anna Harwell Celenza, complements the commonly accepted and scientifically supported view that participating in music—as a listener, performer, or composer—can increase individual well-being. Instead of focusing on music as a performing art, this volume examines music as a humanities discipline, emphasizing the importance and value of music scholarship for fostering individual and collective human flourishing. How can music scholars (musicologists, ethnomusicologists, and music theorists) strengthen the effects of music on flourishing through a consideration of broader cultural, social, and political contexts? Contributors explore how processes of contemplation, critique, and communication within music scholarship can deepen the experience of music, resulting not just in the enhancement of individual well-being but in the more effective cultivation of wisdom and the greater realization of social justice.

Visual Arts and Human Flourishing, edited by Selma Holo, begins with the experience of artists themselves and the function of art in our society. If well-being is thought of as the happiness of self-satisfied complacency, then it would seem to be the antithesis of art, which is often disruptive, unnerving, and unsettling in that it asks viewers to question their assumptions and invites them to see the world in new ways. But if well-being is understood more deeply as the flourishing that can arise from the full range of human experience, including the discomfort of contending forms of meaning and contested visions of reality, then it is difficult to think of it without art. Contributors to this volume consider the overwhelming personal need that artists have to create, the role of well-being in art history, the increasing emphasis on human flourishing in architecture and public art, and salient questions of ethics, accessibility, and social justice in the context of art museums.

The Humanities and Human Flourishing, for which I serve as editor, is an interdisciplinary, capstone volume that contains contributions from the editors of the eight disciplinary volumes. After the disciplinary meetings were concluded, we gathered to discuss what we had learned through the process. We considered both similarities and differences across the disciplinary discussions on human flourishing, identifying social justice and pedagogy as two common themes that emerged in the meetings. Like the other volumes in the series, this volume does not pretend to provide simple solutions or even unified answers to questions of how the humanities are or should be connected to the conceptualization and cultivation of human flourishing. Rather, it provides thoughtful questions and perspectives, distilled as it is from a deliberate process of extended engagement from diverse groups of scholars across eight different arts and humanities disciplines.

I would like to welcome you, the reader, to this book series. I hope you find it stimulating and even inspiring in its explorations into the complexities of the relationship between the humanities and human flourishing. And I hope that you read across the volumes, as they are written in an accessible style that will yield valuable insights, whether or not you have particular expertise in the discipline of the author whose work you are reading. To whatever degree you immerse yourself in this book series, though, I am sure of one thing: you will find it incomplete. As deep and as broad ranging as we tried to be in our explorations, none of the participants is under the illusion that the discussions and volumes brought it to a conclusion. We are keenly aware that a group of a dozen scholars, no matter how diverse, cannot speak for an entire discipline, and we realize that a focus on eight disciplines does not cover the entire domain of the humanities. Furthermore, our discussions and most of the writing were completed before the COVID-19 pandemic, which has made the nature and importance of flourishing all the more salient and has raised a host of new questions about well-being. Instead, we think of our work as an important beginning, and we would like to invite you to join the conversation. We hope that a greater number of diverse scholars, researchers, creators, practitioners, students, leaders in cultural organizations and creative industries, office holders in government, philanthropists, and members of the general public will bring their interests and expertise to the conversation, perhaps leading to new volumes in this series in the future. Investigations into human flour-ishing contribute to our knowledge and understanding of the human con-dition, and they have practical implications for the well-being of scholars, students, and societies. We hope that our ongoing work together will en-able the humanities to play a greater role in these investigations and effect changes in scholarship, research, pedagogy, policy, and practice that will make them more supportive of human flourishing in academia and in the world at large.

Background and Rationale

For readers interested in more information on the background and ra-tionale of this book series, I am happy to share further details on the perspectives, aims, and hopes that motivated it. A key catalyst for the devel-opment of this series was the dual observation that individuals and organi-zations are increasingly focused on human flourishing and that most of the headlines in this domain seem to be coming from the social sciences. Yale psychology professor Laurie Santos, for example, made the news when she developed a course on Psychology and the Good Life—and some twelve hundred students (nearly a quarter of Yale's undergraduate population) signed up for it.[1] As of this writing, her subsequent podcast, *The Happiness Lab*, has reached sixty-five million downloads.[2] On an international scale, dozens of countries around the world have adopted psychological measures of subjective well-being as a complement to economic indicators, and the number continues to grow of nations that have embraced well-being, hap-piness, or flourishing as an explicit governmental goal.[3] The Organization for Economic Co-operation and Development (OECD), founded in 1961

[1] David Shimer, "Yale's Most Popular Class Ever: Happiness," *The New York Times*, 26 Jan. 2018, https://www.nytimes.com/2018/01/26/nyregion/at-yale-class-on-happiness-draws-huge-crowd-lau rie-santos.html.

[2] Lucy Hodgman and Evan Gorelick, "Silliman Head of College Laurie Santos to Take One-Year Leave to Address Burnout," *Yale News*, 8 Feb. 2022, https://yaledailynews.com/blog/2022/02/ 08/ silliman-head-of-college-laurie-santos-to-take-one-year-leave-to-address-burnout/.

[3] Wellbeing Economy Alliance, 2002, https://weall.org/; "UK Measure of National Well-Being Dashboard," *Office for National Statistics*, 11 Aug. 2023, https://www.ons.gov.uk/peoplepopulationa ndcommunity/wellbeing/articles/measuresofnationalwellbeingdashboard/2018-04-25; "History of GNH," *GNH Centre Bhutan*, 2022, https://www.gnhcentrebhutan.org/history-of-gnh/; World Bank, "Bolivia Wants to Duplicate Bhutan's Happiness Index," *The World Bank*, 24 Oct. 2013, https://www. worldbank.org/en/news/feature/2013/10/24/Bolivia-quiere-replicar-el-indice-de-felicidad-de-Butan; "Happiness," United Arab Emirates, 17 Jul. 2023, https://u.ae/en/about-the-uae/the-uae-gov ernment/government-of-future/happiness/.

to stimulate economic progress and world trade, has acknowledged the insufficiency of economic indicators alone for tracking progress. It launched its Better Life Initiative in 2011 to measure what drives the well-being of individuals and nations and to determine how countries can best support greater progress for all.[4] The United Nations publishes the World Happiness Report every year, releasing it on March 20, the UN International Day of Happiness.[5]

These are examples in the social sciences of what I have elsewhere called a *eudaemonic turn*, an explicit commitment to human flourishing as a core theoretical and research interest and a desired practical outcome.[6] Over the last several decades, there has been a growing interest in human flourishing in economics, political science, psychology, and sociology, and in fields influenced by them, such as education, organizational studies, medicine, and public health. Perhaps the most well-known example of this eudaemonic turn in the social sciences occurred in psychology with the advent of positive psychology. Martin Seligman and his colleagues launched the field of positive psychology, which reflected perspectives that had developed in humanistic psychology in the mid-twentieth century and which built on increased empirical work in self-efficacy, self-determination theory, subjective and psychological well-being, optimism, flow, passion, hope theory, positive emotions, and related areas. During a 1998 presidential address to the American Psychological Association, Seligman pointed out that mainstream psychology had become fixated on understanding and treating psychopathology. He argued that, although extremely important, healing mental illness is only part of psychology's mission. More broadly, he claimed, psychology should be about making the lives of all people better. He noted that this requires the careful empirical study of what makes life most worth living, including a deep understanding of flourishing individuals and thriving communities. Such study, he believed, would both increase well-being and decrease ill-being, since human strengths are both important in their own right and effective as buffers against mental illness. Known as "the

---

[4] *Measuring Well-Being and Progress*, OECD Better Life Initiative, Mar. 2020, https://www.oecd.org/sdd/OECD-Better-Life-Initiative.pdf.

[5] World Happiness Report 2023, Sustainable Development Solutions Network, https://worldhappiness.report/, accessed 16 Oct. 2023.

[6] James O. Pawelski, "What Is the Eudaimonic Turn?," *The Eudaimonic Turn: Well-Being in Literary Studies*, edited by James O. Pawelski and D. J. Moores, Fairleigh Dickinson UP, 2013, p. 3; James O. Pawelski, "The Positive Humanities: Culture and Human Flourishing," *The Oxford Handbook of the Positive Humanities*, edited by Louis Tay and James O. Pawelski, Oxford UP, 2022, p. 26.

scientific study of what enables individuals and societies to thrive,"[7] positive psychology has had a transformative effect on psychology and has deeply influenced many other fields of research and practice.

What role do the humanities play in all of this? What role could and should they play? How can the humanities help us conceptualize human flourishing more deeply, cultivate it more effectively, and critique it more insightfully? As a philosopher working in the field of positive psychology for more than twenty years, I have been concerned that there are not more voices from the humanities centrally involved in contemporary work in human flourishing. One of the core aims of this project and book series is to make a way for humanities scholars to play a larger role in this domain by inviting them to consider explicitly what contributions their work and their disciplines can make to the theory, research, and practice of human flourishing.

Historically, of course, human flourishing is at the root of the humanities.[8]

The humanities were first defined and developed as a program of study by Renaissance scholars dissatisfied with scholasticism, which they perceived as leading to an overly technical university curriculum that was removed from the concerns of everyday life and unable to guide students toward human flourishing. They advocated, instead, for a return to the Greek and Roman classics—to reading them for insights and perspectives on how to live life well. Indeed, the Greeks and Romans had developed comprehensive programs of study (*paideia* and *artes liberales*, respectively) that were designed to teach students how to flourish individually and how to contribute to collective flourishing by participating effectively and wisely in civic life.

This emphasis on the understanding and cultivation of human flourishing that was so important to the Greeks and Romans was also of central concern to other philosophical and religious traditions that developed in the ancient world during what Karl Jaspers called the Axial Age.[9] Hinduism, Buddhism, Confucianism, Daoism, and Judaism, for example, along with the later Christianity and Islam, addressed the problem of human suffering and offered ways of promoting individual and collective flourishing. Although different in their cultural context and specific details, each of these traditions counseled against lives exclusively devoted to pleasure, wealth, power, or

---

[7] Constitution of the International Positive Psychology Association, art. 1, sec. 2.

[8] Pawelski, "Positive Humanities," 20–21; Darrin M. McMahon, "The History of the Humanities and Human Flourishing," *The Oxford Handbook of the Positive Humanities*, edited by Louis Tay and James O. Pawelski, Oxford UP, 2022, pp. 45–50.

[9] Karl Jaspers, *The Origin and Goal of History*, Routledge, 2011, p. 2.

fame. They held that such lives only magnify suffering and that flourishing is fostered through a cultivation of virtue that allows people to transcend narrow, individual concerns in favor of a connection with the larger social world, the broader universe, or even the divine. Cultural forms such as literature, music, visual art, architecture, theater, history, and philosophical reflection were deployed in the cultivation of virtue and the establishment of the broader and deeper connections that are valued for human flourishing.

Today, the humanities tend to be thought of less as a comprehensive program of study or means to cultivate virtue and more as a collection of academic disciplines. These disciplines are located largely within colleges and universities and are thus shaped by the values of these institutions. Much of higher education is driven more by the aim of creating knowledge than by the goal of applying wisdom. To succeed in such an environment, scholars are required to become highly specialized professionals, spending most of their time publishing books and articles for other highly specialized professionals in their discipline. The courses that they teach often focus more on the flourishing of their discipline than on the flourishing of their students, requiring students to learn *about* course content but not necessarily to learn *from* it. When human flourishing is addressed in the classroom, it is all too often done in a way that makes it difficult for students to apply it to their lives, and in many cases, it focuses more on obstacles to flourishing than on the nature and cultivation of well-being. It is important, of course, to understand and resist alienation, injustice, and malfeasance in the world and to expose corrosive ideologies that can permeate texts and other forms of culture. But it is also important to understand that flourishing is more than just the absence of languishing. And the argument has been made that "suspicious" approaches in the humanities need to be balanced by reparative approaches[10] and that critique needs to be complemented by a "positive aesthetics"[11] and a "hermeneutics of affirmation."[12] Meanwhile, students in the United States, at least, are reporting astonishingly high levels of anxiety, depression, and suicidality[13] while at the same time coming under increasing economic pressure to select courses of study that will directly help them find

[10] Eve K. Sedgwick, "Paranoid Reading and Reparative Reading: Or, You're so Paranoid, You Probably Think This Introduction Is about You," *Novel Gazing: Queer Readings in Fiction*, edited by Eve K. Sedgwick, Duke UP, 1997, pp. 1–37.

[11] Rita Felski, *Uses of Literature*, Blackwell, 2008, p. 22.

[12] D. J. Moores, "The Eudaimonic Turn in Literary Studies," *The Eudaimonic Turn: Well-Being in Literary Studies*, edited by James O. Pawelski and D. J. Moores, Fairleigh Dickinson UP, 2013, p. 27.

[13] "Publications and Reports," American College Health Association National College Health Assessment, https://www.acha.org/NCHA/ACHA-NCHA_Data/Publications_and_Reports/

employment. Students who in the past might have followed their interests in the humanities are now more likely to major in STEM fields or to enroll in pre-professional tracks. Consequently, the number of students earning bachelor's degrees in the humanities is decreasing significantly.[14]

Would a eudaemonic turn in the humanities be helpful in addressing these obstacles of narrow professionalism, imbalanced focus, and student pressure? Would it help with what Louis Menand has called a "crisis of rationale" in the humanities, with scholars unable to agree on the fundamental nature and purpose of the humanities and thus unable to communicate their value clearly to students, parents, philanthropists, policymakers, and the general public?[15] Could the eudaemonic turn provide a unifying rationale in the humanities? Of course, there is a sense in which such a turn would actually be a eudaemonic *return*. This return would not be a nostalgic attempt to recover some imagined glorious past. Although the human flourishing that was historically supported by the humanities was significant, as mentioned above, it was also far from perfect and often embraced perspectives that supported unjust power structures that excluded many people—including laborers, women, and enslaved persons—from participating in flourishing and that enabled the exploitation of these individuals to the advantage of those in power. Tragically, our society suffers from some of these same injustices today. Instead of a glorification of a problematic past, which could well reinforce these injustices, a eudaemonic (re)turn would invite us to focus our attention on perennial questions about human flourishing by building on wisdom from the past but committing ourselves to a search for more inclusive answers that are fitting for our contemporary world.[16]

Not surprisingly, there is disagreement among scholars in these volumes, with some contributors endorsing the eudaemonic turn in the humanities and working to advance it and others putting forward a variety of concerns about the limitations and potential dangers of such an approach—and some even doing both. Scholars supporting a eudaemonic turn believe that it could

---

NCHA/Data/Publications_and_Reports.aspx?hkey=d5fb767c-d15d-4efc-8c41-3546d92032c5, accessed 11 Dec. 2021.

[14] Jill Barshay, "Proof Points: The Number of College Graduates in the Humanities Drops for the Eighth Consecutive Year," *The Hechinger Report*, 22 Nov. 2021, https://hechingerreport.org/proof-points-the-number-of-college-graduates-in-the-humanities-drops-for-the-eighth-consecutive-year.

[15] Louis Menand, "The Marketplace of Ideas," 2001, American Council of Learned Societies Occasional Paper no. 49, http://archives.acls.org/op/49_Marketplace_of_Ideas.htm.

[16] Pawelski, "What Is the Eudaimonic Turn?" 17 and "Positive Humanities" 26; McMahon, "History" 45, 54.

revitalize the humanities by encouraging deeper investigations into the eudaemonic hopes that initially gave rise to their disciplines and the various
ways in which contemporary work can support and develop these hopes.
They believe that these investigations could bring together scholars across
the various humanities disciplines to create a common understanding and
language for an examination of questions of human flourishing that are appropriate for our times. To be successful, such a project would not require
complete agreement among scholars on the answers to these questions. On
the contrary, diverse perspectives would enrich the inquiry, opening up new
possibilities for human flourishing that are more equitable and widespread
and that support the flourishing of the nonhuman world as well. Some
contributors see significant potential in collaborating with the social sciences
in their eudaemonic turn, a process that can be facilitated through the positive humanities, a new, interdisciplinary field of inquiry and practice that is
focused on the relationship between culture and human flourishing.[17]

Scholars endorsing a eudaemonic turn in the humanities believe that it
could also inform, inspire, and support the work of museums, libraries, performing arts centers, and even creative industries (in music, movies, publishing, and other domains) to advance human flourishing more broadly in
our society. They see a eudaemonic turn as also being of potential value to the
millions of students who study the humanities each year. Without expecting
humanities teachers and professors to take on therapeutic roles, they see con-
siderable possible benefits in a pedagogical focus on how human flourishing
can be understood and cultivated, with resulting courses that are intentionally designed to promote and preserve students' well-being and to mitigate
and prevent their ill-being.[18] Indeed, these scholars believe that the volumes
in this series might serve as useful texts for some of these courses.

Scholars with misgivings about a eudaemonic turn, however, raise a
number of important concerns. Some contributors wonder whether human
flourishing is a proper ideal in a world with so much suffering. Would such an
ideal raise false hopes that would contribute to that suffering? Furthermore,

---

[17] For more information on the positive humanities, see Louis Tay and James O. Pawelski, editors,
The Oxford Handbook of the Positive Humanities, Oxford UP, 2022. The first three foundational
chapters of that text are especially relevant. See also *Humanities and Human Flourishing*, University
of Pennsylvania, www.humanitiesandhumanflourishing.org, accessed 15 Oct. 2023.

[18] Furthermore, would students who perceive real-life value in humanities courses be more likely
to make room for them in their schedules, as suggested by the large numbers of students who enrolled
in Laurie Santos's course Psychology and the Good Life? If so, could a side benefit of the eudaemonic
turn be greater numbers of students who sign up for courses in the humanities?

are there more valuable things than human flourishing (e.g., ethics, the environment), and should flourishing be limited in favor of these greater goods? Is human flourishing inextricably linked to problematic ideological perspectives, perhaps ones that place too much emphasis on the individual and downplay or ignore issues of systemic injustice, or perhaps ones that serve the interests of a small number of persons in power and that encourage everyone else to conform to the status quo? Is human flourishing a false universalism that might result in a failure to see and acknowledge deep cultural differences—or worse, that might see these differences as deviances that need to be suppressed and punished? Could an emphasis on well-being be deployed to exploit individuals or groups of people, as notions of happiness have sometimes been used in the past? Are there other unexpected harms that might arise from a eudaemonic turn?

The unresolved tensions among the various chapters are part of what makes these volumes compelling reading. Are there ways to overcome concerns about the eudaemonic turn by clarifying its nature and aims, avoiding the dangers raised? Or will these concerns always persist alongside efforts to achieve individual and communal betterment through a theoretical and practical emphasis on flourishing? I welcome you, the reader, to join this discussion. What are your views on the perspectives expressed in these volumes? What points might you contribute to the ongoing conversation?

Process and People

I would like to conclude with a fuller account of the process by which the various volumes were created and an acknowledgment of the individuals and institutions who have made this book series possible. With the desire to give contributors ample time to reflect on how their work and their discipline relate to human flourishing, as well as to create opportunities to discuss these ideas with colleagues, we put into place an extended process for the creation of these volumes. After deciding on the eight disciplines in the arts and humanities that we would be able to include in the project, we invited a leading scholar to chair the work in each of these disciplines and asked them to bring together a diverse group of around a dozen noted scholars in their discipline.[19] For each group, we provided participants with some background

---

[19] For a full list of project participants, see *Humanities and Human Flourishing*.

reading[20] and asked them to prepare a draft essay on how their scholarly work informs the conceptualization and cultivation of human flourishing. Many participants chose to address the background reading—appreciatively, critically, or both—in their papers, although none was required to address it at all. We then circulated these drafts to the entire group in preparation for a three-day, face-to-face meeting, during which the disciplinary chair led a discussion and workshopping of the drafts. These disciplinary consultations, held in 2018 and 2019, were also joined by a junior scholar (usually a graduate student) in the field, one or two social scientists who had done work on relevant topics, and the core team.

Following these meetings, participants were asked to revise their drafts in light of our discussion, with the chairs serving as editors for the resulting disciplinary volumes. Given the nature of the project, I also read each of the contributions, providing comments along the way. From beginning to end, the process for creating and editing each of the volume manuscripts took well over a year and allowed for deep engagement with the subject matter and with other scholars. The disciplinary chairs and I were careful to emphasize that these discussions were intended to be robust and the writing authentic, with no foregone conclusions about the nature of human flourishing or the value of exploring it, and we were pleased by the range and depth of thinking undertaken by each group.

As mentioned above, after we held the eight disciplinary consultations, we held a ninth meeting in which we invited the chairs of each of the disciplinary groups to present and discuss drafts of essays for a ninth, interdisciplinary volume that would share what they and their colleagues had learned through the process. We also invited a few humanities policy leaders, including past National Endowment for the Humanities Chairman William Adams, to join us and to help think about the broader implications of this work.

[20] Martin E. P. Seligman and Mihaly Csikszentmihalyi, "Positive Psychology: An Introduction," *American Psychologist*, vol. 55, no. 1, 2000, pp. 5–14; Darrin M. McMahon, "From the Paleolithic to the Present: Three Revolutions in the Global History of Happiness," *e-Handbook of Subjective Well-Being*, edited by Ed Diener et al., DEF, 2018, pp. 8–17; James O. Pawelski, "Defining the 'Positive' in Positive Psychology: Part I, a Descriptive Analysis," *The Journal of Positive Psychology*, vol. 11, no. 4, 2016, pp. 339–56; James O. Pawelski, "Defining the 'Positive' in Positive Psychology: Part II, a Normative Analysis," *The Journal of Positive Psychology*, vol. 11, no. 4, 2016, pp. 357–65; James O. Pawelski, "Bringing Together the Humanities and the Science of Well-Being to Advance Human Flourishing," *Well-Being and Higher Education: A Strategy for Change and the Realization of Education's Greater Purposes*, edited by Donald W. Harward, Bringing Theory to Practice, 2016, pp. 207–16; Louis Tay et al., "The Role of the Arts and Humanities in Human Flourishing: A Conceptual Model," *The Journal of Positive Psychology*, vol. 13, no. 3, 2018, pp. 215–25.

The compiling of the volumes was organized and overseen by the Humanities and Human Flourishing (HHF) Project at the University of Pennsylvania. HHF was founded in 2014 to support the interdisciplinary investigation and advancement of the relationship between the humanities and human flourishing. As the founding director of HHF, I am pleased that it has developed into a growing international and multidisciplinary network of more than 150 humanities scholars, scientific researchers, creative practitioners, college and university educators, wellness officers, policy experts, members of government, and leaders of cultural organizations. In addition to the disciplinary consultations described above and the resulting book series, we have published a number of conceptual papers and systematic reviews, developed conceptual models to guide empirical research, and created and validated a toolkit of measures. Designated a National Endowment for the Arts Research Lab, HHF has developed ongoing programs of research (including on art museums and human flourishing and on narrative technologies and well-being) to understand, assess, and advance the effects of engagement in the arts and humanities on human flourishing. We have published *The Oxford Handbook of the Positive Humanities* to help establish the positive humanities as a robust field of inquiry and practice at the intersection of culture, science, and human flourishing. For more information on HHF, including each of these endeavors as well as its current undertakings, please visit the *Humanities and Human Flourishing* website.

I am deeply grateful to all the individuals and institutions whose collaboration has made this book series possible. I would like to begin by thanking Chris Stewart and the Templeton Religion Trust for the generous grants that have underwritten this work. Thanks also go to the University of Pennsylvania for its robust institutional and financial support. (Of course, the views expressed in these volumes are those of the authors and do not necessarily reflect the views of the Templeton Religion Trust or the University of Pennsylvania.) I am grateful to the more than eighty contributors to these volumes for accepting our invitation to be a part of this work and for bringing more depth and richness to it than I could have imagined. I am especially grateful to the chairs of each of the disciplinary groups for their belief in the importance of this work and for their long-term dedication to making it a success. I also wish to express my appreciation for the hard work of the entire HHF core team, including Research Director Louis Tay, postdoctoral fellows Yerin Shim and Hoda Vaziri, Research Manager Michaela Ward, and especially Assistant Director Sarah Sidoti, who meticulously planned and oversaw each of the disciplinary consultations and used her expertise in academic publishing to help shape this book series in countless crucial ways. Most of the disciplinary consultations took place on the beautiful grounds of the Shawnee Inn and Golf Resort along the banks of the Delaware River. I am grateful to Charlie and Ginny Kirkwood, John Kirkwood, and all the folks at Shawnee for their gracious support and hospitality. Additionally, I am grateful to Jonathan Coopersmith and the Curtis Institute for donating space for the music group to meet, and to Bill Perthes and the Barnes Foundation for similarly donating space for the visual arts group. Thanks to the Penn Museum for a beautiful setting for the first day of our chairs consultation and to Marty Seligman and Peter Schulman for donating further space at the Positive Psychology Center. Finally, I am grateful to Peter Ohlin and all the staff and reviewers at Oxford University Press for their partnership in publishing the volumes in this book series. I hope that these volumes inspire further conversation, welcoming more people from a larger number of disciplines and a greater range of nationalities and cultural and ethnic backgrounds to inquire into what human flourishing is, how its potential harms can be avoided, and how its benefits can be more deeply experienced and more broadly extended.

James O. Pawelski
February 19, 2022

Editors and Contributors

Ellen T. Charry
Princeton Theological Seminary
Ellen T. Charry is the Margaret W. Harmon emerita professor of theology at Princeton Theological Seminary, where she was on the faculty from 1997 to 2017. Prior to that, she was on the faculty at Perkins School of Theology at Southern Methodist University, Dallas, Texas (1991–97), following a Henry Luce postdoctoral fellowship at Yale Divinity School (1989–91). She was a member of the Pursuit of Happiness project at Emory University and a senior advisor to the project on Happiness and Well-Being: Integrating Research across the Disciplines at Saint Louis University, in the Department of Philosophy. Both projects were sponsored by the John Templeton Foundation.

She holds a bachelor of arts from Barnard College at Columbia University, a master of social work from the Wurzweiler School of Social Work at Yeshiva University, and a master of arts and PhD from Temple University.

Her two main interests are the relationships among theology, human flourishing, and interfaith theological reconciliation, particularly between Christianity and Judaism. Her work on theology and human flourishing includes *By the Renewing of Your Minds: The Pastoral Function of Christian Doctrine* (1997) and *God and the Art of Happiness* (2010). Her current book project attempts interfaith theological reconciliation and is tentatively titled "Who Is the Israel of God?" It will reconstruct the theological relationship between these two heritages.

Her additional books are *Franz Rosenzweig on the Freedom of God* (1989), *Inquiring after God: Classical and Contemporary Readings* (2000), *The Austin Dogmatics of Paul M. van Buren* (2012), and *Psalms 1–50: Signs and Songs of Israel* (2015).

Pamela Cooper-White
Union Theological Seminary
Pamela Cooper-White is the Christiane Brooks Johnson Professor of Psychology and Religion at Union Theological Seminary, New York, since 2015, after many years as a professor at Columbia Theological Seminary, the co-director of the Atlanta Theological Association's ThD program in pastoral counseling, and the 2013–14 Fulbright-Freud Scholar of Psychoanalysis in Vienna, Austria. She is the author of seven books, including *Shared Wisdom: Use of the Self in Pastoral Care and Counseling*, *Many Voices: Pastoral Psychotherapy in Relational and Theological Perspective*, *The Cry of Tamar: Violence against Women and the Church's Response*, and most recently *Old and Dirty Gods: Religion, Antisemitism, and the Origins of Psychoanalysis*. She has published over seventy articles and chapters and has lectured frequently across

the United States, Europe, and Israel. She serves on the board of the International Association for Spiritual Care, the steering committee of the Psychology, Culture, and Religion Group of the American Academy of Religion, and the editorial board of *The Journal of Pastoral Theology*. Cooper-White holds two PhDs, one from Harvard (historical musicology) and one from the Institute for Clinical Social Work in Chicago (psychoanalytic practice and research), and she is an ordained Episcopal priest.

Matthew Croasmun
Yale Center for Faith and Culture
Matt Croasmun is an associate research scholar and the director of the Life Worth Living Program at the Yale Center for Faith and Culture and a lecturer in divinity and humanities at Yale University. His first book, *The Emergence of Sin: The Cosmic Tyrant in Romans* (Oxford UP, 2017), addresses questions of individual and collective agency within the writings of the apostle Paul in light of emergence theory in philosophy of science. His second book, *For the Life of the World: Theology That Makes a Difference* (Brazos, 2019), coauthored with Miroslav Volf, calls readers to a renewal of Christian theology that is centered on discerning, articulating, and commending Christian visions of flourishing life.

Hector Kilgoe
University of Pennsylvania
Hector Kilgoe is a doctoral candidate in the Department of Religious Studies at the University of Pennsylvania. He studies religion, race, and politics in the United States in the 19th and 20th centuries, with particular interest in Black nationalism, formations of Black and other identities, and narratives and rhetoric associated with ideas of affective belonging, kinship, and citizenship as they relate to systems of power. His dissertation research is on African American emigrationist thought in the 19th century and settler colonialism in Liberia. Hector received his Graduate Certificate in Africana Studies in 2019 at the University of Pennsylvania. He received his Master of Theological Studies degree in African and African American Religious Studies from Harvard Divinity School, where he was a junior fellow in the Science, Religion, and Culture Program, and his BA in Religious Studies, with minors in Jewish Studies and East Asian Languages and Civilizations, from the University of Pennsylvania, where he was a Benjamin Franklin Scholar. His intellectual interests also include affect theory, science fiction, media studies, and queer theory.

Justin Thomas McDaniel
University of Pennsylvania
Justin Thomas McDaniel's research foci include Lao, Thai, Pali, and Sanskrit literature, art and architecture, and manuscript studies. His first book, *Gathering Leaves and Lifting Words* (U of Washington P, 2008), won the Harry Benda Prize. His second book, *The Lovelorn Ghost and the Magic Monk* (Columbia UP, 2014), won the Kahin Prize. He has received grants from the National Endowment for the Humanities, the Andrew W. Mellon Foundation, the Rockefeller Foundation, the Fulbright Program, University of California Pacific Rim Research Program (PACRIM), the Henry Luce, and the Social Science

Research Council (SSRC), among others. He is the co-editor of the journals *Buddhism Compass* and *Journal of Lao Studies*, and he is the associate editor of the *Journal of Asian Studies*. He has won teaching and advising awards at Harvard University, Ohio University, and the University of California, Riverside, and he has won the Ludwig Prize for Teaching at the University of Pennsylvania. In 2012, he was named a Guggenheim Fellow, and in 2014 he became a fellow of Kyoto University's Center for Southeast Asian Studies. He has published edited books on Thai manuscripts, Buddhist biographies, Buddhist Material Culture, and Buddhist ritual. He also has recently published three new books on modern Buddhist architecture called *Architects of Buddhist Leisure* (U of Hawaii P, 2018), Wayward Distractions: Studies in Southeast Asian Buddhism (Kyoto University and National University of Singapore Press, 2022), and on Thai Illuminated Manuscripts called *Biologies and Cosmologies: Siamese Manuscripts from the Fogg Collection* (Holberton Press, 2024).

Mary Clark Moschella
Yale Divinity School
Mary Clark Moschella is the Roger J. Squire Professor of Pastoral Care and Counseling at Yale Divinity School. Prior to joining the YDS faculty in 2010, she taught at Wesley Theological Seminary in Washington, DC for ten years. Before that, she was a pastor in United Church of Christ congregations in Massachusetts for thirteen years. Her work includes *Ethnography as a Pastoral Practice: An Introduction* (Pilgrim Press, 2008), *Caring for Joy: Narrative, Theology, and Practice* (Brill, 2016), and *Pedagogy in Practice: Qualitative Research in Theological Education* (SCM, forthcoming). Mary teaches courses in pastoral care, qualitative research methods, feminist and womanist pastoral theology, narrative therapy, and joy in the ministry and in life. One of her new projects involves developing an inside-out course to bring divinity students and incarcerated persons into a classroom together. She is married to Douglas Clark and is the mother of Ethan and Abbey Clark-Moschella. In her spare time, Mary enjoys hikes, fiction, art museums, theater, the Red Sox, the beach, and forays into her perennial garden.

Leela Prasad
Duke University
Leela Prasad is an associate professor of religious studies at Duke University. Her research spans the anthropology of ethics, the colonial anthropology of India, narrative, gender, and the South Asian diaspora. Leela is fluent in Telugu, Kannada, Marathi, and Hindi. Her work examines the lived, expressive dimensions of ethics in Hindu and other Indic contexts through various lenses such as narrative, art, material culture, ritual, and everyday practice. Her book *Poetics of Conduct: Narrative and Moral Being in a South Indian Town* (Columbia UP, 2007) won the American Academy of Religion's prize for Best First Book in the History of Religions. She co-edited *Gender and Story in South India* (SUNY P, 2006). In 1999, she served as guest curator of the first exhibition on Indian American life for the Balch Institute and the Historical Society of Pennsylvania, and she edited the exhibition's catalog and co-directed an accompanying documentary film called *Back and Forth*. Leela's next book is *The Audacious Raconteur: Sovereignty through Storytelling in Colonial India* (Cornell UP, forthcoming). She is also co-directing *Moved by Gandhi*, an ethnographic film that

explores how Gandhi exists, beyond the biographically known figure, in the emotional imaginary of individuals, moving them one way or the other.

Noah Salomon
Carlton College

Noah Salomon is an associate professor of religion and the director of Middle East studies at Carleton College. His first book, For Love of the Prophet: An Ethnography of Sudan's Islamic State (Princeton, 2016), winner of the Middle East Studies Association's 2017 Albert Hourani Prize and the 2017 Award for Excellence in the Study of Religion in Analytical-Descriptive Studies from the American Academy of Religion, is a meditation on the religious dimensions of the modern state through an analysis of the production of civic desire in Sudan's political history and present. His subsequent research has focused on the establishment of state secularism in the new nation of South Sudan as a mode of unraveling the Islamic state and on the construction of a Muslim minority as a concomitant project of nation-building. Salomon is a 2018 recipient of a Mellon New Directions Fellowship, which will extend his work into Shi'i contexts, and he has been part of recent collaborative grants from the Deutsche Forschungsgemeinschaft (on Islamic epistemologies in Africa) and the Islam Research Programme, in the Netherlands (on religious minorities in the two Sudans following partition). He was a member at the Institute for Advanced Study in Princeton University's School of Social Science for the 2013–14 academic year.

Jeffrey Samuels
Western Kentucky University

Jeffrey Samuels is a professor of Buddhist studies and the interim department head in the Department of Philosophy and Religion at Western Kentucky University. He is author of Attracting the Heart: Social Relations and the Aesthetics of Emotion in Sri Lankan Monastic Culture. He has also co-edited two books, the most recent one being Figures of Buddhist Modernity in Asia (with Justin Thomas McDaniel and Mark Rowe), and he has written over two dozen articles focusing on Buddhist monastic culture in South and Southeast Asia. He is currently working on writing a social history of Buddhism in Malaysia.

Steven Weitzman
University of Pennsylvania

Steven Weitzman is a professor of religious studies and Jewish studies at the University of Pennsylvania, specializing in Jewish antiquity. His recent publications include Solomon: The Lure of Wisdom (Yale UP, 2011), part of the Jewish Lives series, published by Yale University Press, and The Origin of the Jews: the Quest for Roots in a Rootless Age (Princeton UP, 2017). Although his training is in Jewish studies, he also has a side interest in how scholars of religion relate to the government, as reflected in The FBI and Religion (U of California P, 2017), co-edited with Sylvester Johnson. Weitzman is the Abraham M. Ellis Professor of Hebrew and Semitic Languages and Literatures and serves as the Ella Darivoff Director of the Katz Center of Advanced Judaic Studies at the University of Pennsylvania.

Introduction

Aporias and Affordances

An Introduction to the Study of Religion, Theology, and Human Flourishing

Justin Thomas McDaniel

The Setting

I am not a good listener. I am a terrible "team player." Most humanities scholars are trained to think alone, research alone, and write single-authored articles and books. We lecture in front of students in courses on Baldwin, South Indian ritual, Duchamp, and Peruvian music. We preserve old books and translate poems, often alone in a quiet room. We participate in conferences, where four to five of us each give individual talks and then field our own individual questions. We are alone in a community and are quite good at that. Social scientists, engineers, and natural scientists are much better at working together; they need to deal with big data, longitudinal surveys, laboratory budgets, workflow charts, and collaborative grant applications. Their work is "applied" and functional. Their publications often have multiple authors, they regularly work with postdocs, and they become adept at Zoom and Go-To-Meeting online conversations and conference roundtables. Now, while there are many humanities professors who are great listeners and team players, who are experts at prodding students to share and listen in small seminars, who model engaged and cooperative research, and who bring together students and faculty to work on group editing on Google Docs, I am not one of them. I am suited for the archive, for long hours translating old manuscripts, for presenting my research, fielding a question or two, and walking back to the library or to the hotel. I have mastered the lecture in front of 150 students on Buddhist history or Thai literature, but I have never felt comfortable in a small seminar with students who haven't done the reading.

Justin Thomas McDaniel, *Introduction Aporias and Affordances* In: *Religious Studies, Theology, and Human Flourishing.*
Edited by: Justin Thomas McDaniel and Hector Kilgoe, Oxford University Press. © Oxford University Press 2024.
DOI: 10.1093/oso/9780197658338.003.0001

I am becoming an artifact of the past. I was created in a small PhD program (so small that for two years, I was the only student in the program, and later the department was renamed and moved to attract more students) in the tradition of German-style philology. However, the "real-world setting" in which I find myself now is forcing me to change. I don't always welcome it and am often resentful. I am an extreme case, but many other scholars in the humanities are like me. The world of research and teaching is changing around us. It is becoming more collaborative, public, connected, and socially engaged. The humanities wing of universities that, for so long, has been a collection of individual scholars has become a place more and more focused on interdisciplinary work, faculty workgroups, and active, in-class learning environments. These are mostly good changes, in my mind. We have been forced to listen, to respond, and to work with others.[1] I think that as long as we don't have to conform to a particular model of proper scholarship and aren't reduced simply to job training, collaboration and a consideration of impact is important. I was ready for a change. A few years ago, frankly, I became sick of hearing myself lecture, of researching more and more about less and less (my most recent article, for example, explained Chettiar temple architecture in the 1870s in Saigon, which I find fascinating, but I don't think it will fly off the shelves at Barnes and Noble), and of writing for an audience of three to four experts in my small field. Not that I considered my subject matter irrelevant or that I couldn't learn and teach things of value from what I was reading, but I felt that it was a bit self-serving. I started off by changing the way that I teach most of my courses and by exploring different methods and approaches to scholarship. Although it is important to research and expose new materials for the sake of contributing to global knowledge, there must be a way of making my work more relevant to my students and the general public. Although I didn't know what I was looking for, I found that many scholars in the humanities were seeking the same thing—to make a broader impact, to be more responsive and attentive to student needs, and to think about the social, ethical, and affective ramifications of our role as researchers, mentors, and teachers. We seek to expose our rich material in art, literature, and religion to a wider audience who crave wisdom in an often disturbing, competitive, and violent world. Therefore, the main theme of this volume is to explore what we can learn from religious studies and

---

[1] Hopefully, our tenure and promotion system will respect these changes and reward collaborative, interdisciplinary, and socially engaged work. So far, it has not.

theology for the conceptualization and cultivation of human flourishing. The scholars gathered here come from many different subfields in (Islamic, Jewish, Buddhist, Christian, etc.) religious studies and theology studies as well as other approaches (ethnographic, textual, sociological, historical, philological, etc.), but they are all invested in exploring how we might transform our classrooms and writing to enhance the experience and well-being of our interlocutors, colleagues, and students.

As an editor of this volume, this is quite a personal endeavor as well. A few years ago, I decided I needed to make a change in the way that I approach research and teaching after learning more and more about the growing suicide rates, the increase in the number of students needing mental healthcare, and the impact of the high-stakes admissions process and competition at elite and selective universities. I also simply wanted to learn to listen better and to work with others on more impactful scholarship and teaching. I wanted not only to produce detailed scholarship (artifacts) in my field but also to start to listen more to the needs of my students and to understand the pressure that they are under. I wanted to start to think about what the Jesuits would call the "whole person" when I teach. I started teaching two experimental courses (see my chapter in this volume, "Lab Courses for the Humanities," which describes those courses) and then, through these courses, came into contact with the world of positive psychology and the eudaemonic turn in the humanities and social sciences, especially the work of James Pawelski. Pawelski's work and the eudaemonic turn are described well in the Series Editor's Foreword to this volume, and I won't elaborate on that here, but what is important to understand is that through our conversations and his leadership in winning a major three-year grant from the Templeton Religion Trust, we were able to collaborate in a workshop and on this edited volume to bring together a group of theologians and religious studies scholars to better understand how to incorporate issues of "well-being" and a concern for "human flourishing" into our scholarship and teaching. The fields of religious studies and theology were the first of the eight humanities disciplinary consultations (followed by philosophy, history, cinema and media, literary studies, theater, music, and visual arts). Our task was to see what our disciplines—and our work within those disciplines—could contribute to the contemporary understanding of human flourishing, and how they—and we—could be more effective (if, indeed, we should try to be) in fostering purpose, meaning, and other well-being benefits for readers of research and for students in the classroom.

The result of this workshop and book: unintended consequences.

The Players

Enter: Hector Kilgoe. I have known Kilgoe since he was an eighteen-year-old freshman at the University of Pennsylvania. Now, after earning his master's at Harvard Divinity School, he is back at Penn as a PhD candidate in the Religious Studies Department. Although we are in different fields, mine Buddhist studies and Indic literature, his African American religious history and religion and social justice, I saw in his approach a much needed perspective on applying a serious attentiveness to eudaemonia in the classroom. Moreover, Kilgoe has been a resident advisor in student dormitories for many years, guiding undergraduates. He sees them not only during the day in classes and office hours but in the evenings as he runs programming and study breaks and as he listens to their emotional concerns. He truly has a perspective on a student's whole person that many professors do not have.

Kilgoe and I worked with project director Pawelski and research director Louis Tay, along with project manager Sarah Sidoti and research manager Michaela Ward and two postdoctoral fellows (Yerin Shim and Hoda Vaziri), to bring together a widely different group of theologians and religious studies scholars (Pamela Cooper-White, Matthew Croasmun, Leela Prasad, Mary Clark Moschella, Noah Salomon, Jeffrey Samuels, Steven Weitzman, and Ellen T. Charry) for an extended project to explore the relationships among eudaemonia and religious studies and theology teaching and research, culminating in a three-day workshop in which we discussed previously circulated drafts of our chapters. We were also joined by Kenneth Pargament, a leading empirical researcher on the psychology of religion. Now, I could end the introduction here with a brief summary of each of these chapters and be done with it. However, something unexpected happened in this workshop. We actually listened to each other and changed our perspectives, reimagined the project, and surprisingly left the workshop thinking differently. It wasn't a series of presentations with polite responses. We didn't simply wait for our turn to talk and to try to impress more than express. I have been at dozens and dozens of conferences and workshops throughout my career, and this was truly the first one in which I changed the way that I thought about my career, my scholarship, and my teaching. While I cannot speak for everyone, the difference for me in this workshop was palpable and the intellectual engagement visceral, contentious, sincere, and often uncomfortable. All of us, it seemed, were at a point in our career in which we needed to change something, not quite knowing what it was. With ideas and arguments flying around the room and spilling over into coffee breaks and meals, Kilgoe and I frantically tried to keep the experience documented.

Act One: Aporias

Immediately, since we had read each other's papers, the stage was set to start with disagreement. There was no natural easing in to the discussion, and it was clear from the beginning that the players were not speaking each other's language. Translation and a bit of trans-creation needed to take place first. Aporias are pauses, moments, interstitial encounters that arise out of puzzlement or an impasse in communication. They aren't merely essential states of confusion, but there is a temporal element in which people exist in a state of befuddlement for a time. That time, if used productively, can be illuminating. There were two major periods of productive aporia when we met.

The first concerned the very idea of scientific measurement and its application to religious studies. Social scientists, especially ones who design quantitative studies and mine big data, often seem to humanists to speak a foreign language. When social scientists apply their methods of assessment to art, music, literature, religion, and the vaguely defined affective/emotional realms of a human life, humanists become befuddled and even feel threatened. Teleological and instrumental techniques of analysis, when applied to an abstract painting or a funerary ritual, seem to cheapen its purpose or corral its possibilities. Why limit the emotional range, the creative drive, and the messy sides of life? Why instrumentalize feelings and explain "away" intellectual struggle? Why document tears? Why analyze laughter? Why place novels into pie charts and sculptures into spreadsheets? Shouldn't there be parts of a human life that are permitted to remain complex, contingent, and confusing? Sometimes humans don't want to be told why they feel a certain way and to learn how to package and replicate that feeling. They just want to feel.

This was the first contentious discussion. On one side of the stage, you had philosopher turned social scientist and pioneer in the field of positive psychology James Pawelski; Kenneth Pargament, a world-renown psychologist and clinician; and Louis Tay, a psychometrician and expert in organizational research methods. On the other, you had Noah Solomon, Leela Prasad, Steven Weitzman, and Jeffrey Samuels—all scholars of religious studies (Islamic studies, Hindu studies, Jewish studies, and Buddhist studies, respectively). The argument settled around this main issue—what is the point of measuring subjective religious experience or religious motivation in research or of assessing "learning outcomes" in religious studies courses? There is a problem, the scholars of religious studies argued, with looking at agents through the approach of computational models and psychometric tools that are designed by sociologists and social engineers. They have a tendency to focus on outcomes. Their systems model biological and mechanical behavior to produce solutions for issues of inefficiency, heat loss, reduced profits, or material stress. Most humanists have never been concerned much with outcomes. They proudly practice a woefully inefficient and unprofitable craft. Most religious studies scholars, myself included, are not really concerned (although I understand why other, more social scientifically and managerially minded scholars would be) with studying ideal exemplars or artistic or religious movements that successfully achieve optimal outcomes—great books, paradigm-shifting buildings, revolutionary theories, and inspirational epitaphs. Instead, we often look at how certain agents "get stuck at local optima."[2] They settle on a series of small "goods" and abandon the optimal "perfects" that they initially wanted to reach in the end. Scholars of religion often study struggle, suffering, perseverance, and disquiet. Even if religious leaders, ritualists, visionaries, and spiritual guides want their followers to achieve certain outcomes, their visions are regularly compromised by emotional struggle, the death of spouses, moral compromise, and spiritual awe. Along the way, many religious practitioners and believers have to develop alternative plans or, in computationalspeak—"low-level adaptive algorithms"—and give up ideal outcomes or overarching models. Sometimes lives and material creations are simply the product of a series of local optima. Why limit fractured human experience that is in a continual state of unfolding without any definite goal to stages, steps, and pathways with defined goals? Why put a mushroom cloud in a mason jar or pin a butterfly to a wall chart?

However, quite provocatively, the psychometricians and psychologists argued that humanists used tools of assessment, analysis, and definition frequently; it was just a problem of optics. Religious studies scholars (whether

---

[2] For more about local optima, see McDaniel (esp. the introduction).

they approach their field using literary, text-critical, phenomenological, ethnographic, poststructuralists, or other methods) aren't averse to conclusions, outcomes, and systematic assessment, but since their publications (which often are not the product of grant-funded projects, institutional review board sanctions, or collaborative work) do not have charts and graphs and do not deploy surveys and designated control groups and are often single authored, they are conditioned to be averse to the organizational and rhetorical tools of social scientists and psychologists. Visually, the covers of humanities books (or the simple fact that humanists tend to value single-authored monographs more for tenure and promotion than they value collaborative articles in top-flight journals) are different. The formatting of the text is simply different. Humanists often use many fewer section and subsection headings; they don't have a section on methodology, and they don't cite the same types of journals and studies in their publications. Data-rich charts are replaced by visually evocative field photographs or archival facsimiles and so on. For example, Pargament argued well that religious studies scholars trace the impact and reception that religious texts have over time by studying commentaries, scribal copying, artistic depiction, sermons, and social movements that are inspired by religious texts. By studying, for example, the ways in which writings by Aquinas or Shinran inspire homilies, murals, civil law, or political decisions or policies, humanists are studying outcomes. By showing how religious prophets, cult leaders, and visionaries gather together followers and launch social, ascetic, or reform movements, they are studying outcomes. By looking at the symbolic and rhetorical techniques of religious art and the way that art is interpreted by communities of believers, they are assessing effectiveness. What religious studies scholars often value as evidence—anecdote, rumor, individual emotional reaction, dedication, seemingly irrational truth or belief claims, impractical and seemingly unprofitable ritual activity, undefinable beauty—is not often the more systematic quantitative evidence that social scientists might use, but the goals are often less dissimilar than might be apparent. Scholars of religion do wonder why certain pieces of religious literature, certain pieces of art, and certain doctrines and ideas persist and are received and responded to over time. In their conclusion, they often argue or speculate on why. While every religious belief or tradition, every expression of spiritual joy or pain, every ritual action, and every seemingly illogical act of martyrdom, ascetic physical austerity, or moral purity can't be summarized, assessed, replicated, or measured, that doesn't mean that religious studies scholars and theologians aren't interested in knowing why certain religious pieces of literature or art persist and inspire and why some fade into obscurity, why some religious social movements grow and some stagnate, why some moral rules, traditions, spiritual exercises, and ritual practices easily transfer and influence new practitioners and some remain unique to small groups. Religious studies scholars and theologians often do want to know why the teachings and practices of the Kabbalah, for example, have not been widespread but yoga and insight meditation has been, why female and male circumcision persists in some communities but cannibalism has almost completely disappeared, why Buddhism spread easily while Shinto and Sikhism did not, why some groups remain exclusive and others embrace pluralism, why the writings of Saint Theresa have been translated into dozens of languages but the writings of Mirabai have not, why some people practice sky burial and others cremate, why heaven is often considered up and hell down. Moreover, many scholars of religious studies and theology want to know how to teach their students better and more effectively—to not simply learn about different religious beliefs and practices but to take these religions seriously as spiritual and intellectual worldviews and to understand how, even though often unprovable, certain beliefs and traditions persist and even thrive. What these conversations impressed upon social scientists, psychologists, and humanists alike was that while we may never be able to fully capture (and may not even want to) the full range of motivations, emotions, and experiences of a religious person and their cultural expressions, it is important to try to understand—through deploying new methods, more nuanced tools of analysis, and more evidence—why people remain religious in the face of an increasingly technological and secular world and why certain practices, beliefs, and religious artifacts still inspire hope and faith in a world of human suffering, environmental degradation, violence, poverty, and ethnic division. The question of why humans are religious remains.

The second major aporia concerned the nature of the terms *eudaemonia* and *well-being*. This was a major source of contention. Mainly, the problem was the supposedly "universal" claims that scholars of positive psychology seem to make about humanity and that humans all wanted to be "happy" and to participate in human flourishing. As is clear from the chapters in this volume by Weitzman, Cooper-White, Croasmun, and Salomon, there was a general sense of apprehension, if not downright rejection, of the very idea that well-being and eudaemonia were generally desired by all religions, all cultures, and all humans. This seems counterintuitive. Don't all humans want to be happy? Is that the one thing, besides our mortality, that binds us and crosses religious, class, and ethnic lines? Not necessarily. As Salomon argued, if a religious person sees her life as completely dedicated to God, as completely powerless, and she craves to return to God in this life or the paradise hereafter, then the motivation for earthly happiness may be an affront to her ethical agenda, whether she sees happiness as the pursuit of the whims of the ego-self or as shirking social responsibility. Many a practitioner believes that we should be working to return to God, not necessarily to create realms of general well-being in this human life. Human well-being, human flourishing, and the creation of the conditions that foster human happiness could be seen as antithetical to being dedicated to God's plan. Being happy on earth could suggest a resistance to the Creator, an individuation that bucks his collective purpose. That is to say, the assumption that religion's primary or sole purpose is (or is it that *it should be*?) to make people happy is a false one from its first principles. Furthermore, social scientists often want to flatten the world and assume all terms, whether they be from Sanskrit or Arabic or Latin, are somehow all translatable and understandable across cultures. Sometimes, Salomon argued, cultures and religions don't want to be subsumed under other people's terms and methods of inquiry. There is a certain kind of arrogance in assuming that whatever our subjects are saying is just a poorly articulated version of our own categories, into which they can be subsumed (e.g., they might call it "struggle against the self" but what they really mean is "human flourishing"). It is a radical notion in a neoliberal and technologically connected world, but some people just don't seek to be understood. Moreover, Weitzman argued in the meeting that there is also a political and social danger to universalizing and creating effective systems of measuring well-being. For example, in large surveys about national happiness, religious worldviews, and the like, Judaism, Orthodox Christianity, and Hinduism are often at the lower end of the happiness scale.[3] Buddhists and Mormons are often seen in these survey results as happier than practitioners of other religions are. Could these types of social scientific quantitative and qualitative studies be used and abused in the future to promote government policies or educational curricula that promote Mormonism or Buddhism over Judaism or Hinduism? There is a danger of using neuroscientific studies

---

[3] See, for example, https://www.pewresearch.org/fact-tank/2019/01/31/are-religious-people-happier-healthier-our-new-global-study-explores-this-question/; https://theconversation.com/are-religious-people-happier-than-non-religious-people-87394.

involving MRIs and other types of brain scan technology to study the effects of prayer or meditation in order to create work policies or school programs like Google's use of mindfulness training or the introduction of meditation in public schools.[4] On the one hand, it is hard to argue against programs and studies that promote wellness, health, and feelings of meaning, purpose, connection, and fulfillment so as to reduce rates of suicide, depression, and addiction. On the other, there is a danger in assuming that well-being is the same in every culture and that religion, more broadly, is designed the make an individual "feel good." Furthermore, Salomon argued, what the study of religion offers is the overarching perspective that, in many cases, meaning making and the measurement of human flourishing seemed to be "very much individuated in the study of positive psychology. One might argue that it is precisely the insistence on a psychological model of well-being (rather than a collective, social healing one)" that is a major difference between the two fields and that this is a place where they could learn from each other. If psychologists and social scientists (economists, sociologists, political scientists) assume that the desire for a happiness is universal, then it might lead to a complete lack of understanding of (or even efforts to legally ban) religious practices like fasting, celibacy, clothing restrictions, and ascetic physical austerities and self-torture. It could also lead to assumptions about the universality of well-being that is used to create laws that ban such religious practices or that judge religions as backward or dangerous. Religious studies scholars in the workgroup were all concerned that studies that tracked the ways in which certain religious practices increased well-being and certain ones didn't could be "weaponized" by social workers, politicians, educators, and clinicians as a tool against certain religious people. These objections, these skeptical outcries were received well and vigorously discussed. We listened, not to come to a consensus but to try to productively learn from the aporia thus occasioned.

Connected to these issues with the universality of the concept of well-being was the problem with how we define *well-being*. Generally, scholars and clinicians of positive psychology have defined well-being as being connected to physical health and economic security (not necessarily wealth) but also more vaguely to a general sense of "purpose" and "meaning," a feeling of being "connected" to others or valued or even admired by others, a feeling of wholeness and harmony among the body,

---

[4] See, for example, Sun.

the mind, and the environment, a feeling of being able to be creative and have emotional depth. Well-being involves traceable and recordable neurological and physiological outcomes like the activation of multiple brain areas, healthy cardiovascular systems, and positive affect valence as well as psychological and affective outcomes of self-efficacy, emotional depth, civic engagement, and integrative complexity. However, pastoral theologian Pamela Cooper-White argued that what was missing in studies of well-being was the question of social justice and freedom. For many oppressed peoples, she argued, fighting for liberation for others and yourself even at the cost of your own freedom and physical safety was more important than feeling happy and healthy. Responsibility to others, fighting for human dignity, not just human flourishing, was missing in the eudaemonic turn in positive psychology. Awareness and acknowledgment of others' suffering might not lead to a general sense of wholeness or harmony and certainly might not promote physical health, but they are a part of the study of religion and theology, and, as she titled her chapter, "sometimes a little pessimism is good for the soul."

Charry and Croasmun, while not solving this dilemma, did offer some much needed perspectives from the field of theology, which has been systematically ostracized and institutionally separated or removed from many universities, not only from the other humanities and social sciences but also from the field of religious studies. Charry ("Augustine of Hippo's Eudaemonic Counsel," this volume), offers an urgent call to return the field of Christian theology to the humanities, and more specifically, the "arts." For example, she writes:

> With the arts and other humanities, theology aims to strengthen one's grasp of the meaning and purpose of reality and one's self in it. . . . Theology is an art in the humanist sense of the word. It understands that information is processed through what Gadamer names a *Wirkungsgeschichtliches Bewusstsein* (an "effective historical consciousness"), which a reader of texts brings to them. Before applying this to Christian theology, a caveat must be registered. Christianity reflects on human possibilities and limitations by assuming a flawed moral nature that cannot be fully eradicated but that with care can be modestly reshaped so that individuals become better examples of the species. The church is what Derrida calls an interpretive community. It offers communicable wisdom for "playing well with others." . . . Here is where Christian (Jewish and Islamic) theology deepens Gadamer's description of

historical consciousness to include its moral conscience. Synagogue and church interpret "Am I my brother's keeper?" (43–44)

Moreover, she argues that theology can be seen as enriching and supporting the goals of positive psychology, and therefore her chapter provides an excellent example of how the humanities fields, such as religious studies and theology, can be effective conversation partners with psychology, whose practitioners are concerned with human flourishing, not just human fixing. She continues:

> *Salus* (as in *salute* and *salutation*) means 'health' or 'well-being.' Christianity's goal is to enable people to become spiritually and morally healthy when ravished by the splendorous goodness that is the truth that God is and wanting to become it. Here is the naked desire for God that has eluded many modern seekers. Christianity holds that having God completely in this life is not possible. But journeying into the transcendentals to the extent that one can is celebration of self whereby they, personified as God, celebrate being enjoyed by creatures. This is positive theology. (47)

In this way, positive psychology needs theological approaches, unless it simply wants to develop methods and policies that are designed to make people simply feel happy, not for them to have a sustained sense of well-being. One cannot be isolated in their well-being. Positive psychology can learn from theology not to be just a self-help system.

Croasmun held that theology is perhaps much better suited for social scientific approaches to well-being because it was concerned with the nature of the "good life" and it has long tried to remain relevant to the humanities, even as it is often seen as limited to the historical study of Christianity. He drew our attention to Pierre Hadot's oft-discussed *Philosophy as a Way of Life* and argued that theology has changed from claiming that Christian theology is a "universalism" or that it is normative or the first of the humanities in the modern academy to seeing that it is one of many "contending particular universalisms" that can stand alongside other particular philosophies that have universal claims, such as those of the psychology of Freud, the Buddhist notions of self, or the philosophy of Nietzsche. They made universal claims as well but are taught as alternatives and interesting possibilities. They are learned from as well as learned about. These particular universalisms "contend" with each other, "laying claims to our allegiance." Therefore, even

Christian theologians, who have long claimed to have some answers about the nature of the "good life," are just one of many resources for students of the humanities. And positive psychology is the same, a particular universalism that can claim to provide methods and even answers for everyone but that must settle on being one voice of many if it wants to build bridges and break bread with the humanities.

Act Two: Affordances

As you can see from the above aporias, the conversational impasses of our particular group of pastoral theologians, scholars of religious studies, positive psychologists, and psychometricians centered on the tension between the naturalistic or universal assumptions that all people want to be "happy" and to have well-being and the ethnographic realities and the normative sets of local laws and ethical reasonings that question the universality of the very idea of well-being and human flourishing. For some, justice and selfless submission are essential to well-being, and that well-being does not necessarily mean "feeling good" or maximizing individual flourishing. For others (as will be clear from the various chapters), freedom from was more important than freedom to. Regardless, while we did not all agree on universal definitions of well-being or even the need to have them, and we certainly didn't agree on the universal need for universally agreed-upon techniques and policies for promoting well-being in the study of religion, we did explore the idea that there is a need to explore the separation in the study of religion between natural and normative approaches to our field and, in turn, to remind ourselves that through our research we take seriously the lives of religious people who are making difficult decisions, and as teachers we guide students who might be making difficult ethical decisions or coming from difficult home lives themselves. How do we both attend to the spiritual struggles and emotional needs of our students and encourage them to remain open and objective in their scholarship? How do we acknowledge and allow our "subjects" to lead lives and to hold beliefs that seem to go against our own sense of well-being while at the same time understanding that our students and readers are looking for guidance on how to lead a good life? How do we balance our training for the podium with the pressures of standing behind a pulpit? How do we acknowledge our students' and subjects' subjective psychological, ethical, and emotional concerns and remain objective commentators on the history and practices of certain religious traditions? Like it or not, every teacher of theology, psychology, and religious studies knows that our students and the reading public don't just look to us for de-tached descriptions of a ritual, a religious law, an ethical debate, an act of faith, or brain structure. They seek answers to profound ethical questions or their own emotional aporias. They don't just want to know what Lacan said or what Buddhist temples look like but how Lacan or *Bodhidharma* can help them make sense of their place in society and help them understand why their parents don't want them to marry their Jewish boyfriend or why their friend can't just stop being depressed. Do scholars of religion and psychology have a professional or ethical responsibility to address these questions and to offer space for conversation, debate, and open emotion, or is bracketing these difficult conversations and referring the student or reader of our articles and books to the counseling services on campus or offering the number of a local therapist or minister the more responsible thing to do? What is the "right" thing to do legally and ethically, and do these overlap, or should they?

What do the situations that we often find ourselves in as mentors, educators, and resident or designated "experts" in psychology and religion afford? Here is where several scholars in our group turned to the idea of affordance. As Webb Keane notes, the idea of an affordance

originated in the psychology of visual perception. As defined by James J. Gibson, "[t]he affordance of anything is a specific combination of the properties of its substance and its surface" in light of what it offers, provides, or furnishes for the animal that perceives it. . . . Gibson stresses that al-though the properties are objective phenomena, they serve as affordances only in particular combinations and relative to particular observers. Thus, "[I]f an object that rests on the ground, has a surface that is itself sufficiently rigid, level, flat, and extended, and if this surface is raised approximately at the height of the knees of the human biped, then it affords sitting-on." . . . Or, as George Herbert Mead had remarked a generation earlier, "the chair invites us to sit down." . . . But as Gibson goes on to say, "knee-high for a child is not the same as knee-high for an adult." . . . Two crucial points in this original definition are, first, that affordances are objective features in contingent combinations, and, second, they only exist as affordances rela-tive to the properties of some other perceiving and acting entity. So another crucial point to stress is (mere) potentiality: a chair may invite you to sit but it does not determine that you will sit. You may instead use it as a step ladder, a desk, a paperweight, a lion tamer's prop, to burn as firewood, to block a door, to hurl at someone. Or you may not use it at all. Affordances are properties of the chair vis á vis human activity. As such they are real, and exist in a world of natural causality (they can hold down loose objects or catch fire), but not they do not cause people to respond to them in any particular way. (Keane, Webb. "Affordances and reflexivity in ethical life: an ethnographic stance." *Anthropological Theory*, 14, no. 1, 2014, pp. 3–26)

Simply put, ethical affordances are, Keane argues, the way of making sense of situations (which are often confronted in ethnography, in his case, but the classroom, blogosphere, court room, or scholarly conference in the case of a scholar of psychology or religion) between the

naturalistic approaches (such as psychology and linguistics) and normative ones (such as philosophy, religion, and law)—without, however, inviting reductionism. . . . Naturalistic approaches describe a world of causes and effects, of mechanisms, or statistical correlations of which people are largely unaware. Normative ones invoke a world of principled, reflexive reasoning and decision-making carried out by self-conscious agents. . . . On the one hand, the Kantian and utilitarian traditions in philosophy and political thought often seek to ground ethics in the rationality of self-aware actors. On the other hand, neuroscience, psychology, evolutionary theory, and economics tend to take the sources of ethical responses to be immanent in biological systems, or individuals, or selective pressures, or populations, in each case more or less independently of anyone's self-awareness. The former stresses reasons and justifications; the latter, regularities, causes, and effects. (Keane, Webb. "Affordances and reflexivity in ethical life: an ethnographic stance." *Anthropological Theory*, 14, no. 1, 2014, pp. 3–26)

In Part II of this book, scholars like Prasad and Moschella look at different situations in which they as scholars have witnessed or even been a part of situations in which naturalistic psychological, biological, linguistic drives to fear, to empathize, to defend, to abhor, and to flee have confronted normative laws, religious traditions, physical spaces, and cultural practices. Ethical affordances come between these two approaches and reasonings. If a chair affords us a chance to sit, does being a scholar of religion or theology afford students an expectation of understanding and care? Does the often conflict-laden and traumatic nature of the subject we study afford us the opportunity to comment critically on it politically, socially, or ethically? Exploring the concept of *sanmati* ("noble-mindedness," "goodwill," "wisdom"), Prasad offers three examples in modern India, where despite historical conflict and seemingly intractable differences between Muslims and Hindus, both ethical systems and highly particular situations afforded "imaginative" moments (not solutions) of ethical engagement and mutual care. Her chapter in this volume, "Sanmati, the Art of 'Generous Disposition,'" is the perfect example of ethical affordances in history. Moschella ("Suffering," this volume) reflects on her own position as a pastoral theologian in relation to both the discipline of religious studies and the academy more broadly as well as in situations in her pedagogy and in working with caregivers, whereby she developed an approach that afforded spaces for joy to emerge, not just a response to suffering. In this way, her work overlaps in interesting ways with positive psychology, which wants to complement the traditional focus of psychology on fixing pathologies and explaining psychological aberrations and "abnormalities" by looking at ways of cultivating well-being. In both cases, by promoting joy, they don't just develop therapies for pain. They ask, beyond the rational and the accepted, what do certain historical situations, certain instances of trauma, and certain moments of their professional work afford the scholar of religion and theology? What do they afford the people involved in the conflict or trauma? What situational solutions that go beyond the instinctual reactions and normative rules have emerged? What do particular, complex, and highly contingent historical and therapeutic moments afford? How have people been creative ethical agents in situations that afford, but that don't determine or demand, certain creative answers? How, despite psychological drives, cultural conditioning, legal frameworks, and deeply held beliefs, have humans in different situations simply "gotten along with" or learned to care for each other? How do people develop sophisticated regimes of care and spontaneous methods of repair? How have they learned to listen to others as well as to lecture in the areas of their expertise? Why have their positions as scholars often led to needs for them to be caregivers?

Samuels and McDaniel turn specifically to the classroom. In their experiences as teachers, like in Prasad and Moschella's experience as scholars, they have pushed the boundaries of what are considered normative pedagogical methods and have walked the thin line between teaching about religions and acknowledging students' need to find answers as they call out into the void. They look at the existential questions that students often bring up in class or office hours and the personal anxiety or trauma that they often bring into the classroom and library, and they wonder if there is a way that students can learn "from" religions. What does their positionality as a professor or expert afford, and what do the questions raised by the religious narratives, practices, and ethical stances that they teach afford? How can one teach religion while not acknowledging that the material taught affords certain ethical and existential moments of concern, of debate, and of wonder in the classroom? They explore alternative pedagogies that, in turn, create certain affordances, that don't deny the power of their subject matter, but that at the same time don't limit the types of student responses or solutions.

Conclusion

As you can see, as a group we failed at finding policies, specific methods, conceptual paradigms, and scholarly models that perfectly understand human flourishing and efficiently advance well-being. For many of us, we considered that a success in itself. Perhaps it is self-selective, perhaps natural, perhaps conditioned, but humanists, as a tribe, in the end, don't like to be confined or told to follow certain methods or "best practices." It causes us to lose out on (or not even to apply for) grants that seek outcomes and pathways. It causes us to be accused of not adequately training students for the "jobs of tomorrow" or of not living in the "real world." We are an impractical guild, it seems. However, we proudly operate in the interstitial (not liminal) spaces of emotions, creativity, disquiet, and reflection. We are concerned not only with how to make a person productive and successful but also with how to encourage them to be attentive, aware, empathetic, and respectful of the complexity and even fragility in themselves and others. We learned, though, that human flourishing, as conceived in the social sciences, including positive psychology, is not concerned with things that are wholly different from the concerns of theologians and religious studies scholars and that social scientists often practice as imprecise a craft as we do. Our methods, approaches, and optics might be different, but the care we have for others and our role as experts, caregivers, and teachers was certainly shared. We learned to listen, and in that act of engaged listening unintended consequences emerged. This joint project afforded us productive reflection and aporias. These aporias and affordances thus occasioned by our interactions made us deeply reflect on our roles as scholars, teachers, mentors, and humans who are concerned with the religious communities we study, the narratives, beliefs, and practices we elucidate, and the students we reach.

Works Cited

Keane, Webb. "Affordances and reflexivity in ethical life: an ethnographic stance." *Anthropological Theory* vol. 14, no. 1, 2014, pp. 3–26.

Marshall, Joey. "Are religious people happier, healthier? Our new global study explores this question." *Pew Research Center.* 31 Jan. 2019, https://www.pewresearch.org/fact-tank/2019/01/31/are-religious-people-happier-healthier-our-new-global-study-explo res-this-question/

Ngamaba, Kayonda H. "Are religious people happier than non-religious people?" *The Conversation.* 21 Feb. 2018, https://theconversation.com/are-religious-people-happ ier-than-non-religious-people-87394

McDaniel, Justin. *Architects of Buddhist Leisure.* U of Hawaii P, 2017.

Sun, Jessie. "Mindfulness in Context: A Historical Discourse Analysis." *Journal of Contemporary Buddhism*, vol. 15, no. 2, 2014, pp. 394-415. https://sites.lsa.umich.edu/webbkeane/wp-content/uploads/sites/128/2014/07/Affordances_reflexivity.pdf.

PART I

APORIAS

Defining and Debating Religious Studies, Theology, and Positive Psychology

1

Sometimes a Little Pessimism
Is Good for the Soul

Human Flourishing and a Plea for Complexity

Pamela Cooper-White

Introduction

The overlapping fields of "psychology and religion" and "pastoral[1] theology and psychology" have long grappled with identifying and cultivating religious beliefs and practices related to existential meaning, purpose, goodness, and human flourishing.[2] Many modern theological movements would maintain that work toward peace with justice and an inductive approach to constructive theology that is grounded in human experience and that emphasizes healing for suffering are central to both the living out of the Jewish Torah and the Christian Gospel. While human flourishing is clearly the eschatological vision for theology, many contemporary theologians would reject an overfocus on well-being as a kind of "prosperity Gospel" that is shorn of its roots in its attempts to address suffering and injustice.

In this chapter, I will present reflections on positive psychology from three interdisciplinary strands that have all had an influence on contemporary pastoral theology—with a plea from our field for holding onto complexity in the exploration of human flourishing: (1) liberation theology and a focus on social justice and the healing of oppression, (2) psychoanalytic theory, drawing on Freud's essay "On Transience" and Melanie Klein's theories on splitting, reparation, and gratitude, and (3) a related appeal to the tragic dimension in postmodern theology, theodicy, and the problem of evil. Given that each

---

[1] The term *pastoral* in relation to care and psychotherapy was defined by the famous midcentury theologian Paul Tillich as "a helping encounter in the dimension of ultimate concern" (22)—a definition that stands up to contemporary expansions of spiritual care into multi-faith and secular arenas.

[2] For examples from the field of pastoral theology, see Scheib; McClure; Doehring.

Pamela Cooper-White, *Sometimes a Little Pessimism Is Good for the Soul* In: *Religious Studies, Theology, and Human Flourishing*. Edited by: Justin Thomas McDaniel and Hector Kilgoe, Oxford University Press.
© Oxford University Press 2024. DOI: 10.1093/oso/9780197658338.003.0002

of these areas represents a discipline with a vast literature of its own, these sections will necessarily be gestures and not fully developed arguments. I am most interested in the points at which these areas intersect and together perhaps offer a pastoral psychology and theology that is neither captive to an unceasing focus on misery nor captive to a version of personal "happiness" that is simplistic or solipsistic. Happiness and hope are not the same things (just as my colleague Mary Clark Moschella[3] has amply described how happiness and joy are not the same things either)—in fact, happiness and hope may appear to be quite contradictory in certain times and places. I will conclude with reflections on realistic grounds for hope and a definition of human flourishing that is both contextual (transcending individualism) and paradoxical (transcending "mere" happiness).

Critical Theory and Liberation Theology: Virtues or Vision?

Pastoral theology has been profoundly influenced by feminist/Womanist (i.e., Black feminist), Latin American, and Black liberation theologies with their emphasis on social justice and oppression as the context for pastoral care and healing. More recently, postcolonial theory has also been an important influence,[4] as has the postmodern methodological turn toward linguistic analysis, particularly via "deconstruction" and the interrogation of dominant discourses (Derrida, Foucault, et al.). Liberation theology in particular, while not sharing Marx's atheism and view of religion as the opiate of the people, always poses the question from critical theory "Who benefits?" and, with it, the postcolonial question "Can the subaltern speak?"[5]

There are certain parallels that we might find in positive psychology's turn away from a clinical focus on psychopathology,[6] toward an investigation of what fosters psychological strengths, character, resilience, and flourishing (if not simply "happiness"). A strong theme of empowerment runs through pastoral theology, care, and counseling. Hope—especially framed theologically

---

[3] See Moschella 2011, "Calling," "Caring," and 2022. In the present volume, Moschella describes how joy is an embrace of divine goodness in oneself and in the created order. For another treatment of joy in pastoral theology, see also Son.

[4] See Lartey; and Nyengele.

[5] See Spivak.

[6] See Seligman and Csikszentmihalyi.

in relation to the hope of God's fulfillment of God's promise of redemption, wholeness, peace, and, yes, flourishing for all life—is the "eschatological" hope for all of this to occur in the "end of days"—sometimes referred to by Christian theologians as the "already/not yet" salvation of the world, already accomplished in God's eternal, timeless *kairos* time but not yet perceived or fully manifested in our daily time-bound *chronos* time.

Far from being a pie-in-the-sky belief in an apocalyptic "rapture," this eschatological hope has been framed by twentieth-century postwar political theologians, notably Jürgen Moltmann,[7] as a catalyst or missional goad to participate and "live into" God's Realm ("Kingdom") in the present time, by working for justice as God's partners in the world. For Moltmann, hope is not equated with optimism. It is, in fact, mobilized by a quite negative if not fully pessimistic postwar view of the world—a political analysis that draws on the Gospel narratives of Jesus's proclamation of the "kingdom of God" as a vision of divine overturning of the political and religious hierarchies of the world as it is and as an announcement that quotes the Hebrew prophet Isaiah in saying, "The Spirit of the Lord is upon me, because he has anointed me to bring good news to the poor. He has sent me to proclaim release to the captives and recovery of sight to the blind, to let the oppressed go free, to proclaim the year of the Lord's favor,"[8] and putting this proclamation in the present tense, "Today this scripture *has been* fulfilled in your hearing."[9]

The Gospels are saturated with narratives and parables in which the rich and powerful are cast down from their thrones and the poor are lifted up. Luke has Jesus's mother Mary sing the "Magnificat," a song of exultation of God's salvation of the poor and the downtrodden: "He has shown strength with his arm; he has scattered the proud in the thoughts of their hearts. He has brought down the powerful from their thrones, and lifted up the lowly; he has filled the hungry with good things, and sent the rich away empty."[10] Jesus's audience in ancient Palestine consisted of oppressed Jews under the thumb of Rome and an elite class of co-opted religious overseers; Moltmann's audience was academic, but his goal was the redirection of academic theology toward the downtrodden poor in the West following World War II and the devastations of globalization.

---

[7] See Moltmann, *Theology, Trinity*, 1981, "Eschatology," *Crucified*.
[8] See Luke 4:18–19, 4:21. Luke records Jesus quoting Isaiah 61:1.
[9] See Luke 4:18–19, 4:21.
[10] See Luke 1:51–53.

Latin American liberation theologians declared that the Gospels point toward "God's preferential option for the poor,"[11] from a context in which roughly two percent of the population in countries like El Salvador and Nicaragua controlled sixty percent of the land and virtually all of the wealth.[12] Their declaration was simultaneously political and doctrinal, as they drew from Jesus's own revolutionary vision. They refused to "spiritualize" faith apart from works for justice, and their vision of the fulfillment of God's kingdom was not one of a mystified "by and by" but an earthly fulfillment in which human flourishing would be restored for all people, not just the privileged few. *Flourishing*, from this perspective, envisions *peace* in a muscular political sense, not at all a solipsistic or individualistic personal tranquility. In his landmark liberation theology text, *Doing Theology in a Revolutionary Situation*, Jose Miguez Bonino writes that

> the biblical and ecclesiastical tradition . . . [has] given rise to two different understandings of peace. . . . The first one equates peace with order, lack of conflict, harmonious integration—one would almost say "ecological balance in nature and society." . . . It dominates the Greco-Roman conception of peace and has shaped the theological tradition since Augustine. The other view of peace is typically represented by the prophets but can be shown, I think, to be the predominant one in the Bible. Peace is a dynamic process through which justice is established amid the tensions of history. The Catholic Latin American Conference of Bishops at Medellín (1968) has summarized well this view of peace as a work of justice, an ever renewed task, and a fruit of active love.[13]

Philosopher and public theologian Cornel West sums this up, from a Black liberationist point of view, as "revolutionary love": "Justice is what love looks like in public, just like tenderness is what love feels like in private."[14]

So in addressing human flourishing from a liberation theology perspective, pastoral theologians would always insist upon a continual focus on context and the social, political, and economic facts on the ground that shape—and also misshape—individual well-being. Drawing on biblical sources as well as contemporary theologians' work, pastoral theologians

---

[11] See Gutierrez, *Theology* xxvi.
[12] See Fitzgerald; Goodsell.
[13] See Jose Miguez Bonino 116.
[14] See West, "Justice."

most often would understand well-being—as did Jesus and the Hebrew prophets before him—as more communal than individualistic. Virtue in this Judeo-Christian model would follow the ancient Hebrew emphasis on justice and "loving your neighbor as yourself,"[15] not as it has so often been reduced in popular platitudes about individuals being nice to other individuals but rather as working for the communal good of *all* others or, in the Hebrew, *tikkun 'olam* ("the mending of creation").

Pastoral psychology and theology, like positive psychology, has largely moved away from a clinical focus on individual pathology (although those of us who are therapists still recognize the ways in which psychopathology can not only distort and disrupt individual lives and intimate relationships but also infect entire communities and even national discourses). This has important implications for a pastoral care and counseling model that emphasizes the strengths of persons and resilience in the midst of oppression and conflict. At the same time, pastoral theology, following the ancient Hebrew prophetic roots of the Judeo-Christian tradition at least as much as it does the later incursion of Greco-Roman thought in the New Testament, emphasizes the importance of political and communal context. The published writings of pastoral theologians, especially from so-called mainline (i.e., liberal) Protestant seminaries and divinity schools in the last decade, have offered important critical perspectives on pastoral praxis from what had traditionally been the margins of both the academy and the church.

To put this in direct dialogue with positive psychology and its assertion that the good life also entails morality,[16] the positive emotions, engagement, relationships, meaning, and accomplishment (PERMA) model of positive psychology[17] developed by Seligman and his colleagues harks back to the "virtue ethics" of the ancient Greeks, which emphasized personal character building as the foundation of *eudaemonia* ("the good life"). Retrieving this longstanding approach to ethics, positive psychologists identify six core virtues: courage, justice, humanity, temperance, transcendence, and wisdom.[18] This is certainly also a long tradition within Christianity, tracing back through Aquinas to Aristotle himself, and it is expressed in the notion of the "cardinal virtues" and the "seven deadly sins." In the Hebrew Bible, the

---

[15] See Lev. 19:18; Matt. 22:37–40.

[16] See Peterson and Seligman.

[17] See Peterson and Seligman; Seligman; Pawelski 360. These are further divided into twenty-four "character strengths and virtues" by Peterson and Seligman.

[18] See Peterson and Seligman 36–40; cf. Moschella, 2011 3–4.

series of prescriptions for behavior in the Ten Commandments, and indeed, the whole notion of the Law itself, can be read as a parallel series of virtues to cultivate (e.g., faithfulness to God, parents, and spouse; honesty; peaceableness). But the Law can also be *mis*read according to modernist sensibilities as exclusively pertaining to individual virtues and norms for behavior. Shorn of its ancient communal roots, the Decalogue (or "Ten Commandments") can be viewed as a set of rules for individual conduct, but this is not true either to the context of the biblical texts or to Jesus's own interpretation of them in his attempt to restore communal practices of justice in his own Jewish community.

I do not dispute on any grounds—religious or psychological—the value of cultivating personal virtues. "Virtue ethics" counters an approach to ethics called *deontological*, from Greek δέον ("rule") meaning dutiful adherence to established rules as the guarantor of the Good. Virtue ethics recognizes the problem of competing goods that can arise by attempting to follow rules and to do one's duty, and it suggests that the cultivation of good character will allow for making better judgments when competing values come into play. However, virtue ethics itself has been critiqued in its turn for being self-centered, fuzzy on ethical norms and principles, and ignoring the role of luck in moral development.[19] And ancient Greek and Roman democracy depended as much upon the dutiful obedience of the *polis* as it did upon individualistic cultivation of virtue. The two went hand in hand.

This last critique of virtue ethics, having to do with luck, the circumstances of one's birth and the presence or lack of social supports to cultivate virtue, could be reframed again in terms of political and liberation theologians' insistence on the importance of *context*. To some extent, the utilitarian ethical premise of promoting the maximum "happiness" within whole groups rather than focusing on individuals[20] resonates with aspects of the turn in pastoral theology toward social and political context. Theologians, however, tend not to use the term *happiness*, favoring the promotion of activism for justice and flourishing for *all* people (and creatures and the planet). In contrast to deontological or virtue or utilitarianist ethics, theologians such as Moltmann, Dorothee Sölle, Bonino, James Cone, Delores Williams, and a host of other liberationist writers have emphasized the Gospel call for justice for the poor and the oppressed. These writers point to the eschatological future as the

---

[19] For a good overview of virtue ethics, its historical iterations, and its critics, see Athanassoulis.
[20] See Lambert et al. 311.

final authority of their moral vision. The "authority of the future"[21] becomes the guiding light for ethics, and the notion of the "good life" is widened to take in the perspective of flourishing for all life, not just the rich, the powerful, or even the "virtuous," as individually defined. Both rules or norms *and* virtues, in this teleological perspective, are derived from both the suffering and needs of the present time, from a wide-angle global lens, and from the longed-for vision of an end to suffering and the inauguration of God's reign on earth. Who gets to define that, on what grounds, certainly opens up another vast territory for debate as well as conflict. This theology stands as an important counterpoint to the dangers of solipsism that inhere in a purely virtue-ethics approach to the good life. And it is an important caveat against a spiritualized New Age pursuit of individual "bliss" without regard for the ways in which our North American lives are predicated on the exploitation of the unseen others in the world who labor to make our pleasure possible. As it is declared in a popular liberationist slogan from the '60s, "No one is free until we all are."

Psychoanalysis: Transient Beauty and the Beauty of Transience

A second perspective, foundational for the field of pastoral care and counseling and still a significant dialogue partner for some of us, particularly in its contemporary forms, is psychoanalysis. The study of the history of psychoanalysis and religion is also an ongoing area of research within the broader field of psychology of/and religion. Psychoanalysis is often regarded merely as a historical relic by scientific psychologists today—and I would agree that its therapeutic value lies not in its scientific method (in spite of Freud's insistence on this) but in its use as a hermeneutical tool for exploring meaning and generating metaphors and narratives that help interpret previously inscrutable patterns of relating, thinking, and responding to the world. Contemporary psychoanalysis has largely taken the postmodern turn of the humanities toward the suspicion of universal truth claims, and in the "relational psychoanalytic" paradigm, a constructivist view has prevailed over a scientific positivist one. The "truths" that emerge in the psychoanalytic consulting room are multiple, dynamic, mutable, and influenced by

[21] Russell 17.

the intersubjective dynamics of the therapeutic relationship—and we like it that way!

While academic psychology (ranging from cognitive science to neuro-psychology) tends to set Freud up as a straw man to argue against, there is a vibrant and even growing community of psychoanalysts who still operate with the foundational assumption (and perhaps this is the strongest point of agreement that remains among the various schools of psychoanalysis today) that there is such a thing (or such a mental process) as the unconscious—although the unconscious itself is now understood to be much more complex and mutable than was taught in classical analytic theory.[22] To quote relational analyst Jodie Messler Davies, relational theory

> has begun to conceive of self, indeed of mind itself, as a multiply organized, associationally linked network of parallel, coexistent, at times conflictual, systems of meaning and understanding. . . . Not one unconscious, not *the* unconscious, but *multiple* levels of consciousness and unconsciousness, in an ongoing state of interactive articulation.[23]

The basic adherence to the notion that consciousness is only the tip of the iceberg of all that a person "knows" or experiences, of course, brings with it the insistence that behind every assertion is at least one counter-assertion, and probably a bundle of them, some of which are too intolerable to admit into conscious awareness. The philosopher Paul Ricoeur coined the term *hermeneutics of suspicion*,[24] and indeed, that is always operating in the way that analysts think about the surfaces of things. Too vigorous a claim about anything, especially when exclaimed with emotional fervor, will send the nearest analyst to beat the bushes for its underlying opposite—the fervent are always suspected of "protesting too much." This of course would suggest that psychoanalysis is always the party pooper, the Grim Reaper standing in the corner of every room waiting to interpret our happiness away. Ricoeur himself in his later works cautioned that such a hermeneutics could itself become hegemonic, and he argued for holding suspicion in balance with possibility and only in proportion to the "false consciousness" that needs to be unmasked.[25] By the same token, positive psychology's deliberate turning

---

[22] For much more on this history as it relates to pastoral psychology, see Cooper-White, *Shared Wisdom*.

[23] See Davies 195, 197.

[24] See Ricoeur, "Philosophical Hermeneutics."

[25] See Scott-Baumann 62–70.

away from pathologizing, or looking for ugly truths behind every clinical phenomenon, is a critique well taken. Pathologizing can be an occupational hazard for clinical psychologists of all persuasions, who have been raised on one or another version of the *Diagnostic and Statistical Manual of Mental Disorders* and are looking for diagnoses under every rock.

It is also quite true that no one was more pessimistic than Freud himself was, especially after World War I and the growth of racial anti-Semitism, culminating in the horrors of the Holocaust. Yet, as Philip Rieff pointed out decades ago, there *is* a moralism in Freud—or in a slightly less critical vein, we might say, an implicit set of values for living.[26] All theory is value laden, and Freud's is no exception. For Freud, the injunction "Where ego was, id shall be" was a call to reason that could overcome the malignant social and political tyrannies of his time. Anna Freud and her generation of analysts were caught up in the activism of "Red Vienna," creating poly-clinics, kindergartens, and public housing. They saw psychoanalysis as a liberating force in a hidebound and repressive society. Their view from the margins of anti-Semitism also shaped their theorizing and their ethical sensibilities. Their marginalization created a psychic need to analyze what dark secrets lay beneath the human psyche—of which sex and aggression were perhaps the most powerful in nineteenth- and twentieth-century Vienna.[27]

Most surprising for many who are unfamiliar with the complexities of Freud's thinking, he also wrote about beauty and its preciousness in the midst of the inevitable decay of things. On a walk with the poet Rilke,[28] documented in his essay "On Transience," Freud was dismayed by the poet's despair.[29] Rilke was lamenting that such beauty in nature would eventually die. Freud, on the contrary, admonished the young poet to recognize that the very fragility of the flowers lent them their preciousness. Rilke's desire to defend against pessimism and to be optimistic could not withstand the "reality principle" that death comes to everything and everyone, and Rilke collapsed in depression. In contrast, Freud's capacity to affirm beauty and worth—precisely *because of* rather than in spite of its transience—allowed his self-avowed pessimism about infantile wishes for *perfect* pleasure to invoke something deeper—a modulated view that recognizes the tragedy of the limitations of life while profoundly respecting the love and beauty that

[26] See Rieff.
[27] See Cooper-White, *Old and Dirty Gods*.
[28] Rilke's identity, disguised in Freud's original essay, is discussed in Von Unwerth.
[29] See Freud.

remain. Freud's view here seems to invoke more hope in the end than does the poet Rilke's wishful thinking that could not withstand disillusionment—a hope that does not flee from despair but stands in full awareness of it and nevertheless proclaims the Good.

In Melanie Klein's elaboration of Freud's theory, the inner world or psyche is filled with contradictory representations, that are based on the mechanism of splitting (the primitive developmental state that Klein called the "paranoid-schizoid position"). In Klein's theory, external figures or events that are experienced as bad are unconsciously split off from good representations of the same figures in order to preserve those figures—especially those on whom the small child depends for survival. Both "I" and "others" are thus preserved in split-off forms—which can be either benevolent or persecutory. From a Kleinian point of view, then, the American "pursuit of happiness" without an accompanying acknowledgment of the tragic dimensions of life would be pure paranoid-schizoid pathology. Maturity, for Klein, would mean the capacity to hold good and bad together, to enact love through a desire for the reparation of what has been caused by the destructive drive rather than its denial and, in the words of her famous analysand D. W. Winnicott, to declare life to be "good enough."

Tragic Theology and the Problem of Evil: Happiness or Hope?

Finally, it is not possible from the perspective of theology to talk about the good without talking about the bad—that is, evil (and its ever-present companion, human sin). There have been two significantly different understandings of evil, *evil as negative* (in the sense of absence or lack) and *evil as positive* (in the sense of presence of agency and/or ontological status).[30] The negative view of evil has its origins in Augustine's concept of evil as *privatio boni* ("privation of the good"). For the mature Augustine, who started out from an opposite, dualistic point of view, as a Manichean, evil could not be accorded an active status in the cosmos because that would elevate it to the level of divinity.

---

[30] See Milbank. For more on theodicy and a theology of good and evil in relation to psychoanalytic theory and pastoral theology, see Cooper-White, " 'I Do Not.' "

As Augustine worked out his Christian theological doctrine, he came to insist upon the absolute original perfection and goodness of both God and creation. Evil, then, became in Augustine's theology not a countervailing force of badness but rather a lack or deficiency of good. For Augustine, evil had no place in God's original plan and was a human artifact. In the garden, Adam (we don't hear much about Eve in a positive light) was endowed with will, which was the perfect desire for God's perfect goodness and (borrowing from Plato) inexhaustible plenitude. The human creature was created to love God and with an innate capacity to apprehend the infinite. For Augustine, free will in its original, natural state meant the will, or desire, for the Good. But after the Fall (Adam's "original sin" in the Garden of Eden, eating fruit from the tree of the knowledge of good and evil), humans are prone to sin, which for Augustine meant the propensity to believe in the delusion of self-control and autonomous will.

According to classical Christian theology, then, humans can no longer perfectly discern what is good and perfect, although we are still able to desire the Good, but now this desire is not automatic but mediated by God's reparative gift of grace. Evil in this conceptualization is not an active force but rather a delusory self-reliance and a deficit or lack of the originally intended capacity to desire only that which truly (that is, infinitely) exists, God and all things pertaining to God's perfection—peace, love, perfect harmony. In this way, sin means that humans are prone to confuse lesser goods over greater goods (for example, to be able to choose a desperate act of risky behavior as the good of self-soothing but, at the same time, to miss the destructive consequences of the same behavior for one's own and another's health and security and thereby to tear at the fabric of community trust and accountability).

In this model, there is no positive—in the sense of active—force of evil. And unlike the ancient Greek view, the flesh was not a particular locus for evil. Both desire for the good, and sin, could originate in the passions of the flesh, depending largely on degree. Even something that is good—for example, the desire to procreate (a large stumbling block for Augustine!) or the desire for food—can, in excess become idolatrous, what Augustine termed (in one piquant translation), "the birdlime of concupiscence."[31] Evil "exists" in this model but not in an ontological sense. It exists as an absence, as a tear in the fabric of creation, or, as in the common explanation, as holes exist in Swiss cheese. Evil in the Augustinian model is emptiness, an absence or

[31] See Meilander 78.

nothingness, in which the desire for good is confused with what turns out only to be an illusion, a chimera, of self-possession.

A second prominent strand in both Christian and post-Christian theology frames evil in a very different way—not as a negation, as a privation of the good, but as a positive (in the sense of active and ontological) force in the universe that competes directly against God's goodness and seeks to undo it.[32] This is the *dualistic* view, the view most opposite to that of Augustine, which had its fullest flower in the Manichean doctrine of the patristic era (and in Catharism in the thirteenth century). Dualism has always been labeled as a heresy by the church, but nevertheless it is prominent in popular folk religion, pitting the Devil against God as cosmic forces competing for human souls. So we have the story of Martin Luther hurling his inkwell at the Devil as he lurked in his study. The idea of an Adversary to the good is certainly biblical, even if in the end of days it would not win out: "Be sober, be watchful. Your adversary the devil prowls around like a roaring lion, seeking someone to devour. Resist him, firm in your faith."[33]

A serious and scholarly contemporary conceptualization of evil as an active force has come from post-Holocaust theologians and modern and postmodern philosophers who contend that in the wake of the mass horrors of the twentieth century, we can no longer subscribe to a view of evil as merely the privation of the good. For many modern and postmodern philosophers, the category of "free will" is not a consequence of some primordial human error but rather intrinsic to the human condition. Ricoeur's idea of "fallible man" opens the way toward viewing the capacity for sin and evil as inherent in human existence.[34] Traces appear in Ricoeur of the idea that evil is not simply a "nothing" but a "something."[35] In *The Symbolism of Evil*, he states,

> Evil is not nothing; it is not a simple lack, a simple absence of order; it is the power of darkness; it is posited; in this sense it is something to be "taken away": "I am the Lamb of God who takes away the sins of the world," says the interior Master. . . . Evil comes to a man [*sic*] as the "outside" of freedom, as the other than itself in which freedom is taken captive. . . . This is the

---

[32] For the sake of concision, I am omitting discussion of another positive, or active, conception of evil, that of the second-century theologian Irenaeus, who viewed evil as an active force but one that is subsumed as a necessary part under God's plan as a means of perfecting an immature creation, a view also espoused in modern times by Hick.

[33] 1 Peter 5:8–9a.

[34] See Ricoeur, *Fallible Man*.

[35] See Ricoeur, *Symbolism* 146.

schema of seduction; it signifies that evil, although it is something that is brought about, is already there, enticing. . . . Evil is both something brought about now and something that is already there; to begin is to continue.[36]

Ricoeur's understanding is not strictly dualistic, however. Evil is always, for Ricoeur, subordinate to original goodness, neither symmetrical nor equal to it.[37] He writes, "However primordial badness may be, goodness is yet more primordial."[38]

Many traditional approaches to theology continue to point toward individuals' morality, and individuals' experiences of suffering—either through experiences of lack or active injury. In fact, a focus purely on individual pathology or sin, from either a psychological or theological perspective, can unwittingly collude with the invisibility and pervasiveness of corporate and political privilege and the ongoing perpetration of systemic evil that results in a *societal splitting* between those with access to power and those excluded from it. As trauma specialist Judith Herman has written, "Repression, dissociation, and denial are phenomena of social as well as individual consciousness."[39]

Feminist and Womanist writers' approach to the subject of evil has tended to de-emphasize classical arguments about the abstract nature of evil and individual sin and atonement and to focus much more on what Noddings calls "cultural evil." Noddings highlights women's experience of suffering and participating in evil through complicity with the cultural conditions of poverty, racism, war, and sexism.[40] Womanist theologians especially have highlighted the systemic, institutionalized aspects of evil.[41] Delores Williams redefines individual sin as participation in the larger social systems that devalue Black women's humanity through a process of devaluation and "invisibilization."[42] So, to return to the importance of context described in relation to liberation theology above, at least one reason, and perhaps the most profound reason, that evil *is* evil is that it not only destroys individuals intrapsychically, but it tears at the fabric of human relationship and confounds the human capacity for community.

---

[36] See Ricoeur, *Symbolism* 155.
[37] See Ricoeur, *Symbolism* 156.
[38] See Ricoeur, *Fallible Man* 45.
[39] See Herman 9.
[40] See Noddings 120–21.
[41] See Townes.
[42] See Williams 146.

A view of the complexity of the moral life incorporates what feminist theologian Wendy Farley has identified as the classical tragic components of human suffering: finitude, conflict, and fragility.[43] This is not to abandon responsibility—on the contrary, to quote another feminist theologian, Kristine Rankka,

> What a tragic view of reality and suffering might do, for example, is move one from self-blame or from the projection of responsibility to change things outside oneself to a more mature realization of one's own appropriate responsibility within a context of limitation and finitude.[44]

This resonates with Klein's "depressive position," in which the realities of good and bad can be held together in the mind. These "tragic" theologians relinquish, albeit with sadness, the possibility of perfection. They acknowledge the seeming inextricability of evil from the very fabric of the good and the ever-present reality of suffering, at least from this side of the eschaton.

Conclusion

We cannot avoid the reality of our vulnerability. As Judith Butler wrote in the aftermath of September 11, we are vulnerable. Our lives are always "precarious": "This is a condition, a condition of being laid bare from the start and with which we cannot argue."[45] It is through mutual mourning and recognition of our human vulnerability and contingency, rather than through denial, that Butler sees the possibility for nonviolence and ethical relating. Virtues and character are no doubt an important aspect of claiming the "good life." Yet this all-too-brief overview of several strands of thought that have informed the interdisciplinary field of pastoral theology and psychology demonstrates, I hope, that flourishing must take into consideration the "good life" of the many and not just the elite few who have either the luck or the leisure to take advantage of cultivating their character strengths. Nor as predominantly white, North American academics and clinicians is it our mission to evangelize for a definitive list of virtues to the so-called developing world—especially if we do not first listen to what persons from the

---

[43] See Farley 27–31; Rankka 174–81.
[44] See Rankka 196.
[45] See Butler 31. See also Adams.

Global South have to say to us about what the "good life" and human flourishing means to them and how they believe they might achieve it.[46] Pawelski
has made a good entrée into this expanded view with his concept of "fractal
flourishing[,] . ˑ. an ideal that holds out for the well-being of individuals *and*
groups, that values happiness in the short term *and* in the long term, and that
seeks approaches that work locally and globally."[47] Precisely how this might
be accomplished is a work in progress.[48]

With this chapter, I am making a plea to "complicate the categories" of
positive psychology—affirming the need to balance an overemphasis in the
past on diagnosing pathology at the expense of recognizing and supporting
strength, growth, and resilience but, at the same time, offering some of the
perspectives of pastoral psychology and theology in order to hold in mind
the importance of political, economic, and cultural context, of global suffering, and of the ways in which our own cultivation of virtuous "happiness" should not be exercised (however naively) at the expense of others.
Sometimes a little pessimism is good for the soul. Our work in psychology,
widely construed, is neither abstract argumentation about the nature of good
and evil nor clinical argumentation about what leads to individual happiness
or suffering, but compassionate solidarity with those who suffer beyond our
immediate sphere and concrete actions for justice and healing beyond the
scope of the self. As theologian Jürgen Moltmann has written, "the question
of theodicy is not a speculative question; it is a critical one[,] . . . the open
wound of life in this world."[49] However we decide to frame the questions of
good and evil or to approach the possibility of improvement in individuals'
capacity to relate 'lovingly and productively' (Freud's *lieben und arbeiten*),
our work must be communal as well as individual. It needs to hold together
the hope of *eudaemonia* with the inevitability of suffering in our personal
lives: "If suffering is not written into our life, it remains a constant interrup-
tion or intrusion. . . .In contrast, finding a place for suffering in our narratives
provides the suffering with meaning or, at a minimum, allows us to claim the
suffering as ours."[50] To reiterate, hope and optimism, or hope and happiness,
are not equivalent. Moltmann writes that "unless it apprehends the pain of

---

[46] One example from a pastoral theologian is found in Nyengele.
[47] See Pawelski 363, emphasis in original.
[48] For an earlier, strenuous critique of positive psychology and its lack of attention to issues of social justice and context, see Beier; Christopher and Hickinbottom.
[49] See Moltmann, *Trinity* 49.
[50] See Hall et al. 120.

the negative, Christian hope cannot be realistic and liberating."[51] Practical theologian Simon Kwan explains,

> Moltmann's theology of hope indicates that hope and hopelessness coexist dialectically. They are both contradictory and coexistent, both continuous and discontinuous. Hope and hopelessness have a close relationship, being mutually generating and subjugating, instead of excluding each other and never coexisting.[52]

Perhaps a shared goal of positive psychology and pastoral theology would be to foster *realistic grounds for hope,* and a definition of human flourishing that is both *contextual* (transcending individualism) and paradoxical or, in Moltmann's terminology, *dialectical* (transcending "mere" happiness). To quote Cornel West once more, "[D]espair and hope are inseparable. . . . [H]ope means wrestling with despair and doubt but never allowing them to have the last word."[53] If collaborative work as pastoral and clinical psychologists attends to both the individual and the social levels of *therapeuo*—therapeutics in the broadest sense—then we do have the potential, I believe, for participating together in the work of *tikkun 'olam.* By so doing, we can participate *positively* in the Good—if not the perfect, then at least the "good enough." And for this human lifetime, that, perhaps, will be enough.

Works Cited

Adams, J. P. "The Just Politics of Mourning and Judith Butler's *Precarious Life.*" Psychology, Culture and Religion Group. American Academy of Religion, Nov. 2008. Chicago, IL.

Athanassoulis, N. "Virtue Ethics." *Internet Encyclopedia of Philosophy,* https://www.iep. utm.edu/virtue/#SH4b. Accessed 24 Mar. 2018.

Beier, M. "'Always Look at the Bright Side of Life?': 'Positive' Psychology, Psychoanalysis, and Pastoral Theology." *Journal of Pastoral Theology,* vol. 24, no. 2, 2014, pp. 3–35.

Benjamin, Jessica. *Beyond Doer and Done-To.* Routledge, 2017.

---

[51] See Moltmann, *Crucified God* 5.

[52] See Kwan 65.

[53] See West, *Cornel West* 554. See also Beier 27–28, 35. Beier (3–28) offers an excellent comparative chart differentiating the views from positive psychology, psychoanalysis, and pastoral theology regarding optimism, wishful thinking, and hope. While I believe he oversimplifies the critique of positive psychology in this essay, his argument offers an excellent counterpoint from the view of psychoanalysis and pastoral theology, particularly in regard to social justice and the importance of cultural and sociopolitical context.

Benjamin, Jessica. *Shadow of the Other: Intersubjectivity and Gender in Psychoanalysis*. Routledge, 1997.

Bonino, Jose Miguez. *Doing Theology in a Revolutionary Situation*. Fortress Press, 1957.

Buber, Martin. *I and Thou*. Translated by W. Kaufman. Free Press, 1971.

Butler, Judith. *Precarious Life: The Powers of Mourning and Violence*. Verso, 2006.

Christopher, J. C., and S. Hickinbottom. "Positive Psychology, Ethnocentrism, and the Disguised Ideology of Individualism." *Theory and Psychology*, vol. 18, no. 5, 2008, pp. 563–89.

Cooper-White, Pamela. "'I Do not Do the Good I Want, but the Evil I Do not Want Is What I Do': Multiplicity—Good and Evil." *Braided Selves: Collected Essays on Multiplicity, God, and Persons*, Cascade Books, 2011, pp. 171–94.

Cooper-White, Pamela. *Old and Dirty Gods: Religion, Antisemitism, and the Origins of Psychoanalysis*. Routledge, 2017.

Cooper-White, Pamela. *Shared Wisdom: Use of the Self in Pastoral Care and Counseling*. Fortress Press, 2004.

Davies, J. M. "Multiple Perspectives on Multiplicity." *Psychoanalytic Dialogues*, vol. 8, no. 2, 1998, pp. 195–206.

Doehring, C. *The Practice of Pastoral Care: A Postmodern Approach*. 2nd ed., Westminster John Knox, 2015.

Farley, Wendy. *Tragic Vision and Divine Compassion: A Contemporary Theodicy*. Westminster John Knox, 1990.

Fitzgerald, E. V. K. "The Economics of the Revolution." *Nicaragua in Revolution*, edited by T. W. Walker, Praeger, 1982, pp. 203–21.

Freud, Sigmund. "On Transience." *Standard Edition of the Complete Works of Sigmund Freud*, edited by J. Strachey, vol. 14, 1957, pp. 303–08. Hogarth Press, London.

Goodsell, J. N. "Rich-Poor Gap Drives El Salvador toward Civil War." *Christian Science Monitor*, 25 Feb. 1980, https://www.csmonitor.com/1980/0225/022537.html.

Gutierrez, G. *A Theology of Liberation: History, Politics, and Salvation*. Orbis, 1988.

Hall, M. E. L., et al. "The Role of Suffering in Human Flourishing: Contributions from Positive Psychology, Theology, and Philosophy." *Journal of Psychology and Theology*, vol. 28, no. 2, 2010, pp. 111–21.

Herman, J. *Trauma and Recovery*. 2nd ed., Harvard UP, 1997.

Hick, J. *Evil and the God of Love*. 2nd ed., Harper and Row, 1978.

Klein, M. "Notes on Some Schizoid Mechanisms." *Envy and Gratitude and Other Works, 1946–1963*, edited by R. Money-Kyrle, Free Press, 1975, pp. 1–24.

Kwan, S. S. M. "Interrogating 'Hope'—the Pastoral Theology of Hope and Positive Psychology." *International Journal of Practical Theology*, vol. 14, 2010, pp. 47–67.

Lambert, L., et al. "Foundational Frameworks for Positive Psychology: Mapping Well-Being Orientations." *Canadian Psychology / Psychologie canadienne*, vol. 56, no. 3, 2015, pp. 311–21.

Lartey, E. *Postcolonializing God: An African Pastoral Theology*. SCM Press, 2015.

McClure, B. J. *Moving beyond Individualism in Pastoral Care and Counseling: Reflections on Theory, Theology, and Practice*. Cascade, 2010.

Meilander, Gilbert. "I Renounce the Devil and All His Ways." *Sin, Death, and the Devil*, edited by C. E. Braaten and R. W. Jenson, Eerdmans, 2000, pp. 76–93.

Milbank, John. "Evil: Negative or Positive?," Paddock Lectures, Oct. 2000, General Theological Seminary, New York.

Moltmann, J. *The Crucified God*. 1973. 40th anniversary ed., Fortress Press, 2015.

Moltmann, J. "Eschatology and Pastoral Care." *Dictionary of Pastoral Care and Counseling.* 2nd ed., edited by R. Hunter and N. Ramsay. Abingdon, 1995, pp. 360–62.

Moltmann, J. *Theology of Hope.* Translated by J. W. Leitch. Fortress Press, 1993a.

Moltmann, J. *Trinity and the Kingdom of God: The Doctrine of God.* London, SCM Press, 1981.

Moltmann, J. *The Trinity and the Kingdom.* Translated by M. Kohl, Fortress Press, 1993b.

Moschella, M. "Calling and Compassion: Elements of Joy in Lived Practices of Care." *Joy and Human Flourishing,* edited by M. Vold and J. E. Crisp, Augsburg Fortress, 2015, pp. 97–126.

Moschella, M. *Caring for Joy: Narrative, Theology, and Practice.* Brill, 2016.

Moschella, M. "Positive Psychology as a Resource for Pastoral Theology and Care: A Preliminary Assessment." *Journal of Pastoral Theology,* vol. 21, no. 1, 2011, pp. 5-1-5-16.

Noddings, N. *Women and Evil.* U of California P, 1989.

Nyengele, M. F. "Cultivating Ubuntu: An African Postcolonial Pastoral Theological Engagement with Positive Psychology." *Journal of Pastoral Theology,* vol. 24, no. 2, 2014, pp. 4-1-4-35.

Pawelski, James. "Defining the 'Positive' in Positive Psychology: Part II, a Normative Analysis." *Journal of Positive Psychology,* vol. 11, no. 4, 2015, pp. 357–65.

Peterson, C., and M. Seligman. *Character Strengths and Virtues: A Handbook and Classification.* Oxford UP, 2004.

Rankka, K. M. *Women and the Value of Suffering: An Aw(e)ful Rowing toward God.* Liturgical Press, 1998.

Ricoeur, Paul. *Fallible Man.* 2nd ed., translated by C. A. Kelbley, Fordham UP, 2011.

Ricoeur, Paul. "Philosophical Hermeneutics and Theological Hermeneutics: Ideology, Utopia, and Faith." *Protocol of the Colloquy of the Center for Hermeneutical Studies in Hellenistic and Modern Cultures,* edited by W. Wuellner, vol. 17, The Center, 1976, pp. 1–56. Originally published as a lecture, Nov. 1975.

Ricoeur, Paul. *The Symbolism of Evil.* Translated by E. Buchanan, Beacon Press, 1967.

Rieff, P. *Freud: The Mind of a Moralist.* 3rd ed., U of Chicago P, 1979.

Russell, L. *Household of Freedom: Authority in Feminist Theology.* Westminster John Knox, 1987.

Scheib, K. "All Shall Be Well: Flourishing and Well-Being in Positive Psychology and Feminist Narrative Pastoral Theology." *Journal of Pastoral Theology,* vol. 24, no. 2, 2014, pp. 2-1-2-17.

Scott-Bauman, Alison. *Ricoeur and the Hermeneutics of Suspicion.* Continuum, 2009.

Spivak, G. C. "Can the Subaltern Speak?" *Marxism and the Interpretation of Culture,* editors Cary Nelson and Lawrence Grossberg, U of Illinois P, 1988, pp. 271–313.

Seligman, M. E. P. *Flourish.* Free Press, 2011.

Seligman, M. E. P., and M. Csikszentmihalyi. "Positive Psychology: An Introduction." *American Psychologist,* vol. 55, no. 1, 2000, pp. 5–14.

Son, A. "Agents of Joy as a New Image of Pastoral Care." *Journal of Pastoral Theology,* vol. 18, no. 1, 2008, pp. 61–85.

Stern, D. B. *Partners in Thought: Working with Unformulated Experience.* Routledge, 2010.

Tillich, P. "The Theology of Pastoral Care." *Pastoral Psychology,* vol. 10, no. 7, 1959, pp. 21–26.

Townes, E., editor. *A Troubling in My Soul.* Orbis, 1997.

Von Unwerth, M. *Freud's Requiem.* Riverhead Books, 2005.

West, Cornel. *The Cornel West Reader*. Basic Civitas Books, 1999.

West, Cornel. "Justice Is What Love Looks Like in Public." *YouTube*, 17 Apr. 2011, Howard University, https://www.youtube.com/watch?v=nGqP7S_WO6o.

Williams, D. "A Womanist Perspective on Sin." *A Troubling in My Soul*, edited by E. Townes, 1997, pp. 130–49. Orbis Books

2

Disenchantment with Disenchantment

Or, Can Christian Theology yet Speak?

Ellen T. Charry

Framing a Conversation

Throat clearing is not a fun way to begin a conversation, but it is warranted in this case for two reasons. One is because the phrase "Christian theology" meets furrowed brows in academic circles. The other is because theology is opaque. Furrowed brows suggest skepticism at including Christian theology in a project on flourishing because secular thought associates it with languishing. Theology's opacity is also understandable because its late antique language is now incomprehensible. It sits in the dustbin of history because theology is now a foreign language. Here I argue that Christian theology can again become an instrument of flourishing and clarifying when we consider its claims on fresh terms and dust off its language.

Christian theology has been a leading interlocutor in the conversation about flourishing since its inception. Today however, its "positive" contribution among the arts and letters remains to be named. The assertion that "human culture should result in human flourishing" (Tay and Pawelski 2) is full-throated if it includes the moral formation that the arts and humanities (including theology) should offer.

This chapter opens with a rationale for having Christian theology in the Humanities and Human Flourishing Project at the University of Pennsylvania.[1] It next explains Christian theology and its contribution to the framing of the "positive humanities" in terms of its understanding of their role in promoting flourishing. It identifies modernity's disenchantment with transcendence as an impediment to human flourishing. Furthermore, it

---

[1] For more information about the Humanities and Human Flourishing Project, see the Series Editor's Foreword to this volume or visit www.humanitiesandhumanflourishing.org.

Ellen T. Charry, *Disenchantment with Disenchantment* In: *Religious Studies, Theology, and Human Flourishing*. Edited by: Justin Thomas McDaniel and Hector Kilgoe, Oxford University Press. © Oxford University Press 2024. DOI: 10.1093/oso/9780197658338.003.0003

discusses disenchantment with modernity and even with postmodernity and suggests terms on which transcendence may be reclaimed using a small but significant piece of standard Western Christian theology. Finally, it applies the method proposed to see how Christian theology could come to life, again facilitating both personal and societal flourishing.[2]

Why Theology?

The short answer to this question is because it cannot go away. That is because people need meaningful lives that offer comfort, hope, and guidance. All meaning-making offerings have their own *paideia* and structures for providing productive citizens with skills within their cultural or religio-cultural sphere. Because beliefs about how it is with the world and one's self in it power behavior, it is even more important to study them. To tend to theology is to help the philosophical, religious, and ideological traditions (including secularism) that it cares for to be as safe as possible.

Furthermore, it is not a courtesy to invite Christian theology to join in reflecting on the irrepressible interest in thriving since antiquity. Indeed, it is an insult, because Augustine of Hippo effectively transmitted the Greek philosophical heritage to the West as Christianity came into power. His first extant writing is "The Happy Life." He received it from ancient Western philosophy, Christianizing it for mass consumption. Ancient Greek philosophy in its late antique expressions shaped European civilization's understanding of reality until modernity. Within that, Augustine of Hippo shaped flourishing based on love.

All modalities of meaning can become deformed and abusive. I became interested in Christian theology precisely for that reason. I study it hoping to contribute to making it safer. I call my contribution to "shoring up" Christian theology strength-based theology. Like standard theology, its starting point is sinfulness, but it is differently oriented. Defect-based theology counsels humility as the way away from sinfulness. Its standard ethic is sacrificial self-giving (agapism), the moral life is a sort of zero-sum game of penitential self-sacrifice that expresses humility that pleases God. But humility can become not just a virtue but a virtuosity. I name my alternative Asherism. It

---

[2] For a complimentary approach explaining the role that Christian theology can play in supporting contemporary human flourishing, see Croasmun, "Discerning," this volume.

is a biblically grounded eudaemonism arguing that enhancing the common good upbuilds the self, which contributes to one's flourishing. To improve the common good is to self-enhance, not self-empty (Charry, *God*).[3]

To be honest, however, by some respects theology is not even counted among the humanities and should not be permitted in the academy.[4] That is a dangerous thought. It is precisely the academic study of religion and theology that gives religions a wider intellectual environment than that of a monastery (or its equivalent). It presses the devout to think new thoughts. Moving theology into the University of Paris in mid-twelfth century was done precisely for this end.

Christian theology, queen of the sciences in medieval Paris, is now at best the scullery maid of the humanities or is ousted from the kitchen altogether and considered rubbish that has been sitting too long and become malodorous. Driving disdain is that theology is a normative not a descriptive undertaking as are the social sciences that use empirical data. Being a normative enterprise can be disturbing to those who assume that normative intellectual claims are inherently oppressive because such claims tell people what they should think and how they should live.

Theology and the social sciences look in different directions. The social sciences crunch numbers in order to support or oppose political or public policy. The humanities are rapidly becoming social sciences. On its own terms, mediating literature, music, architecture, paintings, sculpture, language, and thought intends to shape beholders' tastes, interests, values, and even desires. In writing about poetry, H. D. Lewis puts it this way:

> [P]oetry has to do with reality . . . that is foreign and alien, in which we detect . . . a structure that belongs to the ideas themselves. . . . [In] this contact with reality as it impinges upon us from outside . . . we can touch and feel a solid reality which does not wholly dissolve itself into the conceptions of our own minds. It is . . . the revelation of something "wholly other" by which the inexpressible loneliness of thinking is broken and enriched. (154–55)

Lewis is pointing to an adventitious sphere of truth that is not of one's own making. Theology, like poetry, drama, architecture, and art, discloses a denser reality, a grammar below ground level. Discovering reality to be thicker than

---

[3] See also Charry, "Moral," "Academic Theology," *By the Renewing*, "Spiritual Formation."

[4] In my orientation to the doctoral program in the religion department at a secular university, one of the professors poked at us by saying that if we came to the religion department wanting to pray, we should go upstairs to the philosophy department! We took his warning seriously. Religion was to be examined, not practiced.

assumed reshapes those who meet it. Therefore, theology must be in any conversation on flourishing. Religion is ubiquitous and powerful outside the halls of secular academe.

Somewhat later, Paul Ricoeur directed Lewis's point to God:·"Naming God . . . is what the texts of my predilection do when they escape from their authors, their redactional setting, and their first audience, when they deploy their world, when they poetically manifest and thereby reveal a world we might inhabit" (Ricoeur 168). I would emend that to "that might inhabit us."

With the arts and other humanities, theology aims to strengthen one's grasp of the meaning and purpose of reality and one's self in it. The Deuteronomist, Zeno, Plato, and Aristotle are all theologians. In considering Christian theology in particular, a caveat must be registered. Ideologies and religions require supervision. They change and are changed over time. As cultural, geographic, social, and demographic conditions change, they adapt both intentionally and inadvertently. That requires a tradition's intellectuals to be the watchmen who tend both to adapting the heritage to changing circumstances and to offering its gifts to the wider society as appropriate. The introduction to *The Oxford Handbook of the Positive Humanities* points to theology as a humanistic discipline indirectly: "At the societal level, the arts and humanities can provide large groups of people with the shared meaning and common purpose necessary for collective thriving" (Tay and Pawelski 1).

Although religion, like ideology, can become malignant, it need not. In the Christian case, the need is for a dynamic and nuanced theological psychology that enables people to develop salutary habits of mind and virtuous social skills that can slowly eat untoward ones. The theory is that people will enjoy themselves as they become adept at enhancing their community's thriving. Successful living upbuilds one. This requires theology to examine itself and to make repairs as needed.

What Is Christian Theology?

Theology is an art in the humanist sense of the word.[5] It understands that information is processed through what Gadamer names a *Wirkungsgeschichtliches Bewusstsein* (an "effective historical consciousness"), which a reader of texts

---

[5] In the twentieth century, the Barthian school of theology treated the discipline as if it were a science in order to defend its right to a place in the modern research university. Other humanities disciplines did the same for themselves as well. That strategy has now faded, although the removal of theology from the university is still desired in some quarters.

brings to them. Before applying this to Christian theology, a caveat must be registered. Christianity reflects on human possibilities and limitations by assuming a flawed moral nature that cannot be fully eradicated but that with care can be modestly reshaped so that individuals become better examples of the species. The church is what Derrida calls an interpretive community. It offers communicable wisdom for "playing well with others." For Christian, Jews, and Muslims, one's horizon is shaped by their tradition's theological vision of reality before God and the place of humanity in it. Here is where Christian (Jewish and Islamic) theology deepen Gadamer's description of historical consciousness to include its moral conscience. Synagogue and church interpret "Am I my brother's keeper?" as a sword that should pierce every effective historical consciousness shaped by the Bible's plentiful testimony to moral ugliness. Genesis 4:9 aims to press people to control anger and jealousy and thereby to improve themselves and the common good.

Using a funnel-shaped image, in its broadest sense, theology interprets master construals of reality that locate one in them. More narrowly, it helps traditions and communities that are structured around cultural narratives help those who define themselves through them navigate their lives adeptly, so that they and the communities to which they contribute might flourish. Specifically, Christian theology interprets God and the things of God to help the church help people know, love, and enjoy God by embedding themselves in the Christian story of God and "his" relationship with humanity.

God, referring to the God of biblical Israel, has always been an ambiguous word, and fortunately no decision ever prevailed that ruled out others. Several lament psalms are unsure of what *God* means because the speakers scratch scorched earth looking for hope, so abandoned do they feel. The Nazis' victim, God, hanged on the gallows.[6]

Long before undeserved suffering gained a voice, Anselm of Canterbury (1033/4–109) taught that God is perfection personified. What can top that? In a Platonic framework, perfection was specified as being univocally good, having absolute power and knowledge, being spatially and temporally illimitable and immutable. In an age in which perfection may be even less comprehensible than God is, the divine attributes of perfection may seem fantastical. They had a long shelf life because locating perfection is both desired and feared.

---

[6] The allusion here is to Elie Wiesel, *Night* 71.

A complementary suggestion comes from Albert the Great (ca. 1200–80) who defined God through the transcendent categories singularity, goodness, and truth. Others add beauty. Augustine emphasized sagacity. The constituent relationships among the transcendentals are like facets of a diamond. God is the reification of truth that is wise, truth that is good, truth that is beautiful. It is wisdom that is true, wisdom that is good, wisdom that is beautiful. It is goodness that is true, goodness that is wise, goodness that is beautiful. It is beauty that is true, beauty that is wise, beauty that is good. Or one might say that goodness is truly beautiful and wise, or that beauty is truly good and wise, that the truth is wise, beautiful, and good, and that wisdom is truly good and beautiful. The transcendentals are rich fare. Discovering them opens a new and unique way of being in the world. It is living through refreshed eyes. John 9 speaks of restoring sight to the blind. They are everyone.

Plato, of course, pointed us to the transcendentals, but his theory of the forms confused his readers into thinking that in addition to being real they exist in some immaterial place. I agree that the transcendentals are real, but they do not exist apart from experiencing them as the arts and humanities help disclose them. That they are sharable demonstrates their truth, because people can bond with one another in exciting ways, which impresses God's reality on us. The transcendentals happen adventitiously and momentarily. When they impress themselves and we internalize them, they may be said to exist in us. Perhaps we might say that they are eternal in the sense that another art form or experience may disclose another example of beauty or sapience. In this regard, it is more accurate to say that God happens by expanding our enjoyment rather than that God is.

If, previously, Christian adherence was on intellectual grounds, here the moral dimension of enjoying God enters the Christian bloodstream. The transcendentals are powerful both because they carry the imagination into the interstices of the cosmos in unanticipated ways and because they invite one to become them. Stated invitingly, the transcendentals lure mind and emotions to their doorstep. Wanting to know, love, and enjoy God is truly wanting to be beautiful, sapient, and good. As Psalm 29:2 puts it, "[W]orship the Lord in the beauty of holiness." Here is divine revelation. It is not a text or an individual—although Jews claim it in the Exodus and Christians claim it in and through Jesus of Nazareth—but reality itself appears quite serendipitously even though life is "red in tooth and claw" (Tennyson, "In Memoriam" canto 56). God can just as easily vanish. The challenge of Psalm 29:2, indeed of the entire Psalter, is to hold on to such experiences of God, to share them with others, and to organize oneself around them. Augustine put it this way:

How shall I call upon my God, my God and Lord? Surely when I call on him, I am calling on him to come into me. But what place is there in me where my God can enter into me? "God made heaven and earth" (Gen. 1:1). Where may he come into me? Lord my God, is there room in me which can contain you? Can heaven and earth, which you have made and in which you have made me, contain you? Without you, whatever exists would not exist. Then can what exists contain you? I also have being. So why do I request you to come to me when, unless you were within me, I would have no being at all? . . . I would have no being, I would not have any existence, unless you were in me. Or rather, I would have no being if I were not in you "of whom are all things, through whom are all things, in whom are all things" (Rom. 11:36). Even so, Lord, even so. How can I call on you to come if I am already in you? Or where can you come from so as to be in me? . . . What has anyone achieved in words when he speaks about you? Yet woe to those who are silent about you because, though loquacious with verbosity, they have nothing to say (Augustine 3, 4, 5).

Karl Barth called God the "wholly other" precisely to forestall Augustine's desire—to be entered by God. Yet Barth's warning is valuable. To be entered by God in the sense of becoming the transcendentals, to become God in this sense, one must assume that God is an "other" made accessible as a gift. Here the holy other both enters an unsuspecting beholder and beckons her into itself. This is but one example of the words that that malodorous old rubbish is trying to speak, but they are gobbledygook in a world unplugged from transcendence. Secularism abandoned an enchanted universe that Lewis and Ricoeur assume and that the arts and other humanities were designed to disclose. From this perspective, artists who disclose themselves instead of the transcendentals have either abandoned their post or have untowardly mistaken themselves for God as understood here. Lewis understands theology better than he knows even as he, along with so many others, dismisses it as smelly rubbish. Listen:

The very soul of art is . . . to make us see things as we have never seen them before, see the familiar for the first time. . . . All things are made new in art, they are made for the first time, they count for their own sake instead of being pointers by which we move about in our own orbit. . . . There is a feeling of wonder, an inexpressible delight in being alive. . . . The light in a picture . . . must make us see what we could not normally see . . . by making us aware of the familiar as we are not normally aware. There must be a miracle. (155)

Shaping oneself through such miracles is to become the "new creation" that Paul enticed his pagan targets into (2 Cor. 5:17).

Neither Anselm's nor Albert's definition of God accounts for evil, however. That poses a problem for Christianity, and theology has struggled mightily with it refusing to acknowledge evil either as a divine property or as a divine creation that would unseat the transcendentals. The Bible depicts God anthropomorphically, but post-biblical Christian theology insists that God *in se* is not a person but confoundingly became one for a short time to rescue humanity from itself by carrying it to himself that humanity might become truly beautiful, sagacious, and good. The church names this divine transformative operation *salvation*.

Salus (as in *salute* and *salutation*) means 'health' or 'well-being.' Christianity's goal is to enable people to become spiritually and morally healthy when ravished by the splendorous goodness that is the truth that God is and by wanting to become it. Here is the naked desire for God that has eluded many modern seekers. Christianity holds that having God completely in this life is not possible. But journeying into the transcendentals to the extent that one can is celebration of self whereby they, personified as God, celebrate being enjoyed by creatures. This is positive theology.

To enact this, the Christian narrative wraps around posthumous reports about an untutored radical Nazarene who itinerated around the Galilee warning people of an impending terrible Day of the Lord that would divide the righteous from the impious. The reports consider those who follow Jesus as godly and those who do not as ungodly, disobedient. Jesus confused people. Some thought him a charlatan, but others read him as sent by the God of Israel. Some understandably expected him to rescue them from Roman military occupation. Others believed that he was a miracle worker who could heal the sick and raise the dead. Others were grateful that he preached repentance so that on the terrible Day of the Lord they would escape punishment.

He gathered a following among the restive Judean populace. The Romans, fearing that he was plotting an uprising against them, executed him. It may have prevented a bloodbath. But it did not crush his party, either. His followers did not organize a military offensive but organized around his life and teaching. They claimed that he was sent by God and that his death was not final but that he was resurrected by God and returned to him. They believed that by following Jesus's teaching and believing that he did overcome death, they would, too.

Various reports about this Nazarene and the amazing stories about his message, miracles, execution, resurrection, and return to God merged into a powerful package of ideas, images, and possibilities that spread rapidly not among Judeans but among pagans who thus became worshippers of the God of Israel. Jesus was understood as carrying his followers to God as he went back to God after his resurrection. As the Gospel according to John implies, he was not only sent by God but was God!! He will dwell in those who adhere to him and his teaching by loving him and one another, and so they, too, will be in God. Three centuries later, Christian leaders voted that Jesus is God and, a century after that, that humanity is en-godded through him. The first Christian writer, Paul, taught that those who live according to Jesus's teachings and holiness experience life transformed unto godliness, the beautiful wisdom and goodness of God. To give this theology subsequent reflection is to facilitate finding one's way into the divine life through the story that formed around this Jewish artisan.

While the church uses the arts and humanities to evangelize to and to educate people, that is not theology's contribution to the self-understanding of the emerging positive humanities. It is rather that the arts and humanities are to lure people into a morally re-enchanted world where the transcendentals can reshape one's character and interests. Furthermore, theology encourages reflection on that reality beyond self and on what becoming it means for being in the world. In the case of the Christian transcendentals, theology grows that transformed self through spiritual exercises and practices that socialize novices into communities living from and through the Christian story.

The theological undertaking is one with the call of arts and humanities generally, as laid out in the introduction to *The Oxford Handbook of the Positive Humanities*. Seriously encountering them forms people through five psychological mechanisms: reflecting on one's habits, character, values or worldview; building new positive skills, competencies, and perspectives; being so immersed in the experiences given by these encounters that one loses oneself in them; taking on various roles and identities offered by the communities and cultures in which one becomes embedded; and being able to express one's growing identity in various ways and settings (Tay et al. 5–6). To sustain attention to the divine transcendentals is to meet another way of understanding the world whereby one finds oneself redefined through the intellectual, moral, or spiritual narratives of the community that lives through them or perhaps of a new community that one does not know. This is encountering an enchanted world.

Yet even beyond enchantment with God through the transcendentals discussed above, Augustine of Hippo spent decades urging people to enter the further truth that is God: love. Yet, having argued on behalf of theology within the humanities and particularly within the positive humanities, it is important to appreciate the disgrace of transcendence and the dismissal of the sacred.

Disenchantment with Disenchantment

Assigning transcendence to the dung heap of history and dismissing the sacred as an excrescence of ecclesiastical clericalism and European colonialism are understandable. Any attempt to reconsider them must take modernism and postmodernism seriously. It is not necessary to elaborate that history here, but the arguments on behalf of secular atheism are as cogent as they are arresting. The position taken here is that in the ardent desire to liberate humanity from a monstrous, punishing God and his ordained henchmen, something essential for human thriving has been lost. The arts and humanities can address that loss because when they produce true beauty, wise goodness, and good wisdom, something alluring hangs tantalizingly in the air after the show is over.

Transcendence and sacrality were banished along with God when religion was seen to be emotionally harmful and life inhibiting and its institutions as power hungry. Some consequences of the three religions that have descended from the biblical God are indeed ugly. At the time of this writing, the unpretty underside of Christianity continues to be exposed. Religious verve is certainly dangerous, but the fact of abuse is not conclusive. Theology's and religions' abuse of people indicts human self-promotion by those who interpret God and the things of God self-servingly. But religions have no monopoly on this. Ironically, harmful theology both betrays the calling of religions to promote human well-being and illustrates the significance of Christians being convinced of human sinfulness. Whether interpreters betray God is another question because all we know of God is through them. It seems to be a vicious circle.

The thought of reigniting interest in transcendence and the sacred begins from a doubly disenchanted world, then. The first wave of disenchantment came with the modern hoisting of secularized reason to the top of the intellectual flagpole. It displaced trust in tradition, authority, and the social structures built on them. Similarly, Watergate disenchanted trust in public leadership. In the case of religion, modernity shifted trust from God to reason, from the church to the university. Disenchantment with the ontotheological world posited by the Platonic and eventually the Aristotelian worlds was for the sake of intellectual, social, and political freedom. Reason was detached from God, who was disappeared by its modern scion that birthed modern science, advanced technology, and modern democracy. The power, presence, goodness, and knowledge of God were superseded by secularized reason that was untethered from the church's shackles.

High modernity's claim to universal reason's unlimited benefits and one of its most vaunted children, progress, held sway for two centuries as STEM ascended to privilege, honor, and power. Trust in secularized, reason-produced STEM yielded control of society to highly skilled elites who redefined and now control knowledge and access to institutions of government, the corporate sector, and education that enable them. Yet, even minds as taut as those of Marx, Feuerbach, Nietzsche, and Freud debunked God and the sacred in order to advance the quality of life in this world. That yielded the cynical hermeneutic of suspicion that eventually was used against those very institutions that various publics who were unable to benefit from their offerings relied upon.

Here is a second wave of disenchantment: suspicion of secularized reason.

Those disenchanted with both classical metaphysics and modernity's promises of a better life for everyone responded angrily to being marginalized or simply left out of the advantages of the STEM-dominated world. Women and racially marginalized groups responded with radical feminism and critical race theory. Recently, other left-out publics gravitated to angry alt-right ideologies and now confront left-leaning special interest groups at the cost of civility. Hope that a rising tide would float all boats failed. Being marginalized by forces that promised rescue from the margins is psychologically debilitating. Anger and cynicism take on a life of their own, leaving those left behind doubly burdened.

With trust in God demolished and trust in reason suspected of being a Trojan horse of sorts, the space between social institutions and personal identity has widened. Popular culture, powered by the desire for corporate profits, far outstrips the power of education to shape the young. Where once an alliance between educators and parents could be presupposed (the teacher is always right) there is now tension in some echelons between school and family and detachment in others.

Even when parents and teachers agree about a student's needs and abilities, they compete with pop culture and the peer group for their children's attention. With social supports weakening before the demand for shareholder profits, the formation of the young may be for sale. Children of divorce and blended families face additional stresses. These situations cry out for the arts and humanities to instantiate the healing power of the transcendentals.

Yet one additional constituency that is disenchanted with both classical metaphysics and universal reason proposed postmodernism. Classical metaphysics trusted texts, and modernity sought the mind(s) behind them. Mid-twentieth-century philosophers and literary critics suspected both and turned to interpreting texts, thereby upstaging both text (that classically held sway) and author (when modernity took over). Humanists themselves sought to construct meaning from the acts of reading and speaking. Not only were God and the sacred disappeared and universal reason suspected, but texts and their authors were marginalized by readers and by interpretive communities whose identity was formed from particular suspicious readings of texts and authors (Charry, "Literature"). A text means only what it is thought to mean. No reading can be discounted. Without criteria for adjudication, criticism itself becomes impossible. Only theories about criticism can be interlocutors.

While they disagree with one another substantially, Jürgen Habermas, Hans Georg Gadamer, Paul Ricoeur, Jacques Derrida, Wolfgang Iser, Stanley Fish, and Richard Kearney agree that the Platonic conviction of a "there" beyond empirical data is and always was a fantasy. The only "there" is here where one is. The problem they all struggle with becomes whether beauty, truth, goodness, and wisdom happen beyond my construal of them. That is can they be shared or is there only solipsism? If there is no goodness outside self or one's cultural group or religion but only "what is true for me" is real, communication is impossible and social cohesion a fantasy. On the textless, authorless, meaningless terms of postmodernity where competing interpreters only clash, there are no grounds to say *no* to Hitler. He was, after all democratically elected and took most of the German church and many intellectuals, including leading philosophers and theologians, with him. If the only there is here; it is only self-interest that defeated him and not the truth, beauty, goodness, and wisdom of God that powered the weapons deployed against him. The final sentence of Abraham Lincoln's famous Cooper Union address of 1860, reads, "Let us have faith that right makes might, and in that faith, let us, dare to do our duty as we understand it" (Lincoln 550).

If, then, the transcendentals can save us by binding us together in wise honesty and goodness—that is, if "God" is beyond any individual determination—on what terms do we encounter "him" and communicate within that truth? The question matters and becomes not whether the transcendentals exist apart from instances of them. That would only make Plato pristine again. The question is whether experiences of them are contagious. It is whether they create transcultural community. Can they be in Esperanto? If they are sharable and do create bonds of unity and community across master narratives (democracy, Islam, Christianity, Judaism, Buddhism) that enable the transcendentals to be disclosed in unfamiliar artistic, literary, and ritual forms in order to penetrate one's comfort zone, we escape selfism and detachment from God. It would be the death of the death of God. It would be a miracle.

Another angle of vision from which to view this suggestion for reclaiming God is that of the artists, theologians, composers, musicologists, dramatists, filmmakers, and performers who cannot be themselves, cannot do what they are called to do with their gifts if minds and emotions cannot ingest their insights and wisdom because deep cannot call to the deep (Ps. 42:7). If Blake does not pierce us by contrasting the innocence of "The Lamb" with the ferocity of "The Tyger," we live in a half-truth about ourselves. If Henry Ossawa Tanner's *Christ and His Mother Studying the Scriptures* does not teach parental devotion, our children are doomed. If Uriah Heep does not convict Dickens's readers of the transparency of their hypocritical "humbleness," we remain self-deluded. If insouciant men are not nailed by Janáček's *Jenůfa*, what will stop them from abusing the women they love and the children they sire? If Picasso's *Guernica* does not slow the race to war, people blind themselves to its reality. If Eli Wiesel's *Night* does not skewer sadism, what could? If Kurosawa's *Rashômon* does not undermine thinking that we alone know what happened, what might? If Sir Michael Tippet's *Child of Our Time* does not condemn racism and anti-Semitism in one great exhalation, hope for honor is banished. If Bach's six solo *Cello Suites* do not captivate the listener with its sonorousness, deafness has the last word. If Spike Lee's *Jungle Fever* does not confront viewers with their confused and conflicted racial, social, and sexual convictions, they are doomed to perpetuate them. If the incessantly pounding guillotine in Poulenc's *Dialogues des Carmelites* does not condemn the Reign of Terror, we are doomed to terrorize. If Bernstein's "Chichester Psalms" do not galvanize the young into hope for confronting the lust of the powerful, what is the hope for art? If artists cannot speak, God despairs of creation and mourns shut human eyes and ears.

When, however, an audience member is met by an alluring, unanticipated truth that hangs in the air after the performance concludes, artist and audience rejoice together although separated by centuries or miles. Here is Lewis again: "The light in a picture . . . must make us see what we could not normally see, not by superimposing something on the ordinary scene, but by making us aware of the familiar as we are not normally aware. There must be a miracle" (155). Lewis goes on:

> The genuine artist is never "true to life." . . . [H]e sees what is real, but not as we are normally aware of it. . . . [T]he rages or the sorrows in which he traffics, and the moods by which the *dramatis personae* of his world are shaken, are not those we normally experience. . . . [I]t is and it is really, but it has both these at a new power. (162)

The Original Psychologist

Concern for *felicitas* entered Christian thought with Augustine of Hippo. He wrote more than anyone before him and perhaps more than anyone after him. He drank from philosophy's eudemonic wells and the Christian Bible to father the Western Christianity that sustained civilization for a millennium.

He discusses *felicitas* and *beatitudo* frequently.[7] His earliest extant work is a dialogue among eight friends (including his brilliant mother) conducted over three days, as a birthday present to himself in November 386. *A Happy Life* (the same title as Seneca's earlier essay but of quite different orientation) presents themes that Augustine would rework throughout his four-decades-long career. In this early work, a blessed person is sagacious. Sagacity turns on a morally and spiritually nourished *psyche* who enjoys God.

---

[7] Charry, *God* ch. 2. See also Beierwaltes; Burt 1999, ch. 4.

To be spiritually mature is to gain the ability to love better as sagacious love slowly overcomes self-serving love. Loving better is loving another in ways that enhance her well-being. That requires seeing the other in her own terms not as an extension of or implement for one's own advancement. When one is able to meet another's needs and to enhance her flourishing, one's own flourishing is enhanced, and confidence in one's ability to strengthen others strengthens. The point is that one becomes sapient when stepping back from one's immediate interests and recognizing them as intimately tied with those of others. Yet one inadvertently advances one's proper self-interest by becoming adept at loving successfully:

> [T]wo things are required to make you happy: to wish well and to be able to do what you wish. . . . [T]he perversion should be avoided of a man choosing to be able to do what he wants and neglecting to what he ought, since the first thing he ought to have is a good will, and only after that great power or authority. The good will, of course, has to be cleansed of faults, because if a man is overpowered by these the result is that he wills badly, and then how can his will be good? So, it is right to desire power to be given to you now, but against your faults; men hardly ever want to be powerful in order to overpower these, they want it in order to overpower men. What does this mean but that truly speaking they are overpowered, and their overpowering of others is deceptive, and that they are not victors in truth but only in repute? Let a man will to be sagacious, will to be brave, will to be moderate, will to be just, and by all means let him want the power really to manage these things, and let him seek to be powerful in himself and in an odd way against himself for himself. (Augustine, *Trin* 357)[8]

Frederick Douglass's *Narrative of the Life of Frederick Douglass, an American Slave* exemplifies what Augustine and other theologians of his day were teaching. This historical narrative depicts a master beating a slave, Douglass's aunt. From this, some readers have thought that the master dishonored her. But the reverse is the case. The master abused her. He injured her body, but her honor and dignity are untouched. The slave owner conceded his dignity and honor literally by his own hands. For he seeks mastery over others when he should be seeking the dignity of self-mastery. Similarly, the dust jacket of

---

[8] In "Teaching," this volume, Noah Salomon draws on al-Ghazali to make similar points about the importance of the disciplining of the self. Salomon astutely asks whether human flourishing might be just as much a function of struggling against the self as it is one of bolstering it.

Elie Wiesel's *Night* reads, "For Wiesel, his monstrous degradation was having endured to the point of caring more for one more hour's or minute's survival than for all the other considerations in the world rolled together." Like the slave, Wiesel was traumatized, not degraded. The Nazis degraded themselves by mistaking might for right.

Augustine put the point clearly in the case of rape: "[S]o long as the [woman's] will remains steadfast and unshaken, nothing that anyone else does with the body or to the body—and that cannot be avoided by the person who suffers it without some sin on his own part—brings any blame to the one who undergoes it" (*City of God* 1.10.19). In the crucible of patriarchy, Augustine defended raped women against the Roman assumption that "she enjoyed it"! The victims are innocent. The men who abuse them degrade themselves. Augustine makes a proposal.

Augustine's Moral Psychology

Augustine inherited the notion of an internal private self and an external public self from the ancients. We present ourselves differently as circumstance warrants. The inner self may shift a bit over time or simply emerge more clearly with age, but a persistent personality and temperament endure. Augustine did not use the ancient medical theory of the four temperaments or humors (optimistic, gloomy, irascible, and unflappable). Rather, he proposed a single personality type that characterizes everyone. Lumping us all together as morally bruised ignores significant differences of course but has the advantage of binding people together who face a common plight.

Being a malefactor is the counterpart to being the *imago dei*. Augustine understood the importance of recognizing both features of human identity, one that energizes and one that cautions. The self is divided against itself, and each aspect struggles for control. It is one if not the most powerful of his lasting gifts. The goal of the internal struggle is self-mastery that the *imago* triumph. This is happiness.

Augustine did not expatiate on how to balance both aspects of the self in these terms, however. Rather he grapples with the problem of the divided self in his numerous discussions of happiness: what is it and how to achieve it. Happiness is knowing what you want and having it. The path to it is loving well—that is, loving things as is best for them. Loving some things and loving them well uplifts one while loving good things wrongly or loving things that should not be loved degrade one. In the cases of slavery, genocide, and rape, the perpetrators are enamored with power over others. They have the truth backward. They know not the transcendentals. *Caritas* is the salutary way of loving something for its own sake, not instrumentally. It is strengthening; *cupiditas* exposes one's worst self. For Augustine, the only thing worthy of being loved for its own sake is God because God cannot be snatched away by fortune or death. Banking on these breeds fear of loss and losing them brings grief (Babcock). Perhaps this is like the Buddhist opposition to craving that brings misery. Understanding God in terms of the transcendentals brings life to Augustine's insistence on loving only God and other things for God's sake.

Unfortunately, Augustinian psychology was not received in terms of this universal struggle between being in the divine image and being morally bruised but as bequeathing distinct categories of good and bad people to the Western church. It is one of the tragedies of Western Christian theology. But as the first to teach us to identify, explore, and develop the inner life, his gift endures.[9]

Healthy selves become genuinely happy as they become wholesome. At the same time, people are conflicted and confused as they wrestle with their better and worse tendencies.[10] Thriving depends on which way of loving predominates. Healthy selves love the right things and love them well. Unhealthy selves love the wrong things and love them inordinately or love the right things badly. He presented everyone as tilted toward unhealthy loving whereby both individuals and society flounder.

Society languishes because human love is torn, twisted, sick.[11] Disheartening as it is, everyone suffers from spiritual scoliosis. He concluded this from recalling himself as an adolescent and by observing infants screaming for attention. From this he posited that everyone is at least a tad egotistical and processed the observation using scriptural imagery. The biblical doctrine of creation teaches that everything is "very good." Yet Genesis 3

---

[9] Leroy S. Rouner asked a group of philosophers from various cultures and religions to answer the question "Is there a human nature?" No consensus emerged; each contributor wrote according to a specific subculture or agenda. It is another example of the modern discovery or invention of the isolated individual or community pursuing their self-interest. The jacket design by Juanita Dix captures it well. A black and white photograph of a forest in winter with very tall, slender trees and some snow on the ground is projected onto a black background. The top part of the photograph is cut into the shape of seven people whose heads and shoulders form the forest's canopy. The figures stand next to one another, joined below the shoulders.

[10] See also Hill 261.

[11] Augustine's psychological axiom and his principles, strategies, and tactics are analogous to the Buddhist axiom that suffering is caused by craving, to its path to alleviate it that is the eightfold path, and to the four noble truths.

confirmed what he saw in himself as an adolescent and in petulant babies. He concluded that although knowing what would ennoble them, Life (Eve) and Earth (Adam) succumb to shame themselves.[12]

Everyone is beset with at least a smidge of narcissism that needs to be carefully channeled. The way toward that begins with recognizing the problem. The thought that people are inherently imperfect is indigestible from a selfist perspective. For Augustine, the next step is realizing that one needs to wrap oneself around something larger and better than self. That may be evident to observers of strong narcissists, but modern psychology overruled Augustine's insistence on the ubiquity of narcissism (Lasch).

Narcissism is not readily recognized by those afflicted with it.[13] Those who try to point it out to the seriously impaired may only incur their ill will, as we saw with Donald Trump. The disorder impedes its recognition.[14] Augustine put that resistance in theological terms. Recognizing that one needs help and that help is available is a divine gift. It is a gift of wisdom. Even today, psychopharmacology has nothing to offer narcissists, even were they do recognize their need of it. Augustine concluded that the something larger and better than self can only be God. Any other option only plunges one into the deeper misery of seeking bad things powerfully and good things inadequately.

Classical Christianity, relying on Augustine's insistence that we reflect God (are the image of God or in the image of God), assumed that a conscience, the voice of God within, or the seed of religion that Freud named the superego is innate. But that is fading into history as it becomes evident to even the most casual observer that conscience and its corollary, contributing constructively to society, require socialization into a stable, healthy family and society that educates its citizens well. We are back to William Golding, who takes Augustine's position, which was forged as the Roman Empire was imploding and a new foundation for civilization was needed.

---

[12] This story is usually interpreted as being about disobedience. God gave a command, but they did not heed it. But an Augustinian read of it is better. The primal parents disgraced themselves when they could have honored themselves by trusting God. See 2 Peter 5:8–5:9a: "Be sober; be watchful. Your adversary the devil prowls around like a roaring lion looking for someone to devour."

[13] If another personal anecdote be permitted, two men have personally asked me if they are arrogant. It was true that they were, in both cases. Obviously, others had tried to help them to no avail. Neither understood what was being said. For a less anecdotal account, see Kay and Shipman.

[14] *Superbia* is Augustine's word of choice. It is often translated as 'pride,' but that is a dangerously confusing word because it tends to white out proper pride at being in the divine image. 'Vanity' is better.

Augustine advocates of seeking God because divine beauty, goodness, and wisdom reorient the mind to noble desires and pursuits that press one toward a fine way of being. The theocentric turn is to the truth that transcends self that one must now consider and locate oneself within or that unselfconsciously enters one and begins to take over. It is a radical re-orientation for a narcissist. Arrogance is blinding. Augustine's thousands of sermons were popular for their entertainment value, but that was not his intent. They must have hit some targets, however, because people were flocking to the baptismal font. He trained teachers to prepare inquirers for this mighty undertaking, because at that time, although it was legal, Christianity was consequential. Baptism was not undertaken promiscuously.

Augustine taught that *caritas* is the medicine for narcissism. It is proper love of God. I suggested that God personifies the transcendentals. As Augustine put it, " 'What is loved necessarily affects its love with something of itself': and the eternal, as the object loved, will tincture its love with eternity" (*De div quaest.* 35.2, qtd. in Babcock 56).

It took Augustine many years to get himself to the baptistry. He had shopped around and wanted to be sure that Christianity was both cogent and salutary. In pondering, he eventually confronted his own narcissism, in his case wanting to be recognized as the smartest person around (which he was). Realizing how difficult it is to recognize and admit one's need of help, he saw even that limited beginning as a gift of divine grace. A millennium later, Teresa of Avila spoke of this breakthrough as crossing the bridge sur-rounding the moat of the "interior castle" where one begins the inner journey to God. Personifying the transcendentals, God makes what we call a thera-peutic alliance with the patient. Augustine names this enabling grace. God enables the desire for himself that in turn enables the godward turn. Ricoeur spoke of it as "a world we might inhabit."

While this turn is necessary, it is not sufficient because transformation into a better self is long and arduous. On one hand, psychodynamic psy-chotherapy is needed. Self-scrutiny is key in the Christian life that has a six-week liturgical season dedicated to it. On the other hand, the church also provides cognitive behavioral therapy through a community of companions who can model what the patient wants to become. Its task is to mentor those who know that they can benefit from help. Augustine well understands that the reforming narcissist needs friends (not pals) who can mentor the patient as they take two steps forward and one back or perhaps one step forward and two back.[15] Most of this is now lost from the church that relinquished its psychological responsibilities to modern secular psychology.[16] It remains its own skeleton.

Languishing is remediable by learning to love well. Coming to want to learn to love well and to love all things well is the foundational transformation that Christian spirituality seeks. Loving God is the chief plank in Augustine's platform for happiness (Augustine, *Doc. Chr.* bk. 1). Although God is the only hugely enjoyable and utterly lovable "being," all creation is enjoyable and lovable for his sake, as noted previously. Creatures belong not to themselves but to God and flourish truly only as such where they are free to love others for the sake of their beauty, wisdom, and goodness. Although Augustine says that creatures are to be loved for God's sake, after Kant he is read as pitting loving God against loving creatures who should be loved for their own sake. But loving God for God's sake and loving creatures for their sake severs creatures from God and would horrify Augustine. To love creatures for God's sake is to love them in a way that enables them to actualize the transcendentals of which they are capable. That is the soteriology proposed here.

Not surprisingly, Augustine's primary tactic for implementing his strategy for loving well requires interpreting the Bible judiciously. And he knows quite well how daunting a task that is. The work in which this strategy is concentrated is that mentioned just above. *De doctrina Christiana* is his brilliant treatise on hermeneutics. Although he was not able to follow his own advice, he proposes that biblical texts be interpreted through the lens of love. The interpreter is to read the texts so that they teach loving well because it enables the beloved to enter and be entered by God. That may be by reading the texts to illustrate how God loves so that other readers (and unlettered hearers of his sermons) may do likewise. It may also be by putting his own readers into the text whereby interpretation shows them both that they are loved by God and how to love as God does. Interpreting Christian scripture in service of the transformation of society in late antiquity was the center of Augustine's thought throughout his career. The thrust of all his work is to have people do what he did: embed themselves in God so that they come to love themselves

---

[15] It is a central theme in one of his earliest works, *On Order*.

[16] During my tenure on the seminary admissions committee, therapists would occasionally refer patients to us hoping that it would be a therapeutic environment. But it is an academic institution.

wisely, well, and beautifully and to love others in the same way. Though it require tough love at times, it is nonetheless love.

Can Christian Theology yet Speak?

Being among the oldest of the *Geisteswissenshaften*, theology contributes to shaping sapient people and societies by offering a way of life that encourages becoming beautiful by loving adeptly. Granting that that has at times been un-artfully articulated, the church (excepting some forms of Protestantism) supports the arts in surrounding people with personalities and behaviors that will awaken and provide skills for the new creation that they can "taste and see that the Lord is good" (Ps. 34:8).

When introducing oneself at a social gathering, many will forward their vocational, national, or ethnic identity. For example, one might say, "I am a food service worker" or "I am a Bangladeshi" or "I am Hispanic." But they would hesitate to say, "I am in the image of God." Theological identity is in the rubbish bin. Yet further it would be considered rude, perhaps outlandish, to say "I am in the image of God, and you are, too." Self-identifying through one's vocational, national, or racial markers differentiates one from others. It presupposes the modern or postmodern self that is isolated from God. Such distinctions feed binary oppositions that can become power struggles.

Christians will hide their theological identity because locating themselves in the rubbish bin is thought to be not only divisive but embarrassing. Certainly, other aspects of one's religious identity such as "I believe that the angel Gabriel dictated the Qur'ān to Muhammed" or "I believe that Jesus Christ is the Son of God" or "I believe that my people are the chosen of God" certainly are divisive. But these beliefs make historical claims about events that are believed to have happened in time. Being in the image of God and being morally compromised, by contrast, are inclusive. They are assertions about how it is with humankind. They refer not to beliefs about historical events but to human identity as such.

Introducing oneself using one's theological identity does the opposite of introducing oneself with reference to historical events, nationality, or ethnicity. It unites rather than divides people.[17] Even though the phrase

---

[17] People often confuse "I am in the image" with "I am a child of God." They are quite distinct terms. The former is in that part of the Bible that Jews and Christians share. The latter is from Romans 8:14 in the Christian Bible that Jews and Christians do not share.

"image of God" is familiar only to those who know Genesis 1, they believe that it applies to everyone. The unity formed from being bound together in the divine image yet being fallen is the foundation of the church, certainly, but it binds all people together. Babcock, again: "In this love, far from finding others a threat or wishing to exclude them, [Augustine] wants as many as possible to join with him in desiring and enjoying wisdom. The more wisdom is loved in common, the more its lovers are linked in friendship (*Sol.* 1.13.22)" (57). These two sentences summarize the argument herein.

What then does naming theological identity call forth? It is the proper source of one's dignity. One honors oneself by living from and into that nobility. Scripture shared by Christians and Jews says that "God is merciful and gracious, slow to anger and abounding in steadfast love and faithfulness, keeping steadfast love for the thousandth generation, forgiving iniquity and transgression and sin" (Exod. 34:6–7a). Being in the divine image then is serious business. If God is even close to what Exodus claims, and if Genesis does locate all people in intimate relation to God, these biblical verses are one's deepest identity. Taking it and the implications and corollaries that follow therefrom seriously affects how one cares for self and others.

Although Muslims, Christians, and Jews do not share scripture, the Qur'ān teaches Muslims to embrace the prior Jewish and Christian revelations: "Say: 'We believe in God, and what has been sent down on us, and what been sent down on Abraham, and Ishmael, and Isaac, and Jacob, and the tribes and what was given to Moses, and Jesus, and the prophets from their Lord. We make no distinction between any of them, and to Him we submit'" (Sura 3:84, House of 'Imrān). If this verse rings in Muslim ears, both Genesis 1 and Exodus 34:6–7 holds meaning for Muslims, too. Jews, Christians, and Muslims comprise about sixty percent of the world's population.

Introducing oneself by saying "I am in the image of God, but I do not always live up to it well" is an Augustinian way of introducing oneself that invites friendship across traditions race, gender, sexuality, and so on. Inviting people to explore together the truth of knowing beauty, wisdom, and goodness through which one tries to live enables everyone to enhance their own and one another's well-being. Such friends will enable one another to become the people they truly want to be. As they grow in flourishing, enjoying one another as they go, God smiles.

Works Cited

Augustine. *City of God (Books 1–10)*. Translated by William Babcock, vol. 1, New City Press, 2012.

Augustine. *Confessions*. Translated by Henry Chadwick, Oxford UP, 1991.

Augustine. "The Happy Life." *Augustine of Hippo: Selected Writings*, edited and translated by Mary T. Clark, Paulist Press, 1984, pp. 165–93.

Augustine. *On Christian Teaching*. Oxford UP, 1997.

Augustine. *On Order*. Translated by Michael P. Foley, vol. 3, Yale UP, 2021.

Augustine. *The Trinity*. Translated by Edmund Hill, New City Press, 1991.

Babcock, William S. "Cupiditas and Caritas: The Early Augustine on Love and Human Fulfillment." *The Ethics of St. Augustine*, edited by William S. Babcock, Scholars Press, 1991, pp. 39–66.

Barnes, Jonathan. "Rhetoric and Poetics." *Cambridge Companion to Aristotle*, edited by Jonathan Barnes, Cambridge UP, 1995, pp. 259–85.

Beierwaltes, Werner. *Regio Beatitudinis: Augustine's Concept of Happiness*. Villanova UP, 1981.

Burt, Donald X. *Friendship and Society: An Introduction to Augustine's Practical Philosophy*. W.B. Eerdmans, 1999.

Charry, Ellen T. "Academic Theology in Pastoral Perspective." *Theology Today*, vol. L, no. 1, 1993, pp. 90–104.

Charry, Ellen T. *By the Renewing of Your Minds: The Pastoral Function of Christian Doctrine*. Oxford UP, 1997.

Charry, Ellen T. *God and the Art of Happiness*. Eerdmans, 2010.

Charry, Ellen T. "Literature as Scripture: Privileged Reading in Current Religious Reflection." *Soundings*, vol. 74, no. 1–2, 1991, pp. 65–99.

Charry, Ellen T. "The Moral Function of Doctrine." *Theology Today*, vol. 49, no. 1, 1992, pp. 31–45.

Charry, Ellen T. "Spiritual Formation by the Doctrine of the Trinity." *Theology Today*, vol. 54, no. 3, 1997, pp. 367–80.

Lasch, Christopher. *The Culture of Narcissism: American Life in an Age of Diminishing Expectations*. Warner Books, 1979.

Lewis, H. D. "On Poetic Truth." *Philosophy*, vol. 21, no. 79, 1946, pp. 147–66.

Ricoeur, Paul. "Naming God." *Rhetorical Invention and Religious Inquiry*, edited by Walter Jost and Wendy Olmsted, translated by David Pellauer, Yale UP, 2000, pp. 162–81. *JSTOR*, https://www.jstor.org/stable/j.ctt32bqqd.13.

Rouner, Leroy S., editor. *Is There a Human Nature?* U of Notre Dame P, 1997.

Tay, Louis, et al. "The Role of the Arts and Humanities in Human Flourishing: A Conceptual Model." *The Journal of Positive Psychology*, vol. 13, no. 3, May 2018, pp. 215–25. *EBSCOhost*, https://doi.org/10.1080/17439760.2017.1279207.

Tennyson, Alfred. "Canto 56." *Tennyson: In Memoriam,* edited by Susan Shatto and Marion Shaw, Oxford UP, 1982, pp. 79–80.

Wiesel, Elie. *Night*. Hill and Wang, 1960.

3

Discerning the Shape of Flourishing Life

Theology and the Humanities

Matthew Croasmun

Thinking about the relationship between Christian theology[1] and the university can have something of a "here we go again" feeling to it.[2] There are at least two stubborn sticking points that immediately come to mind. First, there is the issue of theology's normativity and the way it makes theology a misfit for religious studies, and if a misfit in religious studies, then a misfit within the humanities, and if a misfit in humanities, then a deposed queen without a place in the modern university. No doubt, there have been strategies for resolving the "problem" of theology's normativity. The primary strategy for the last century has been to suppress the normative dimension of theological reflection, transforming theology into a knowledge-generating discipline better suited to the modern research university and the ascendancy of the research ideal.[3] The subject matter of theology, in this mode, is no longer God and all things in relation to God but rather Christian thought and practice. The result, in the extreme, is to render Christian theology a parochially narrow subfield of religious studies. Suffice to say, this is an unsatisfactory solution for many theologians—and for their ecclesial audiences.[4] Alternatively, one could point out the universal scope of theological normativity for Christians

---

[1] I will regularly use the term *theology* to designate *Christian theology*, not because other religions' modes of reflection are unimportant to the questions being examined—indeed, they are central, as will be demonstrated in this chapter—but rather as a matter of expediency and in the knowledge that many other traditions choose not to use the term *theology* to describe their reflection inasmuch as the label can exert a "Christianizing" force on the conception of such reflection.

[2] McCutcheon 13. By way of situating myself, I should say that I come to this conversation with allegiances on all three "sides" of this debate: I received my PhD in what would traditionally be described as a "theological" discipline (New Testament studies) from a university department of religious studies, and my current post has me in a Christian theological research center (the Yale Center for Faith and Culture), though I do all of my teaching in an interdisciplinary humanities program in a pluralistic undergraduate college (Yale College).

[3] For the ascendancy of the research ideal, see Marsden 153; Kronman 91–136; Delbanco 67–101.

[4] Kathryn Tanner (200–02) assesses multiple attempts to work a compromise.

Matthew Croasmun, *Discerning the Shape of Flourishing Life* In: *Religious Studies, Theology, and Human Flourishing.* Edited by: Justin Thomas McDaniel and Hector Kilgoe, Oxford University Press. © Oxford University Press 2024. DOI: 10.1093/oso/9780197658338.003.0004

and, therefore, demand that Christian theological normative commitments serve as the foundation for the entire university. It's not hard to see why, while this might fit within a particularly Christian account of the university, it is a nonstarter in pluralistic institutions. So the problem persists.

Second, both theology and the humanities are facing legitimation crises. Much of theology's legitimation crisis within the university has to do with the "problem" of the fact of its normativity. But this is an intramural crisis that, as significant as it might be (and, given bureaucratic academic structures, intramural crises can quickly become *existential*), there is a broader legitimation crisis with theology's various publics, whether the church more narrowly or the reading public more broadly.[5] And this broader crisis wouldn't be solved even if theology were able to justify a seat on the humanities boat, for this vessel, too, is sinking. The humanities are also facing a legitimation crisis. Witness Rita Felski's litany of recent books that attempt to legitimate literary studies by trying to make a case that literary studies "matters."[6] The external questions about legitimation have arisen because the humanities no longer know their purpose. "The humanities disciplines are facing a crisis of rationale," argues Louis Menand. "They are institutionally insecure because they appear to have lost their philosophical roots."[7] This legitimation crisis has as much if not more to do with *teaching* than it does with research.[8] The public's perception of the legitimacy (or lack thereof) of the humanities hinges on its perception of the legitimacy (or lack thereof) of the pedagogical mission of the humanities, the core of liberal arts education.

Adding *human flourishing* to the mix might only seem to further muddy the water, but I want to argue that placing flourishing life[9] at the center of

---

[5] Both publics are a concern for Kathryn Tanner 199.

[6] Felski 14.

[7] Menand, 1. James Pawelski interacts more deeply with Felski and Menand in articulating the humanities' legitimation crisis.

[8] Menand argues that "research in the humanities is essentially a byproduct of the production of college teachers" (5). Granted, there are many points of overlap between pedagogical and research goals and ideals. Yet it is likely that the public legitimacy of humanities research hangs on the perception of humanities education. If the public understood what a humanities *education* has to offer, research that fits with that pedagogical mission would be received favorably in light of that mission.

[9] I will use *the good life, flourishing life,* and *human flourishing* somewhat interchangeably. Of these three, I have a preference for *flourishing life* inasmuch as it is less likely to be conflated with the images of revelry and conspicuous consumption that *the good life* can sometimes have in contemporary culture, and it wards off the potential anthropocentrism of *human flourishing*, a concern that I share with many humanist thinkers. (As far as I can tell, the term *human flourishing* in something akin to the sense in which I use it here was coined by Elizabeth Anscombe in her landmark essay "Modern Moral Philosophy." Ecofeminist thinkers like Chris J. Cuomo especially have emphasized the way that the language of flourishing could encompass the flourishing of individuals, human societies, environments, and nonhuman organisms. See for example Cuomo's Feminism and Ecological

Christian theology, religious studies, and the humanities solves these stubborn problems because the quest to *discern, articulate, and commend* flourishing life lies at the heart of all three.[10] In this light, Christian theology's normativity makes it not an outlier but rather a "standard" if undoubtedly *particular* humanistic discipline, one whose legacy of sturdy constructive normativity can help the humanities as a whole recover their raison d'être. Two things are required of theology for it to play this role. First, Christian theology itself must embrace its purpose to *discern, articulate, and commend* visions of flourishing in light of the life and teachings of Jesus Christ. Together, Miroslav Volf and I have argued this in our book, *For the Life of the World: Theology That Makes a Difference*, and sketched a path forward for theology to conceive of itself in this manner. Second, Christian theology must embrace its role as one of multiple particular discourses that articulate visions of flourishing life within the modern pluralistic university and, indeed, in the emerging pluralistic global society.

The careful reader will note that religious studies has begun to fall away from the picture. This is intentional. Religious studies has a crucial role to play in inquiry into human flourishing but not as the middle term between theology and the humanities nor as the intermediate "membrane" within which theology fits and is rendered acceptable to the broader humanistic project of the university. Indeed, there is a sense in which some modes of religious studies don't properly fit under the heading "humanities" but are rather a better fit in "social" or "human sciences."[11] This is all to say that theology, religious studies, and humanities are not a set of nesting dolls. Religious studies is an extraordinarily important resource for theology, both when religious studies is functioning as a mode of humanistic inquiry of the sort that Tyler Roberts writes about but also in its mode precisely *as* a human science, offering not normative visions of flourishing life but rather truthful

Communities. For humanists concerned about the anthropocentrism of the language of *human flourishing*, see Roberts 92–93).

[10] I find myself in agreement with the case that James Pawelski makes for the unifying role of human flourishing across the humanities and for a transformation of the humanities curriculum that is in line with the theoretical and practical importance of human flourishing in his Well-Being and Higher Education. See also Pawelski, "Positive Humanities."

[11] See Roberts, *Encountering* 89. Roberts places this conception of religious studies in contrast to the "humanistic study of religion" for which he advocates. However, religious studies need not shed these more third-person, descriptive, even "scientific" modes of inquiry in order to make room for humanistic work. There are, I take it, modes of religious studies that rightly *ought to be* "human sciences."

descriptions of the word. Christian theology in particular, given the centrality of the Christian faith's claims about historically contingent reality (chiefly, the incarnation), must be accountable to truthful accounts of the world as it actually is. But because theology in all its various forms is a field of humanistic inquiry, it will be most fruitful for the purposes of this chapter to focus just on theology and the humanities without the various complications that keeping religious studies in view would require.

This chapter, then, will first briefly review the current cultural state around the question of the shape of flourishing life, describing an opportunity for theology and the humanities to answer their legitimation crisis by embracing their (sometimes latent) normative impulses. Second, I will describe the key intellectual reframing that the humanities would need to undergo in order to orient themselves—and, in particular, their *teaching*—around the question of flourishing life in a way that is analogous to the reframing of theology that Volf and I have proposed. Finally, I will return to consider Christian theology's role as one among multiple distinct voices that are contesting the nature of flourishing life within the framework of a renewed conception of the humanities. Throughout, we will see theology and the humanities helping students and society as a whole learn to *discern* the *substance* of human flourishing—what it means for life to be led well, go well, and feel as it should.[12]

The Status of the Question of Flourishing Life

The question of the shape of flourishing life is pressing today in ways it has not previously been.[13] In ages past, a vision of flourishing life[14] was largely written into the conditions of lived lives—in the perceived givenness of the cosmic and social orders, in accepted rituals and traditions, in the ways in which communities engaged in the cultural, economic, and political reproduction of life. For a large and increasing portion of the world, this is

---

[12] For another perspective on how Christian theology can shed light on what human flourishing is and on how it can be fostered, see Charry, "Disenchantment," this volume.

[13] This section, as much of this chapter does, draws extensively on writing I have done with Miroslav Volf in For the Life of the World.

[14] "This, then, is what we mean by a vision of flourishing life: a set of explicit or implicit convictions about what it means for us to lead life well, for our life to go well, and feel right, convictions that guide—or should guide—all our desires and efforts, a sketch of human fullness and of a journey into it" (Volf and Croasmun, *For the Life* 16).

no longer the case. In cultures shaped by modernity, we have come to live "disembedded" lives.[15] Because we no longer see ourselves as constituents of a meaningful cosmos and parts of a social collective, meaning for us can no longer be "read off" of our social and cosmic locations. Visions of the good life that we once inherited we are now free to choose, construct, and/ or assemble from various available fragments with which we work.[16] More than this, we are *forced* to choose.[17] Even if one were to make the (increasingly uncommon) decision to adopt a vision of flourishing "off the shelf" from our favorite religious, philosophical, or cultural source, this would be a *choice* that we would have to make and one for which we would have to be responsible.

This choice is not a matter of choosing among more or less desirable objects but rather choosing to adopt "reflexive standards" by which we decide what kind of human it is worth being and what kind of world is worth inhabiting; in short, these are the standards by which we decide what it is that is truly *worth wanting*. This is the most important question of our lives, a question about which we can never become experts but which we have an inalienable responsibility to answer. All of us—our students, our neighbors, as much as ourselves—are in this situation together.

To be clear, the problem isn't just that collectively we're lacking *strategies* to realize the flourishing life, though often this problem is conceived of in precisely this way.[18] Rather, the problem is that we have lost the ability to reason *about* flourishing life, lost the ability to choose wisely among multiple competing visions of what flourishing life *is*. Better to have ineffective than effective strategies of achieving dubious ends, if we have no access to the sort of normative inquiry that would help us refine and, indeed, *change* our goals.

Yet just as the question of flourishing life is most pressing, reflection about this most important question is waning. Some of our most important schools of the good life—colleges and universities—have largely "given up on the meaning of life."[19] Rather than the normative inquiry demanded by the

---

15 Taylor 146–58.

16 Willie James Jennings's language of "fragment work" (23–46) has given me greater hope for the creativity of this work; we necessarily work in fragments and the fruit of this work needn't be demeaned as arbitrary "bricolage."

17 Peter Berger has described this choice as a "heretical imperative."

18 Indeed, Hartmut Rosa (6–7) has accurately described the way in which much of late modernity conspires to make the case that all we are lacking is the *means* to the good life—health, wealth, education, various forms of social capital, and so on—rather than the good life itself. Focusing on these means, we then confuse them for life's proper ends.

19 I borrow this phrase from the subtitle of Anthony Kronman's Education's End. While I find myself sympathetic to some of Kronman's diagnosis of the problem ("giving up on the meaning of life"),

question of flourishing life, our universities prize the incremental increase in the knowledge of the world and advances in technological know-how. These are the goods that STEM fields offer students; it is sometimes difficult to make the case that the humanities constitute a necessary component of *that education*—hence the crisis of legitimation. The result is that today's colleges and universities serve primarily to equip students with skills to be able to secure resources for any kind of life they may decide to live but offer little to no help in reflecting on the *nature of that life*, no tools for discerning and articulating what sort of life it is that is most worth living.

Given the crises of legitimation facing both theologians and humanists, scholars of both fields are incentivized to cast their disciplines primarily as providing knowledge and know-how. But this recasting is doubly doomed to failure: First, it has proven unlikely to succeed. The knowledge and know-how produced by the humanities is seen as having less immediate instrumental value in the world than that offered by the sciences. Second, even were this disguise to work, the "reward" that humanists and theologians would receive would be the privilege to contribute as equals to a vision of education that is failing our society on the most crucial question of our day. As it is, the humanities often contribute as second-class citizens to an education that with each passing day looks easier and easier to replace with technical training.

Renewal

Rather than chasing after new ways to legitimate themselves on terms foreign to their disciplines, theologians and humanists have an opportunity to solve their legitimation crises by reorienting their fields around discerning, articulating, and commending visions of flourishing life—what James Pawelski has called a "eudaimonic turn."[20] In both fields, the transformation

---

I do not see "multiculturalism" as a threat to taking up the meaning of life, perhaps because I am not at all convinced that the "Western" tradition has the best answers to life's big questions. Accordingly, our proposals also diverge in terms of whether to center the Western canon (I argue that we should not). And, of course, I'm inclined to think that theological visions of flourishing can and should be included in pluralistic conversations about flourishing (on this last point, see the discussion of CPUs in Volf and Croasmun 95–107.

[20] Pawelski, "Bringing" 209. The language of *eudaemonic turn* is adopted from Pawelski's use of the term in Pawelski and Moores.

would have primarily to do not with shifting the topics taken up but rather with transforming the prevailing thought style. That's not to say that there wouldn't be shifts in the topics that receive the most attention. Long-neglected topics like joy, hope, and resilience need to be examined—by theology and other humanistic disciplines—in light of holistic accounts of flourishing life.[21] Nevertheless, genuine transformation will come through three fundamental shifts in how the humanities understand themselves: moving beyond the mere negation of unending critique, embracing their normative dimension, and engaging a hermeneutics (and pedagogy) of encounter. These shifts are equally required for both theology and the humanities more broadly because they have to do centrally with making possible the sort of rigorous normative inquiry that each set of disciplines requires.

The crux of the matter is the hermeneutics of suspicion that is embedded in the ascendancy of critique in the contemporary humanities. By *critique*, I don't mean *criticism* in the generic sense of careful analysis but rather a particular intellectual posture that has taken tearing down an argument, breaking the aesthetic spell of a work of art, or unraveling a historical explanation to be the very pinnacle of intellectual achievement. I mean what Christopher Castiglia has called "critiquiness" and Felski has described as "an unmistakable blend of suspicion, self-confidence, and indignation."[22] This is a different problem than psychology's focus on pathology in the days before positive psychology. This isn't about a focus on negative content but rather a more fundamental difficulty: negativity as an undying opposition to all closure that would allow *any* normative assertion or, in the extreme, any assertion at all.[23] This disease both thwarts humanistic inquiry internally and also mars the humanities' reputation externally. When a training in critique is all that a humanistic education seems to be able to offer, it's not hard to see why the humanities have such poor public standing:

---

[21] Mary Clark Moschella ("Suffering," this volume) offers a sketch of her important work on joy of just this sort.

[22] Felski 187–88.

[23] Eagleton writes, "Politically speaking, this is a latently libertarian theory of the subject, which tends to 'demonize' the very act of semiotic closure. . . . It occasionally betrays an anarchic suspicion of meaning as such; and it falsely assumes that 'closure' is always counterproductive. But such closure is a provisional effect of any semiosis whatsoever, and may be politically enabling rather than constraining; 'Reclaim the night!' involves a semiotic and (in one sense of the term) ideological closure, but its political force lies precisely in this. . . . Whether such closure is politically positive or negative depends on the discursive and ideological context. . . . [A] certain provisional stability of identity is essential not only for psychical well-being but for revolutionary political agency" (197–98).

"Isn't this fabulous? Isn't it really worth going to graduate school to study critique? Enter here, you poor folks. After arduous years of reading turgid prose, you will be always right, you will never be taken in anymore; no one, no matter how powerful, will be able to accuse you of naïveté, that supreme sin, any longer? Better equipped than Zeus himself you rule alone, striking from above with the salvo of antifetishism in one hand and the solid causality of objectivity in the other." The only loser is the naïve believer, the great unwashed, always caught off balance. Is it so surprising, after all, that with such positions given to the object, the humanities have lost the hearts of their fellow citizens, that they had to retreat year after year, entrenching themselves always further in the narrow barracks left to them by more and more stingy deans? The Zeus of Critique rules absolutely, to be sure, but over a desert.[24]

What Latour describes might be called a *pedagogy of negation*. His depiction, of course, is intended to make us recoil. Yet we should pause and consider also the "goods" that Latour notes the pedagogy of negation offers to students and teachers alike. Principally, it offers *power*. The one who can effectively wield the weapon of critique can win just about any intellectual battle. As master of critique, the instructor has power not just over the texts on the table but also over the students. Inasmuch as critique so often turns on insights drawn from obscure historical, cultural, or theoretical insights known only to experts (it is, in this sense, the logical extension of what Frank Kermode has called the interpreter's commitment to the "superiority of latent over manifest sense"[25]), critique only heightens the power arrogated to the instructor in her role as *expert*.[26] The result of this power is security. In academic institutions that so often run on the anxious energy of students and faculty alike who are trying adequately to perform what Willie Jennings calls institutionally normative "white, self-sufficient masculinity," critique offers a weapon to wield in self-defense.[27] The greatest tragedy is that critique often

[24] Latour 239.

[25] Kermode writes, "Interpreters usually belong to an institution, such a guild as heralds, toastmasters, thieves, and merchants have been known to form; and as members they enjoy certain privileges and suffer certain constraints. Perhaps the most important of these are the right to affirm, and the obligation to accept, the superiority of latent over manifest sense. It is a preference of great antiquity, though we recognize it as modern when we see it in its Freudian form" (2).

[26] For discussion of the instructor's self-conception as an expert and the (dangerous) power that this posture grants in the classroom, see Palmer 34–40.

[27] On the language of "white, self-sufficient masculinity," see Jennings 6. For the ways that critique contributes ironically to the reinforcement of this ideal, see Jennings's discussion of "emancipatory formation" (108).

succeeds in its tasks. In the extreme, the classroom becomes a place for thickening one's defenses against any and all challenges—proving oneself as the idealized white, self-sufficient, masculine subject.

The result of the absolute rule of critique—when and where it reigns—is a complete loss of the humanities' natural normativity,[28] for it is here where critique has the least patience for stable semiotic closure. Normative claims must be "troubled," destabilized. Make no mistake: there are plenty of normative claims (including many made by Christian theologians!) that ought to be resisted. Histories and structures of oppression *have* distorted regnant regimes of moral reasoning and need to be named as false—or, in theological terms, as *sin*.[29] But the blunt instrument of critique, particularly as it is often offered in the classroom, is often unable to do this subtle work, instead merely teaching students to dismiss normative claims as "socially constructed" rather than to receive the claims as they are—claims to truth—and to evaluate them as such. The consequences for education and the broader society that our students go on to help shape are catastrophic. As Michael Roth notes,

> Once outside the university, our students continue to score points by displaying the critical prowess for which they were rewarded in school. They wind up contributing to a cultural climate that has little tolerance for finding or making meaning, whose intellectuals and cultural commentators delight in being able to show that somebody else is not to be believed.[30]

Education oriented around critique fails the student and the society to which they will contribute.

Let us again be careful to note the particular shape of the problem. One could say that when Roth notes that the education that the humanities are offering our students is leaving them with little—if any—ability to find or make meaning, he's describing a negative outcome for students' prospects for finding their way into flourishing life. This is true, but it's worse than that. "Making and finding meaning" is not merely a *component* of the good life. *Meaning making* is the process of discerning the *shape* of flourishing life and its various components. If we are leaving students unable to do this work, we

---

[28] On the normativity of the humanities, see Pippin 35–43; Roberts, *Encountering* 88–95; Roth.
[29] See Croasmun 124–37.
[30] Roth.

have fallen short of our particular vocation as humanistic pedagogues, for this is the work that humanists alone can do—for the normative is the peculiar domain of the humanist.[31] Scientists can (and should!) help students more accurately *describe* the world as it actually is and how it works. Engineers can (and should!) help students more effectively act in the world to bring about whatever ends they elect to pursue. Psychologists can (and should!) describe what habits, attitudes, and practices correlate with what sorts of emotional, physical, and social outcomes. But only humanists—philosophers, literary theorists, musicologists, and theologians—can help students learn to discern which outcomes are truly to be desired. This is why rehabilitating the normative in the humanities is vital not only to the survival of the humanities but also to the furtherance of flourishing human life.

The solution is not to leave *critical thinking* behind but rather to teach the intellectual habits of what Tyler Roberts calls "critical assent." We need to ask along with our students "[H]ow do we inherit values and traditions, how do we assent to and commit ourselves to normative visions[?] . . . What are the methods, the dispositions, the practices by which we commit ourselves even as we open ourselves to rigorous questioning?"[32] Roberts takes this posture of critical assent to be typical of Christian theology, pointing specifically to scholars like Rowan Williams and Kathryn Tanner.[33] Indeed, at its best, this is Christian theology's strong suit, and it may well be that Christian theology can help point the way here. Theology, at least in its classic sense, requires both negation (the apophatic) and affirmation or assertion (the cataphatic). Theological education ought to cultivate the counterbalancing intellectual virtues of *humility* (in the knowledge of one's intellectual fallibility, holding convictions with a certain degree of provisionality) and *courage* (nevertheless being willing to act for the sake of what one takes to be the good, even in the knowledge that one might be wrong). It seems to me that humanistic education, too, ought to embrace this productive epistemic tension between intellectual humility and intellectual courage. Though we should recognize that even these virtues do not come from nowhere but need to be recast within the particular vision of flourishing embraced by each individual instructor.

---

[31] James Pawelski points in this direction when he insists that the eudaemonic turn would entail a "renewed examination of the question of well-being relevant for our times" ("Bringing" 209).

[32] Roberts, "Response" 5.

[33] Roberts, "Response" 6 and *Encountering* 62. We might add Cornel West to this list, particularly when he insists that cultural criticism be "guided by moral visions and ethical norms that flow from synoptic worldviews," even as "these worldviews are to be rationally scrutinized" in light of their ability to respond to "life-denying forces" ("Historicist" 369).

As we begin to adopt this new posture of critical assent, we find that new pedagogical possibilities open up. Chief among these is the possibility of genuine encounter—and candid existential response—between the student and a focus of inquiry, whether a piece of art, a theological argument, or a work of literature. The pedagogical goal here is not the mere cognition of the object of study but rather an encounter with it.[34] This fundamentally changes the posture of teacher and students alike. The instructor can no longer pretend to be a neutral third-party tour guide, nor can the students feign a "view from nowhere." Each member of the learning community must embrace their particularity and their located-ness such that the moment of existential encounter is one in which *they* themselves, not some fictive character invented for the purposes of the classroom, come face to face with the object of study— and, through it, with themselves. In this "humanistic mode," the pedagogy switches from the third person to address the student directly in the second person.[35] The text is no longer an object of autopsy but rather a "Thou" that confronts the students and teacher alike. Make no mistake: this is a vulnerable posture; there is real risk in each and every genuine encounter.[36] But precisely in this risk is the possibility that, in such encounters, our very humanity is forged.[37]

With this renewed thought style, myriad courses can be taught. A broad humanities course might explicitly engage the question of flourishing life as approached by multiple different religious and nonreligious traditions and thinkers, like our Yale College course Life Worth Living or the Philosophy as a Way of Life courses at Fordham and Wesleyan, or God and the Good Life at the University of Notre Dame. They might require students to lean into *embodying* rather than simply *learning about* different ways of life, as does Justin Thomas McDaniel's course Living Deliberately.[38] A theology course might explore one particular tradition's vision of flourishing life, as

[34] Consider Roberts: "[T]he humanities are not just a matter of making fine distinctions or exposing mechanisms; they are about responding to texts, ideas, visions of the human, artworks, and values, that is, about encountering and engaging the claims and visions embedded in them to ask what they mean for *me* or *us*" (*Encountering* 91).

[35] Robert Pippin makes a similar point using similar language when he notes that "normative questions . . . are irreducibly 'first-personal' questions" (38).

[36] Roth, in "Beyond Critical Thinking," is right to suggest that oftentimes it is the knowledge of the possibility of this change that makes us prefer the typical third-person mode of critique: "As students and as teachers we sometimes crave that protection because without it we risk being open to changing who we are" (#).

[37] Simpson 11.

[38] See McDaniel, "Lab Courses," this volume. For a practice-focused, experiential pedagogy, see also Samuels, "From the Head," this volume.

does our Yale Divinity School course Christ and Being Human. But perhaps even more significant than these particularly focused courses would be the myriad "standard" courses: courses on Russian novels that read the text not just historically but in fact offer the text an opportunity to say something true,[39] courses on Western music of the Romantic period that take seriously the possibility that students might personally discover something about the role of affect in flourishing life, courses engaging the experiences of LGBT persons in communities of color that require existential engagement with issues of sexuality, race, and identity. This last example, of course, is one type of course in which bell hooks and black feminist scholars and pedagogues have long led the way in advocating for the urgency and necessity of existential modes of knowing. The "eudaemonic turn" in humanistic pedagogy advocated for by Pawelski won't have succeeded until all courses are infused with this new hermeneutics of response and with practices of critical assent.

The Role of Theology in a Renewed Humanities

A renewed humanities of the sort I have described is what it would take to meet our society's need to develop once again intellectual muscles and to find the existential courage to discern, articulate, embody, and commend visions of flourishing life. In so doing, the humanities would recover their normativity and, in turn, answer the crisis of legitimation of the humanities. An objection may come at this point: Has theology, in serving as an analogy for the renewal of humanistic pedagogy that I've offered, been pulling the strings behind the scenes, reinstalling the Christian faith as the privileged normative frame for the university? If so, we would have reason to suspect that theology can only ever exist in the university as queen, and so long as we want to live out from under her rule, she ought to be locked outside the gate. But I take it that this is not the case; theology can and ought to be happy to operate within the renewed humanities that I have described, not as queen but as a fellow democratic citizen. Explaining why this is the case will serve to fill out the picture of the renewed humanities that I've been painting.

The simple response is to say that Christian theology ought to be able to coexist alongside any number of other voices that discern, articulate, and commend visions of flourishing life in the modern pluralistic university.

---

[39] Gadamer 303.

However, this is much easier said than done. Visions of flourishing life do not easily sit alongside one another like flavors at the ice cream parlor. Rather, most of these visions are what Volf and I have called *contending particular universalisms* (CPUs). They are *universalisms* in that they make a claim to be true for all humans. The Christian faith is itself one such universalist account—or, more precisely, a quarrelsome family of such accounts of flourishing life. Just about every world religion, at least in some of its rival versions, makes universal claims about its vision of flourishing life. And there are, of course, secular universalisms as well, like the philosophy of Nietzsche or the psychology of Freud. At the same time that they are universal, these traditions are also undeniably particular. They have origins and have undergone significant reformations in particular places and times. Many make claims to be true for all humans, but none is universally accepted. Each is mutable and permeable. Rather than sitting passively alongside one another, these particular universalisms *contend* with one another, laying claims to our allegiance, some even to our ultimate allegiance. That said, contending universalisms are not necessarily violent; rather, each has internal resources such that they can be true to their nature when they both contend and do so without violence.

One of the great challenges of our day, therefore, is to create and to manage public spaces in which particular universalisms can constructively contend with one another. The pluralistic university ought to be just such a space— the humanities in particular.[40] A renewal of the humanities around discerning, articulating, and commending visions of flourishing life would be precisely such a site of contestation. Entering into such a space, each CPU would need to mine its own resources in order to articulate reasons that are indigenous to its own tradition for playing by the rules of the pluralistic university. Christianity has such resources, including theological resources for affirming freedom of conscience (and, therefore, of religion), affirmation of difference, the distinction between God's rule and human rule, and the moral equality of all humans. Christians who are able to marshal these resources should be able to engage constructively in pluralistic spaces *because of* rather than *despite* their Christian convictions. Many adherents to other CPUs have been and will continue to be able to identify and deploy analogous sets of resources that are indigenous to their own accounts of the good life.

---

[40] This vision of the university as a site for the contending of multiple particular universalisms is consonant with the vision advanced in Kathryn Tanner's "Theology and Cultural Contest in the University."

The takeaway is this: We need to foster educational institutions that consider it part of their purpose to facilitate critical discussion and appropriation of visions of flourishing life, including the claims that they make on our self-understanding, our aspirations, and our images of a desirable future for the world. Such educational institutions will need to see themselves as sites of truth-seeking, critical conversation and personal transformation that equip students to do the difficult work of evaluating the truth claims of multiple CPUs and of contending in a responsible give and take on behalf of the universalism that they embrace.[41] In such a space, both theology and the rest of the humanities could find their rationale in meeting one of the most pressing needs of our day, the formation of a new generation of students who are prepared to do the difficult work of discerning, articulating, commending, and ultimately embodying flourishing life.

Works Cited

Anscombe, Elizabeth. "Modern Moral Philosophy." *Philosophy*, vol. 33, 1958, pp. 1–19.

Berger, Peter. *The Heretical Imperative: Contemporary Possibilities of Religious Affirmation.* Anchor Press, 1979.

Castiglia, Christopher. "Critiquiness." *English Language Notes*, vol. 51, no. 2, 2013, pp. 79–85.

Croasmun, Matthew. *The Emergence of Sin: The Cosmic Tyrant in Romans.* Oxford UP, 2017.

Cuomo, Chris J. *Feminism and Ecological Communities: An Ethic of Flourishing.* Routledge, 1998.

Delbanco, Anthony. *College: What It Was, Is, and Should Be.* Princeton UP, 2014.

Eagleton, Terry. *Ideology: An Introduction.* Verso, 1991.

Felski, Rita. *The Limits of Critique.* U of Chicago P, 2015.

Gadamer, Hans-Georg. *Truth and Method.* Translated by Joel Weinsheimer and Donald G. Marshall, 2nd rev. ed., Continuum, 2003.

Jennings, Willie James. *After Whiteness: An Education in Belonging.* Eerdmans, 2021.

Kermode, Frank. *The Genesis of Secrecy: On the Interpretation of Narrative.* Harvard UP, 1979.

Kronman, Anthony. *Education's End: Why Our Colleges and Universities Have Given Up on the Meaning of Life.* Yale UP, 2007.

Latour, Bruno. "Why Has Critique Run Out of Steam? From Matters of Fact to Matters of Concern." *Critical Inquiry*, vol. 30, 2004, pp. 225–48.

Marsden, George. *The Soul of the American University.* Oxford UP, 1994.

---

[41] This requires that such educational settings will welcome—at least provisionally—the various rationalities and epistemologies that CPUs bring with them rather than insisting on a particular set of acceptable methodologies and approaches to rationality.

McCutcheon, Russell T. "The Study of Religion as an Anthropology of Credibility." *Religious Studies, Theology, and the University: Conflicting Maps, Changing Terrain*, edited by Linell Elizabeth Cady and Delwin Brown, SUNY Press, 2002, pp.13–30.

Menand, Louis. "The Marketplace of Ideas," 2001, American Council of Learned Societies Occasional Paper no. 49, http://archives.acls.org/op/49_Marketplace_of_Ideas.htm.

Palmer, Parker. *To Know as We Are Known: A Spirituality of Education*. HarperCollins, 2010.

Pawelski, James. "Bringing Together the Humanities and the Science of Well-Being to Advance Human Flourishing." *Well–Being and Higher Education: A Strategy for Change and the Realization of Education's Greater Purposes*, edited by Donald W. Harward, Bringing Theory to Practice, 2016, pp. 207–216.

Pawelski, James, "The Positive Humanities: Culture and Human Flourishing." *The Oxford Handbook of the Positive Humanities*, edited by Louis Tay and James Pawelski, Oxford UP, 2022, pp. 17–41.

Pawelski, James, and D. J. Moores, editors. *The Eudaimonic Turn: Well-Being in Literary Studies*. Fairleigh Dickinson, 2013.

Pippin, Robert B. "Natural and Normative." *Daedalus*, vol. 138, no. 3, 2009, pp. 35–43.

Roberts, Tyler. *Encountering Religion*. Columbia UP, 2013.

Roberts, Tyler. "Response to Theology and the Good Life." Yale Center for Faith and Culture Joy, Security, and Fear Conference, 23–24 Oct. 2015, Yale University, New Haven, CT.

Rosa, Hartmut. "Two Versions of the Good life and Two Forms of Fear: Dynamic Stabilization and Resonance Conception of the Good Life." Yale Center for Faith and Culture Conference on Joy, Security, and Fear, 8–9 Nov. 2017, Yale University, New Haven, CT.

Roth, Michael. "Beyond Critical Thinking." *The Chronicle of Higher Education*, 3 Jan. 2010, https://www.chronicle.com/article/beyond-critical-thinking/.

Simpson, Lorenzo C. *The Unfinished Project: Toward a Postmetaphysical Humanism*. Routledge, 2001.

Tanner, Kathryn. "Theology and Cultural Contest in the University." *Religious Studies, Theology, and the University: Conflicting Maps, Changing Terrain*, edited by Linell Elizabeth Cady and Delwin Brown, SUNY Press, 2002, pp. 199–212.

Taylor, Charles. *A Secular Age*. Belknap Press of Harvard UP, 2007.

Volf, Miroslav, and Matthew Croasmun. *For the Life of the World: Theology That Makes a Difference*. Brazos Press, 2019.

West, Cornel. "The Historicist Turn in Philosophy of Religion." *The Cornel West Reader*, Civitas, 1999, pp. 360–71.

PART II

AFFORDANCES

*New Ways of Teaching and Learning Religious Studies
and Theology after the Eudaemonic Turn*

4

Sanmati, the Art of "Generous Orientation"

Flourishing amid Religious Difference

Leela Prasad

Prelude

On December 11, 2019, the Indian Parliament approved the Citizenship Amendment Act (CAA), which makes provision for expedited citizenship for Hindu, Jain, Buddhist, Sikh, Parsi, and Christian migrants and refugees seeking to escape from persecution. Significantly, the provision excludes Muslim refugees. The controversial CAA, to be followed by an equally dubious National Register of Citizens (NRC), was widely condemned as flouting the principles of the Indian Constitution, which guarantees equality of religion and secular citizenship. The CAA and the NRC triggered both widespread interfaith protests and police crackdowns in India. But amid the reports of violence, a story reported in mainstream news media stands out. In the city of Kanpur, about eight hours south of Delhi, a wedding in a Muslim family was in jeopardy. The groom's family, who lived three hours away from Kanpur, had called to say that the wedding procession was unable to make it to Kanpur because of the curfew and the risk of being attacked. There was little that either family could do, because they were part of a religious minority community that was often subjected to Hindu nationalist surveillance and assault. The anxious bride, twenty-five-year-old Zeenat Khan, was certain that the wedding was going to be called off. Zeenat's neighbor, Vimal Chapadiya, a Hindu who worked as an administrator at a private school, heard about the predicament and decided to do something about it. He telephoned the groom's family to assure them that no harm would come to the procession and that wedding plans should remain as scheduled. He then gathered fifty friends and escorted the groom's family to Kanpur. As

Leela Prasad, Sanmati, *the Art of "Generous Orientation"* In: *Religious Studies, Theology, and Human Flourishing.* Edited by: Justin Thomas McDaniel and Hector Kilgoe, Oxford University Press. © Oxford University Press 2024. DOI: 10.1093/oso/9780197658338.003.0005

they got off their vehicles at the Khan residence, Chapadiya and his friends formed a protective human chain around the groom's party and took them to the venue of the wedding a short distance away. They stayed on until Zeenat left for her new home. Later, on a visit to her maternal home, Zeenat told a news reporter that Vimal *bhaiya* ("brother") had come to her rescue "like a *farishta*" ("angel"). Chapadiya said that he had simply done what was right. "I have seen Zeenat grow up," he said, "She is like my younger sister. How could I let her heart be broken?" (Mishra). Some might want to argue that basic neighborliness explains these gestures, but during India's Partition (1947), long-time neighbors forgot everyday proximal ties for fuzzy historical enmities and killed and maimed one another. Estimates of lives lost ranged from 200,000 to 2 million. During the 2002 Gujarat riots, gruesome murders and rapes were committed by so-called neighbors.[1] Therefore, the Kanpur story of neighborly care is indeed exceptional.

In this chapter, I dwell on an underlying kinship beyond religious categories that makes such generous action possible. How might we describe the moral orientation that underlies such neighborliness? What is lost by the absence of that orientation, and what can be gained by its practice? Even more powerfully, how does this orientation generate neighborliness between strangers? These questions pivot on conceptions of relationality that are framed broadly across several chapters in this volume. They are implied, for instance, in Mary Clark Moschella's observation that enduring social justice praxis is attentive to promoting ideas of beauty and healing as well as to performing public-oriented, hands-on civic work. The questions of relationality in this chapter also intersect with Noah Salomon's critique of what I will call the "individuality epidemic" in the Anglophonic humanities; as Salomon's chapter does, this chapter, too, will explore how such a thing as "human flourishing," in order to succeed, needs a consciousness that focuses not on the singular human but rather on many humans and that even goes beyond the human.

My inquiry on "orientation" builds on the notion of co-being that I discussed in an earlier essay, in which I proposed co-being as a praxis of the public that is grounded in the recognition that we share our worlds with others and with other forms of life. Pre-fourteenth-century Hindu stories that describe embodied practices of reciprocity and accommodation affirm

---

[1] The case of Bilkis Bano is an example. See https://caravanmagazine.in/vantage/rape-2002-guja rat-bilkis-bano.

the modern philosopher Hannah Arendt's view that the public is that *commonality* which arises when we overcome "our privately owned place[s]" (52). When the private self is able to "undergo an artistic transposition," it is able to evoke a reality in which "the presence of others who see what we see and hear what we hear assures us of the reality of the world and ourselves" (50). Co-being depends on this provision of assurance to *all* members of society, an assurance that is tangible in everyday acts as well as in governance. What we know as "the everyday" spans at least three broad categories of living: place, possession, and pact. How do I occupy space? How do I own things and ideas? How do I enter into tacit and spoken understandings with other persons? To be clear, when I use the word *how* in these questions, I am referring to the manner in which we occupy, own, or come to understand. Our practices around these questions determine how capacious we can make the world; the more accommodating and dialogical we are, the more capacious and assuring the world becomes. Yet it would be a mistake to imagine co-being as a state of utopian togetherness. On the contrary, a harmonious public with equal freedoms for everyone is possible only when individuals and private collectivities endure physical discomfort, risk, and uncertainty. Trial and error are intrinsic to the process of achieving co-being. One exemplar of a society striving for co-being is the Gandhian ashram in pre-independent India. Despite the broad contract of committing to simple and communal living at the ashram, there was plenty of potential for disagreement among the ashram's residents who came from different religions and castes and held differing views on social norms, human-environment relations, and other matters. Yet the ideals of self-sufficiency and resource sharing and a resolute trust in democratic equality made ashramic co-being possible despite occasional failures.[2]

To return to the question at hand, what is the orientation that makes it possible to reimagine personhood so that we can negotiate space, things, and ideas and form pacts that promote human flourishing? To answer this question, I turn to the concept of *sanmati*, a Sanskrit word that means 'goodwill,' 'wisdom,' and 'noble-mindedness.' I will return to the definition shortly. The word became popular through a *bhajan* (a type of devotional song) called *Ramdhun* ("*The Tune of Rama*") that was a favorite of Mahatma Gandhi. It was set to music by Pandit V. D. Paluskar, one of the founding musicologists of Hindustani music, "with the hope that [Gandhi] would take it to the

---

[2] For a fascinating account of trials and tribulations of ashram living, see M. K. Gandhi, *Ashram*.

masses" (Lal 245). The *Ramdhun* was always sung during Gandhi's ashram prayer meetings along with songs and verses from diverse religious texts and traditions. Ecumenical prayers were a cornerstone of Gandhian political praxis.[3] The most quoted stanza of the song goes,

> Raghupati raghava raja ram
> patita pavan sitaram
> Ishvar Allah tero nam
> sabko sanmati de bhagavan.

> Rama, the lord of the Raghu dynasty
> The deliverer of the fallen, Sitaram[4]
> Ishvar[5] and Allah are your names
> We pray that you give *sanmati* to everyone.[6]

The song's origins are debated, but more importantly, Tridip Suhrud points out,

[f]ew remember that it was [Gandhi's grandniece] Manu who fundamentally altered the very nature of Ramdhun by inserting Ishwar Allah tere naam, sab ko sanmati de Bhagwan to the ancient lines Raghupati Raghav Raja Ram in a moment of deep inspiration during a prayer meeting on 22 January 1947 at Paniala village in [riot-stricken] Noakhali [in present-day Bangladesh].

The lines acquired a unique visionary tone when Gandhi embraced them, as he saw it as necessary to remind the Indian public, time and again through song and speech and service, that if there was to be a free and progressive India, Indians would have to respectfully recognize that God has different names or no name and that there are many paths to the divine. In the January 22, 1925, issue of *Young India*, Gandhi writes, "Rama, Allah and God are to me convertible terms" (qtd. in Lal 244). As Vinay Lal points out, Gandhi's *Ram* was not tied to the hero-prince of the *Ramayana*; instead *Ram* signified

---

[3] See Snodgrass for a detailed study of songs and rituals associated with Gandhi and ashram life.

[4] A reference to Sita, Rama's wife, whose commitment to the dharmic path is admired in popular tradition. Sitaram is also another name for Rama.

[5] *Bhagavan* and *Ishvar* are among Hinduism's many words for God.

[6] My translation.

an eternal divinity available within everyone. In a turbulent India that was rapidly polarizing along Hindu-Muslim lines, the prayer for *sanmati* was an urgent one. The song was sung during the historic Dandi Salt March in 1930, a march that turned world attention in India's favor and against British colonial rule. Quite consistent with his famous conviction that "[t]here can be no politics without religion" (by which he meant that there can be no politics without Truth), Gandhi brought the concept of *sanmati* to the secular domain, where he believed it would yield a politics of collective mindedness, one that appreciates and accepts religious differences—and thereby promotes flourishing. For Gandhi, pluralism depended on *sanmati*, which he imagined as a potential that could be awakened in oneself. Philosopher and grandson of Mahatma Gandhi, Ramchandra Gandhi, reminds us that etymologically *sanmati* is the compounding of *sat* and *mati*. *Sat* is 'absolute truth' (read *reality*), and in an nondualist (Advaitic) conception, reality is the essence that suffuses and connects everything. *Mati* is 'mind' or 'mental orientation.' He therefore defines *sanmati* as "reality orientation" (R. Gandhi, "Moksha" 136), an orientation that perceives the fundamental interconnectedness among phenomena, people, and so on. Ramchandra Gandhi's reminder of the etymology of *sanmati* is the foundation of my argument that *sanmati is the art of generous orientation*. The word *generous* helps me underscore the imaginative and active effort it takes to perceive interrelations. The mirroring between oneself and another takes ethical work. I will illustrate the concept of *sanmati* through a staging of three acts, each set within a distinct moment and place, and conclude by suggesting that without *sanmati*, there can be no flourishing.[7]

Act I

On February 13, 2018, a mini-truck refurbished and bedecked to resemble an ornate, pillared Hindu temple began its forty-one-day journey through six states of India. By itself, in a land of pilgrimage traditions and adaptive forms of worship, the glitzy 'chariot's journey' (*rath yatra*) would not have taken headline space. But the chariot's itinerary and intent, engineered by

---

[7] The art of generous orientation is analogous to James O. Pawelski's notion of "sustainable preference," which holds out across many "frames of reference" and leads to a "fractal flourishing" that ripples across widely (263).

the Hindu nationalist organization, the Vishwa Hindu Parishad (VHP), contained multiple ancient and modern refurbished histories that secured it front-page coverage in the Indian media.

The *rath yatra*'s itinerary had been drawn up to trace the southward route of the exiled god-prince Rama, the hero of the popular Indian epic the *Ramayana*—the same Rama in Gandhi's favorite song cited in the "Prelude" to this chapter. Thus, the chariot's starting point was Ayodhya, Rama's birthplace in the north, now a town in the Faizabad district of Uttar Pradesh. Its culminating point was the town of Rameshwaram on the southeastern coast of India, from where, as the epic goes, Rama launched his transoceanic campaign into Lanka (with the help of his beloved devotee Hanuman) to recover his wife, Sita, and destroy her abductor. In effect, though, the *rath yatra*'s intent was to pressure the government of India to consent to building a grand temple to Rama (as envisioned by the VHP) on a site that is sacred to both Muslims and Hindus and to forge public opinion in favor of this demand (Husain).

The 2018 *yatra* visually foregrounded an infamous national memory: the events of December 8, 1992, in which a Hindu mob mobilized by the right-wing political party the Bharatiya Janata Party (BJP), the political arm of the VHP, demolished brick by brick a historic masjid, or mosque, in Ayodhya, driven by the slogan "mandir vahin banayenge," which means, 'we will build the temple on that very site.' More than two thousand people lost their lives across the country in the riots that followed. Hindu nationalists had been claiming from the mid-nineteenth century that the founder of the Mughal Empire, Babur (d. 1530), had destroyed a temple that marked the site of Rama's birth and built an eponymous mosque that came to be called the Baburi (also known as the Babri or Babari) Masjid.[8]

The masjid, with its three domes and three arches, sat on the northeastern corner of a hillock called *Ramkot* ("the fortress of Rama") that overlooks the Sarayu River and in whose vicinity were many shrines associated with the *Ramayana*. In the outer courtyard of the mosque are smaller but important structures such as *Sita ki Rasoi* ("Sita's kitchen"), Ram Chabutra (a platform to mark Rama's birthplace), and a *bhandar griha* ("storage house"). According to the detailed study of the mosque by Ram Nath, a historian of Mughal art, a key inscription in the central arch says that the mosque was built by Mir Baqi,

---

[8] The dispute is called the Ramjanmabhumi-Babri Masjid title case. See Rehman for the implications of this event for India's secularism.

a nobleman in Babar's court. Nath surmises that with unceasing onslaughts from the Afghans, it is likely that Mir Baqi, rather than build a mosque entirely anew, expediently renovated an existing structure in the same manner that he had made other repairs in Ramkot. The basic brick-and-mortar structure of the mosque had several layers of lime-plaster and whitewash, which suggest that the mosque had been restored and renovated several times over time. Nath argues that the mosque's use of black stone for some of its inner pillars, stylized carvings typical of Hindu architecture, and tantric features indicate that the mosque used materials from a despoiled temple. Art historian Catherine Asher observes that the mosque (which some records identify by the name of Masjid-i-Janmasthan, "mosque of the birthplace"), is largely "stucco-covered, over a rubble or brick core but carved black stone columns from a pre-twelfth-century temple are embedded into either side of the central entrance porch" (Asher 29–30). The embedding and reuse of Hindu architectural features on the visible façade of a mosque is "highly unusual" for that time, which suggests that the construction of a mosque at Ayodhya may have served to legitimize Babar's sovereignty in a non-Islamic region.[9] Although Nath is of the view that a temple had been destroyed at some point in history, possibly by the Afghan armies of Mahmud of Ghazni (1001–26) or by the Sultans of Delhi (1206–1526) in order to build a mosque, this view remains controversial (Nath 38).

As this past accrued, with the overgrowth of British colonial records and policy, the site of the mosque turned into a zone of conflict, quietly obliterating the fact that for some time, Hindus and Muslims had prayed amicably alongside each other at the site, as reported by the 1905 *District Gazetteer of Faizabad* (qtd. in Ghosh 24). Also obliterated in the conflict is the fact that an India without its Islamic past would need to tear down its secular infrastructure, give up a vastly popular cuisine, forgo styles of clothing and textile arts, bury its Mughal gardens, and forget influential literary and musical traditions—in fact, sacrifice its soul and substance.

The first recorded clash in Ayodhya, in which 150 people died, occurred in 1855 over the Hanumangarhi temple in the Ramkot precinct. According to

[9] At the same time that we acknowledge that Muslim rulers did on occasion destroy temples, the myopias of rightwing thinking seek to erase the memory of another powerful historical reality: that the demolition and the sponsorship of temples were both part of an emerging political episteme in India from the 1300s, an episteme that has given rise to spectacular fusions and exchanges in language and art, food and dress, governance and love. See Eaton for how "temple desecration" as well as support for Hindu temples by Mughal sovereigns and elites needs to be understood within prevailing practices and rhetoric about religious monumentality and minority subjects.

some versions, the priest of Hanumangarhi constructed the Ram Chabutra on the east side of the mosque (Menon and Varma; also MirrorNow News). Other accounts say that the Ram Chabutra existed well before 1855. The muezzin of the Babri masjid filed a petition objecting to what he perceived to be an encroachment. In 1859, the British segregated areas of worship by building a wall; Hindus entered from the east side while Muslims from the north. Hindus could not access the inner part of the mosque and had to conduct their worship on the outer platform. The history of litigation begins in 1885, when the priest of this makeshift shrine filed appeals many times to build a permanent temple over the platform; the appeal, however, was denied each time. Muslims also continued to file petitions.[10]

In 1949—just two years after the Partition—on the night of December 22, an idol of infant Rama (Ram Lalla) and Sita were clandestinely placed by some Hindus inside the masjid. The city magistrate ordered the masjid to be locked, barring Muslims from the mosque altogether while Hindus were given limited permission to view the images from a side gate. Muslims had not prayed in the mosque since its closure to them in 1949. The Sunni Central Waqf Board of Uttar Pradesh filed a suit to claim possession of the site, as Babur, they argued, was a Sunni Muslim. Hindu organizations—backed openly by governments seeking votes—began petitioning the courts to allow them to worship Ram Lalla. The stalemate continued until 1986, when a district court, prompted by an anxious government, ordered the lock on the mosque to be broken for Hindus to worship inside the mosque. The Babri Mosque Action Committee was formed to protest this move. Through the 1950s and 1960s, contesting suits were filed by the deity Ram Lalla (considered a legal minor whose estate is administered by an organization called the Hindu Mahasabha), the Nirmohi Akhara (a Hindu sect), and the Sunni Central Waqf Board.

After a preliminary GPR (Ground Penetrating Radar) survey reported "the presence of walls, pillars and slab flooring under the ground," the Allahabad High Court directed the state-run Archaeological Survey of India (ASI) to excavate the site in 2003 with the explicit charge of determining whether the Babri masjid was built on a temple that had been destroyed in order to build the masjid (Menon and Varma). Five months later, the ASI presented its 574-page report, concluding that beneath the masjid's floor there was evidence of

---

[10] For a history of the litigation, see Ghosh; Menon and Varma. For a synopsis, see Business Standard.

a temple that had been destroyed. The ASI argued that it had discovered pillar bases (which would have been the base of the stone pillars that supported the alleged temple) that "account for" the pillars used in the masjid, and it also found several architectural fragments characteristic of a north Indian temple. Two archaeologists, Jaya Menon and Supriya Varma, appointed by the counsels to Sunni Central Waqf Board, observed the ASI's digs at the site, and they vigorously disagreed with the ASI's final report.[11] They argued that the ASI's archaeological procedures were fundamentally flawed and politically motivated by the VHP's predetermined convictions. In their view, the ASI's argument about fragments and pillar bases had been fabricated using unreliable surface debris rather than findings from under the ground. If anything, they argued, a Buddhist stupa or smaller mosques remnants lay beneath the floor.

In 2010, the Allahabad High Court ruled that the disputed 2.77-acre site be equally divided among the three petitioners: Ram Lalla the deity, the Nirmohi Akhara, and the Sunni Central Waqf Board. However, the parties contested this judgment, and in 2011, the supreme court of India stayed the order.

What possibilities for resolution does this tangled and thorny dispute present?

In 2019, the supreme court took up its final hearing after a court-mandated mediation panel failed to resolve the dispute, and in February 2020, it declared the following verdict: The disputed land in Ayodhya was to be given to *Ram Janmabhoomi Nyas* ("birthplace of Rama trust") for the construction of a temple. The trust had been formed by members of the nationalist VHP. The Sunni Central Waqf Board was to be compensated with five acres of land for the construction of a mosque in Ayodhya. The politicians who instigated the 1992 destruction of the mosque would be tried in a separate criminal case. This was the legal resolution.[12]

Some have argued that the verdict was perhaps the most pragmatic one possible, considering the contentious nature of virtually all aspects of the case. But the verdict fails in one crucial way. It concedes to an ideology founded on exclusionary principles and tactics, and it offers a compensatory

[11] The not-for-profit web-based news outlet *The Wire* conducted an interview with Menon and Varma after the supreme court's verdict in 2020. See Mahaprashasta.

[12] On August 5, 2020, Prime Minister Narendra Modi (BJP) laid the foundation stone for the construction of the Ram *mandir* at the site. A few months later, all thirty-two politicians accused of instigating the demolition of the Babri masjid in 1992 were acquitted. The temple is projected to open to the public at the end of 2023, ahead of the general elections in 2024.

concession to a community already minoritized by the CAA. It opens other sites to "reparations" that are triggered by agents who are invested in revisionist history. In short, the verdict fails to embody the spirit of pluralism that can heal, assure, and generate co-being. As Gandhi might have put it, in considering the question of wins and losses in the dispensation of justice, unless there is a change in the *mindset* of opponents, there can be little moral victory.[13] In Ramchandra Gandhi's 1992 meditative book *Sita's Kitchen: A Testimony of Faith and Inquiry*, we get a glimpse of how such a transformation of mindset could occur. A prescient foreboding of the demolition runs through *Sita's Kitchen* (it was published before the event). Disturbed by the convolutions of history that made it hard to discern fact from erroneous assumption, Ramchandra Gandhi visited Ayodhya. He stood in front of the mosque and gazed at the main arch, where he saw the "carved lotuses and pitchers on the small pillars supporting it at the bottom, and the hexagonal tantric motifs on the walls above the arches and other unmistakably Hindu features of the structure" (R. Gandhi, *Sita's Kitchen*, 14). And he concludes, "There could be little doubt that sacred components of Hindu temple (or a cognate Buddhist or Jain shrine) had been used in the construction of the mosque in the sixteenth century (1528/29)" (14). He speculates that perhaps an existing temple in fact had been destroyed to build the mosque, or perhaps materials had been brought from a temple destroyed elsewhere, at another time. Ramchandra Gandhi is stricken with grief:

> Whatever be the precise historical truth of this matter, the fact remains that the mosque owes its existence to the despoliation of structures sacred to Indian spirituality and does not hide this fact; adding insult to injury, says my wounded Hindu pride. . . . The child in me grieved. (14)

A few moments later, however, his grief turns into a greater anguish. He writes that

> the adult in me awakened to the reality of the images of Rama and Sita and other deities in the sanctum sanctorum of the house of Allah; to the fact of stealthy trespass with intent which converted the Babari mosque into a Rama temple more than forty years ago; to the fact that the chanting of the

---

[13] See Mohandas K. Gandhi's (*Autobiography* 439) reflections on what he considered a failed satyagraha in Kheda, Gujarat.

names of Rama and Sita—essential nourishment for my Hindu soul—had been used to silence nearly half a millennium's call to Islamic prayer; to the fact that Muslims were not allowed to come anywhere near the mosque under siege, which no doubt was an addition of insult to the injury caused to their pride by the forcible conversion of a mosque into a temple in secular India. (14)

He closed his eyes to meditate on this realization. When he opened them, he saw a sign of contemporary making in Hindi announcing a spot as *Janmasthan Sita ki Rasoi*, or "Sita's kitchen in Rama's birthplace," a spot that a chauvinist media had forgotten to take as seriously as the spot where Rama was supposed to have been born. Sita's kitchen becomes the restorative metaphor, "a magic inscription in crude paint," for Ramchandra Gandhi (15). He finds in the architectural idea of Sita's kitchen an archetypal notion: "It is on earth, in the embrace of the Divine Mother, that all are born, all creatures great and small; all forms manifest, noble and evil; and all are nourished" (16).

Why do I see this shift in Ramchandra Gandhi's response as so powerful? His initial response is clearly a *reaction* to the visuality of the Hindu, Buddhist, or Jain pillars and the imagery in the mosque, and it reflects his internalization of the commonplace narrative that "invading Muslims desecrated our temples." The reaction contains a familiar identification but also a dis-identification. *Me* is most certainly not *the other*. The transition, however, from grief for one's own to anguish for another communicates a special transcendence, which I argue is the essence of *sanmati*, 'generous orientation.' The transcendence is not a removal from contested and unknowable historical events but an overcoming of the me-other divide. The transition in his response presents the question "Can my flourishing come from the abjection of another?" This question shows that what is "my own" now extends to include what was the "other." It is *sanmati*—the precondition for co-being—that allows Ramchandra Gandhi to reimagine the entire site, the Babri masjid and all of Ramkot and all of India, as a place of birth and nourishment for all.

Act II

Sringeri is a Hindu pilgrimage town in south India, about nine hours from the city of Bengaluru, into the western ghats of India. It is most well-known for its temple to Sharada, the goddess of learning and for its *matha*, a monastery that was established by the eighth-century philosopher Shankara. An unbroken lineage of gurus of the *matha* guides the study and propagation of Advaita, Shankara's philosophy of nondualism. For centuries the *matha* has interpreted texts known as the Dharmashastras, codes of conduct and law for Hindus. Hindus across the world who affiliate with this tradition revere the gurus of the *matha*. And residents in Sringeri—of all faiths—specially cherish both the goddess Sharada and the gurus, consulting the latter for everyday matters as well as for spiritual advice. Along the main street, which is Sringeri's commercial street, there are a few temples and a Jain *basadi*. In a neighborhood where Muslims have traditionally lived north of town, there is a major mosque. During my fieldwork in Sringeri in 1994–95, I heard about an incident that involved a wild visitor to town. I translate two tellings of this incident from Kannada.[14]

I first heard about the incident from my landlord, Ramachandra Bhat, a schoolteacher. In his account, the guru, sometime in the 1980s, had sanctioned the reconstruction of the façade of a local temple to Mallikarjuna, a form of Shiva. The temple, which is off the main street, is on a hill. Steep stone steps, flanked by trees, lead up to it. On the top, off to a corner, is also a *mazar*, a shrine to a Muslim saint. During the renovation of the façade, the guru felt that the pedestal of Shivalinga (known as the *pānipītha*) should also be reconstructed. In order to do this, they discovered that the Shivalinga had to be removed from the pedestal.

> Ramachandra Bhat
> While these discussions were going on, a weird thing happened.
> Suddenly there was a leopard in the town.
> We've seen this with our own eyes!
> Right in the town! For five days!
> There was newspaper coverage too.
> Who knows where it came from.
> But, strange thing was, that leopard would go and
> sleep in cattle sheds.
> If you raised an alarm, it slipped away.

[14] I first translated this narration for *Poetics of Conduct*. Here I produce a condensed version, which, for the sake of readability, omits my own interjections.

Pilgrims coming at night got wind of it and were terrified: "There's a
 leopard in this town."
We also saw all this happening. But we could not catch it.
I mean, even with all the advanced technologies in this world, it could
 not be trapped.
It would sleep in some cattle shed at night, or just walk around.
The guru became worried.
[He thought] "Should I not have undertaken the reconstruction of the
 Shivalinga?"
Then he prayed, "Please don't harm anybody. I will finish this task
 quickly. I did not know that I had disturbed something that has been
 there for generations."
Then, soon after that, everybody saw the leopard run up the hill, up the
 steps of the Mallikarjuna temple.
Nobody saw it ever after that.

I heard about the leopard's visit also from Ziya Ahmed, a prominent former
member of Sringeri's municipal council. Since the Ahmed family had lived
in Sringeri for many generations, I had visited them to understand the history of Muslims in Sringeri. He told me the story of the leopard in one of our
conversations.

Ziya Ahmed
Sometime, in 1980s, maybe 1984, a leopard came into town.
It came right into town. It created a real scare, and went straight into one
 school headmaster's house. (He ran out).
It stayed there all day.
The Forest Department showed up and tried different things to catch it.
They couldn't.
Now what had happened meanwhile was that—now this is what I have
 heard; I haven't seen this—
There on the hill is a *mazar* and the plan was made to dig it out.
At the time this decision was made, the leopard appeared.
The *swamiji* ["guru"] came to know about the leopard.
He immediately sent word.
"The *mazar*—don't touch that spot, leave it alone."
And you know, after this, strange thing, nobody knows where that
 leopard disappeared.

It came out of the house, they tried to catch it, but it vanished.
So this is what took place, so we've heard.
You know, the *swamiji* has some *mohabbat* ["love"] for us.
We organized a feast recently and he sent us a message, "You're
doing a good thing; it will go well."

I mentioned to Mr. Ahmed the other story that attributed the leopard's appearance to the Shivalinga's reconstruction. And Ziya Ahmed said, "Yes, that story is also told. They say that, too." When I met Ramachandra Bhat again, I told him the story of the *mazar*. Like Ziya Ahmed, he acknowledged that he had heard it. He said, "Who knows for sure, with regard to such things?"

Despite the political success of right-wing formations in and around Sringeri that try to orchestrate separatist fevers, Sringeri's Muslims and non-Muslim communities have clearly got along. With Shail Mayaram, a historian of modern India, I ask, "What is it that makes coexistence and conviviality possible, so that conflict is minimized?" (Mayaram 276). One answer is that negative interventions in Hindu-Muslim relations have not succeeded in Sringeri because of the resilience of older, more complex ties to each other; they have lived in shared neighborhoods for hundreds of years. In Malerkotla, Punjab, Anna Bigelow finds that a "shared sacred" is indeed a powerful cohesive force. When massacres broke out elsewhere in Punjab at the time of Partition, not a single death was reported in this border town. Bigelow's ethnographic research shows that Malerkotla's Muslims, Hindus, and Sikhs find common ground through their devotion to the Sufi saint Haider Shaikh (who founded the city in 1454). A deliberate commitment to an ethos of peace, enacted through collective representations, rituals, and stories, enables harmonious inter-religious relations (Bigelow). Peter Gottschalk similarly shows that residents of the Arampur area of western Bihar do not lead lives that are truncated along "Muslim" and "Hindu" identities. Their stories, which shape a fluid, "intercommunal public sphere," affirm worlds that are profoundly interrelated and dynamic across contexts, a pervasive fact that should not be surprising yet has been scanty in colonial-era discourse and its modern offspring and thoroughly disposed of by fundamentalist constructions of society.[15]

Violence and oppression justify the culture of disbelief that beleaguers the humanities and interpretative social sciences, making "harmony" suspect.

---

[15] Gottschalk 151. For a broader corrective, see Gottschalk and Schmalz.

Ricoeur's "hermeneutics of suspicion" is a double-edged sword. While it helps uncover embedded power asymmetries and ideologies, it hinders, at the same time, an appreciation of the idealism and interdependence that creates and sustains peace in places such as Malerkotla or Arampur or Sringeri. Put another way, Pamela Cooper-White ("Sometimes," this volume) sees the hermeneutics of suspicion as operating in the cold, analytical dismissal of emotion-based arguments; this dismissal is based, as she says, on surface understandings of issues. But if we set some limits on this hermeneutic and trudge past the culture of disbelief, we are able grasp the ethical orientation that Hindus and Muslims in Sringeri cultivate through their everyday practices to make neighborliness work. We can now ask: How do the two leopard stories demonstrate *sanmati*? The *mazar* and the Shivalinga have coexisted in the same compound for generations with no reason for that arrangement to be altered. Similarly, there seems be little reason for the two stories to encroach on each other. Bhat's and Ahmed's accounts are about more than the space on Mallikarjuna Hill. We can say that they share an understanding about human-divine entanglements: that the divine manifests itself through "signs," that human vision is limited, that cosmic orders can be disturbed by human action, and so on. Yet what is more important is that both narrators were aware of the "other" story. A skeptical view would be to ask why neither of them acknowledged the existence of other telling until I mentioned it. However, we must not neglect to notice that neither Bhat nor Ahmed made an exclusionary claim to truth. As Bhat said, "Who knows for sure with regard to such things?," and Ahmed accepted that there could be other explanations. *Sanmati*, then, comes from the admission that there can be other possibilities, other potential truths. Such admission yields a democracy that is created through everyday humility; a democracy that allows us to acknowledge another person's truth and that does not rely on state policy will be a democracy that lasts.

Act III

In 2013, at age ninety-one, the Indo-French painter Sayed Haider Raza (1922–2016) undertook a series of seven paintings with a Gandhian theme.[16]

[16] The paintings were displayed in a solo show titled *Gandhi in Raza*, by the Kolkata-based Akar Prakar gallery in collaboration with the Raza Foundation on the occasion of Raza's ninety-fourth birthday. Raza passed away in July 2016.

Raza's close friend Ashok Vajpeyi, a poet and critic, muses, "A group of seven paintings is a kind of parikrama (circumambulation) by a painter around a great soul, a Mahatma who always inspired him[,] a noble venture around an ennobling theme" (Vajpeyi 39). The *saptak* (series of seven) is reminiscent also of the *saptapadi* ("seven steps") around a sacred fire that a Hindu couple takes together in the marriage ceremony as they enunciate vows for lifelong friendship and mutual care. Though the *saptapadi* ritual was not part of Raza's inspiration for these seven paintings, the paintings express Raza's own weddedness to Gandhi's values of peace, duty, and truth. Raza was eight years old when he first saw Gandhi, who had come to address a public meeting in Mandla, Madhya Pradesh, Raza's hometown. Raza would never forget the image of the ascetically clad Gandhi, who became a shaping source of his artistic imagination and life. When his extended family's homes were vandalized during the ethnic violence of the Partition, many of his relatives left for Pakistan, but Raza decided not to leave—the reason, he told Vajpeyi, was the Mahatma (Vajpeyi 29). After six decades in France following a career in art, Raza returned to India for good in 2011. It had become a personal tradition for him to visit Gandhi's ashrams in Sevagram and Sabarmati or Rajghat (Gandhi's memorial site in New Delhi) on every visit to India (Vajpeyi 30).

The first of Raza's Gandhi paintings is titled "Hey Ram," after the last words believed to have been uttered by the Mahatma when he was assassinated. The second is the Gujarati phrase "Peed Parai" ("The Suffering of Others"), taken from "Vaishnava Jana To," a famous composition by the fifteenth-century poet Narsi Mehta, another song that Gandhi loved. The other paintings are *Sanmati* (see fig. 4.1), *Satya* (*Truth*), *Shanti* (*Peace*), and "Thoughts of Gandhi Ji." The painting *Swadharm* (*One's Duty*) traces itself to a concept held dear by the freedom fighter and Gandhi's friend Vinoba Bhave. The last two consist of block quotations from Gandhi's and Bhave's writings. The written text on Raza's canvases functions not as exhortation but as invocation (Vajpeyi 35).

Two lines from Gandhi's favorite *bhajan* (the *Ramdhun*), which I translated in the "Prelude" to this chapter, resonate through Raza's *Sanmati*, which is a colorful grid of interlocking squares, rectangles, and triangles, at the center of which is a large, black circle. At the lower right corner is a line in Hindi: "Sabko sanmati de bhagavan" ("O God, give *sanmati* to all," my trans.). It is almost as if the many shapes and colors visually "speak" the other, un-reproduced line, "Ishvar and Allah are both your names," a truth held sacred by Gandhi—and Raza. The painting captures the flow between the aural

Fig. 4.1. Sayed Haider Raza, *Sanmati*, acrylic on canvas, 2013.
Reproduced from Bose et al. 20.

and the visual, manifesting Raza's belief that "a painting must be seen with
the ear" (Raza 25). In other words, art is an all-senses experience, and its
meanings percolate into many domains of life.

Raza's *Sanmati* painting depicts a mandala, a tantric geometrical diagram prominently used in Buddhist, Jain, and Hindu art, ritual, architecture,
and personal spiritual practice. While the symbolism of the mandala varies
across history and tradition, it is commonly understood as a metaphor for individual and cosmic energies and as a tool that can bring these energies into
balance (see Bühnemann). Reflecting on the influence of mandalas in his art,
Raza explains, "I wanted to understand the spirit which fires them. . . . My
preoccupation lies in the arrangement of the colored space. The equilibrium

of forces is as necessary in painting as it in life" (20–21). Such a balance between countervailing subjective forces is the outcome of *sanmati* when it is
an ethical practice of the everyday. It is also an outcome that is immeasur-
able, palpable but beyond the scientific.

The rough brushstrokes leave the work of the brush exposed, and in this ex-
posure, they display an unpredictable blending of solids and shades—browns
mingle with yellows, orange mingles with brown, black into grays, and so on.
The earthy colors, vivid, yet mingling, and the strokes, rough but distinct, play
out the aesthetic of *sanmati*, which recognizes humanity's many-ness, its quo-
tidian state, and its interconnectedness. This symmetrical juxtaposition leads
to the innermost focal point of the diagram: a tiny white dot, the *bindu*, in the
center of the black circle. Raza observes, "The bindu is full of potential. It is
the seed, the very beginning. In the West, one paints that which can be seen by
the retina of the eye. I have gone beyond immediate vision[;] I wished to grasp
Prakriti which is nature [in Hindu thinking]" (20). Seen through these remarks,
sanmati is a foundational orientation that harmoniously accommodates the
diversity of life forms. It is hence the seed of human flourishing.

***

The resolution of communal conflict that I have suggested can only be secured
through a response that requires first an imaginative immersion in history, or
multiple histories, and second (or simultaneously) an ethical orientation that
overcomes the imperialism of history as an adjudicator or arbiter of justice.
The first act concludes with how *sanmati* can be such a timely and timeless
response. The second act further argues that the claim to shared space could
generate narrations that may be different from each other but that are framed
in a way that accommodates each other. In the working of *sanmati*, such narrative frames acknowledge, corroborate, and build mutuality. They provide
assurance to others that they matter. The third act demonstrates an artist's
vision of *sanmati* as the flourishing of an exuberance of pluralism. To conclude, I have argued that *sanmati* is a generous orientation that overcomes
the me-other divide, that admits the truth-possibility of other worldviews,
and that recognizes humanity's interconnectedness across differences and
to other lifeforms. This orientation is the poetry, or the soul of worthwhile
living, the very ground on which co-being is imaginable and achievable. It
is fitting to end this chapter with the words of the scholar and human rights
activist Asghar Ali Engineer, who has written tirelessly on secularism and the

importance of an inter-religious society: "There are no theories, theologies and concepts to quarrel about; there are only problems and difficulties to be shared together. This is real dialogue of life, a dialogue through living together and sharing together."

Works Cited

Arendt, Hannah. *The Human Condition*. U of Chicago P, 1998.

Asher, Catherine. *Architecture of Mughal India*. Pt. 1, vol. 4 of *The New Cambridge History of India*. Cambridge UP, 1992.

Bigelow, Anna. *Sharing the Sacred: Practicing Pluralism in Muslim North India*. Oxford UP, 2010.

Bose, Nandalal, Gopalkrishna Gandhi, Ashok Vajpeyi, and S. H. Raza. *Gandhi in Raza*. Akar Prakar, 2017.

Bühnemann, Gudrun. *Maṇḍalas and Yantras in the Hindu Traditions*. Brill, 2003.

Business Standard. "The Ayodhya Case Timeline: Events Leading Up to the Historic Judgment." https://www.business-standard.com/article/current-affairs/the-ayodhya-case-timeline-events-leading-up-to-the-historic-judgment-119111000010_1.html. Accessed Dec. 11, 2023.

Eaton, Richard. "Temple Desecration and Indo-Muslim States." *Journal of Islamic Studies*, vol. 11, no. 3, 2000, pp. 283–319.

Engineer, Asghar Ali. "On Inter-Religious Dialogue." *Caravan*, May 1999, http://www.alliance21.org/caravan/en/3/pg18.htm. Accessed 29 Jun. 2020.

Gandhi, Mohandas K. *Ashram Observances in Action*. Navajivan Publishing House, 1955.

Gandhi, Mohandas K. *An Autobiography: The Story of My Experiments with Truth*. Translated by Mahadev H. Desai, Beacon Press, 1993.

Gandhi, Ramchandra. "Moksha and Martyrdom." *Selected Essays by Ramchandra Gandhi: The Seven Sages*, edited by A. Raghuramaraju, Penguin Books, 2015, pp. 121–41.

Gandhi, Ramchandra. *Sita's Kitchen: A Testimony of Faith and Inquiry*. State U of New York P, 1992.

Ghosh, Srikanta. *Muslim Politics in India*. Ashish Publishing House, 1987.

Gottschalk, Peter. *Beyond Hindu and Muslim: Multiple Identity in Narratives from Village India*. Oxford UP, 2000.

Gottschalk, Peter, and Mathew N. Schmalz. *Engaging South Asian Religions: Boundaries, Appropriations, and Resistances*. State U of New York P, 2012.

Husain, Yusra. "Ram Rajya Rath Yatra for Ayodhya Temple." https://timesofindia.indiatimes.com/city/lucknow/ram-rajya-rath-yatra-for-ayodhya-temple/articleshow/62844530.cms. Accessed Dec. 11, 2023.

Lal, Vinay. "Raghupati Raghav Raja Ram." *Experiments with Truth: Gandhi and Images of Nonviolence*, edited by Josef Helfenstein and Joseph N. Newland. The Menil Collection, 2014. pp. 244–45. https://southasia.ucla.edu/history-politics/gandhi/raghupati-raghav-rajaram/.

Mahaprashasta, Ajoy A. "Ayodhya: Evidence from Excavation Does Not Support ASI's Conclusion About Temple." https://thewire.in/history/ayodhya-dispute-excavation-evidence-temple-asi. Accessed Dec. 11, 2023.

Mayaram, Shail. "Ramchandra Gandhi: 'The Personal Is the Political Is the Philosophical.'" *Ramchandra Gandhi: The Man and His Philosophy*, edited by A. Raghuramaraji, Routledge, 2013, pp. 275–85.

Menon, Jaya, and Supriya Varma. "Was There a Temple under the Babri Masjid? Reading the Archaeological 'Evidence.'" *Economic and Political Weekly*, 11 Dec. 2010.

MirrorNow News. "Ayodhya Verdict: What are the Existing Structures in the 2.77 Acre Disputed Land?" https://www.timesnownews.com/mirror-now/in-focus/article/ayodhya-verdict-what-are-the-existing-structures-in-the-2-77-acre-land/513245. Accessed Dec. 11, 2023.

Mishra, Ishita. "Hindus Form Human Chain Around Muslim Baraat in Violence-hit Kanpur, Escort Them to Safety." https://timesofindia.indiatimes.com/city/kanpur/hindus-form-human-chain-around-muslim-baraat-in-violence-hit-kanpur-escort-them-to-safety/articleshow/72976520.cms. Accessed Dec 11, 2023.

Nath, Ram R. *Architecture and Site of the Baburi Masjid of Ayodhya: A Historical Critique.* Historical Research Documentation Programme, 1991.

Pawelski, James O. "Defining the 'Positive' in Positive Psychology: Part II, a Normative Analysis." *The Journal of Positive Psychology*, vol. 11, no. 4, 2016, pp. 357–65.

Prasad, Leela. *Poetics of Conduct: Oral Narrative and Moral Being in a South Indian Town.* Columbia UP, 2007.

Prasad, Leela. "Co-Being, a Praxis of the Public: Lessons from Arendt, Hindu Devotional (Bhakti) Narrative and Gandhi." *Journal of the American Academy of Religion*, vol. 85, no. 1, 2017, pp. 199–223.

Raza, Sayed Haider. *Mandalas.* Edited by Olivier Germain-Thomas, translated by Muthusamy Varadarajan and Padma Natarajan, ArtAlive Gallery, 2009.

Rehman, Mujibur. "What Dec 6 Means for India." *The Hindu Centre*, 5 Dec. 2015, http://www.thehinducentre.com/the-arena/current-issues/article7952163.ece. Accessed 20 Mar. 2018.

Snodgrass, Cynthia. *The Sounds of Satyagraha: Mahatma Gandhi's Use of Sung-Prayers and Ritual*, 2007. U of Sterling, PhD dissertation.

Suhrud, Tridip. "The Woman Who Cradled Gandhi." *India Seminar: Women Who Inspire.* Oct. 2021, https://www.india-seminar.com/2021/746/8%20The%20woman%20who%20cradled%20Gandhi-Tridip%20Suhrud.htm. Accessed 4 Feb. 2022.

Vajpeyi, Ashok. "Life, Art and Gandhian Light." *Gandhi in Raza*, edited by N. Bose et al., Akar Prakar, 2017, pp. 29–39.

5

Suffering, Joy, and Wonder

Teaching toward the Fullness of Life

Mary Clark Moschella

The field of pastoral theology and care addresses the formation and preparation of religious professionals in seminaries and divinity schools. The field developed historically out of a religious trajectory known as the "cure of souls" tradition.[1] This field has a long-held concern for human well-being, suggested by the pastoral image evoked in Psalm 23 (*King James Version*), in which "[t]he Lord is my shepherd," who is not only present "though I walk through the valley of the shadow of death" but who also "restoreth my soul" so that "my cup runneth over." Pedagogy in the field of pastoral theology involves teaching students caregiving skills that enable them to accompany care seekers through their own valleys of the shadow and back up into the light, to experience again what Carrie Doehring calls "reconnecting with the goodness of life" (185).[2] The learning of such skills, as Matt Croasmun puts it in his chapter in this volume, "Discerning the Good Life," requires "not the mere cognition of the object of study but rather an encounter with it" (73). Students learn pastoral and spiritual caregiving through reading, practicing, and reflecting not only upon their work but upon their encounters with the Holy. In tending to the spiritual in their own lives, students tap wellsprings of compassion for themselves and others.

In this chapter, I articulate a challenge that I have encountered in teaching in this field, particularly in discovering a lacuna of resources that concentrate on joy and flourishing in the lives of students, practitioners, parishioners, and pastoral care seekers. I then describe a research project that I undertook to explore

---

[1] From the Latin words *cura*, meaning 'care,' 'concern,' 'trouble,' and *curatus*, meaning 'one responsible for souls,' *cure* is also related to *curate*, suggesting the therapeutic dimensions of a religious, caregiving role. See https://www.etymonline.com/word/cure.

[2] Such accompaniment "through the valley" does not imply that recovery from loss or hardship always follows a linear path from sorrow to healing. In reality, while some hardships and sorrows ease over time, others persist. The classic pastoral care functions of sustaining, healing, guiding, and reconciling address the complexities of human spiritual struggles and joys.

Mary Clark Moschella, *Suffering, Joy, and Wonder* In: *Religious Studies, Theology, and Human Flourishing.*
Edited by: Justin Thomas McDaniel and Hector Kilgoe, Oxford University Press. © Oxford University Press 2024.
DOI: 10.1093/oso/9780197658338.003.0006

joy as a spiritual path in caregiving, noting how such a pastoral theological approach both overlaps with and diverges from the study of positive psychology. Finally, I return to pedagogy, describing new strategies that have helped me tilt my teaching more toward the light of goodness, grace, and glory.

Some years ago, while teaching what I considered a comprehensive introductory course called Introduction to Pastoral Theology and Care, I looked up one morning to notice a pained look on my students' faces. We were about three-quarters of the way through the term, and we had covered several serious topics: pastoral responses to grief, trauma, violence, depression, substance abuse, and poverty. And we had discussed many of the harmful social narratives that complicate these experiences and caring ministries: racism, homophobia, sexism, classism, and ableism. As I looked at my students' faces that day, they seemed not only tired but afraid. I imagined that they were thinking to themselves: "What is she going to hit us with today?"

I started to suspect that something might be missing from this introduction to the care or cure of souls. I asked myself: Was there any joy or wonder evident in the room? Was there any sense of what a privilege it might be to offer pastoral or spiritual care? And were the students gaining a feeling of their growing strength and competence for pastoral work? Upon reflection, I did not conclude that the students were completely bereft of joy or confidence, but rather I concluded that these affects had become muted by the overwhelming sadness of the human struggles that we were trying to learn to help alleviate. We had gone all the way down into the valleys of human suffering, but we had not experienced many moments of feeling our souls restored, much less the Psalmist's exalted assertion of "my cup runneth over" (Ps. 23:5b).

This gave me pause. For while all the topics and the literature and skills that the course covered were germane, it struck me that I had not offered enough in the way of replenishing soul care that could sustain students as they learned how to minister to suffering people. Though I had saved one week at the end of the course to talk about self-care, this allotment was too little, too late. Even teaching self-care often degenerated into proclaiming yet another obligation: that religious leaders must keep themselves emotionally healthy and strong lest they allow their woundedness, conscious or unconscious, to cause harm in the congregation. I was piling on one more duty rather than inviting students to take care of themselves with tenderness and holy love out of the knowledge that they themselves are precious beings, beloved of G-d.

These realizations led me to begin thinking and teaching about the importance of joy in the ministry and in life. Noting the paucity of the field's literature on joy,[3] and believing that the work of spiritual and pastoral caregiving
would not be vibrant, effective, or sustainable if caregivers failed to notice or
fully experience joy, I developed a research proposal to study these topics.
A generous fellowship gave me a year off in 2010–11 to work on this project.[4]
I spent some of this time studying positive psychology and offering a preliminary assessment of its relevance to the field of pastoral theology (Moschella,
"Positive").

Ultimately, I decided, in keeping with my field's communal, contextual
model of care (Ramsay), that I wanted to do research that would foreground
lived human experiences of joy, especially in the lives of caregivers. The word
communal in this model refers to the theological notion that the work of caregiving is not reserved for ordained clerics; it belongs to whole communities
of faith. The term *contextual* suggests the importance of social and cultural
dimensions of human lives. Influenced by postmodern understandings of
the social construction of reality and by a diversity of liberation theologies
(Latin American, Black, Feminist, Womanist, *Mujerista*, and so on), the field
of pastoral theology and care has recognized a duty to be attentive to cultural
differences and to injustices resulting from power asymmetries in social, political, and historical systems and institutions.

Working from this standpoint, I deployed a qualitative methodology,
whereby I explored primarily first-person accounts of five particular
caregivers (of various sorts) whose narratives exemplified, expressed, or inspired deep spiritual joy. I define *joy* (and distinguish it from *happiness*) in
two ways: first, as an emotional experience that is felt and expressed in a diversity of ways, and second, as a deeper and more enduring dimension of life
that might be called a spiritual path or a way of living that is characterized
by a sense of being deeply alive and aware (Moschella, *Caring* 97–126).
I wanted to catch a glimpse of this second kind of joy in action. I chose not
to interview people directly, in order to avoid "leading the witness" and
influencing respondents too much. Instead I explored traces of joy in the
published writings of these five paradigmatic figures, three of whom were
living and two, deceased: Heidi Neumark, Henri Nouwen, Gregory Boyle,

[3] Some important exceptions include work by Volney P. Gay, Angella Son, and Peggy Way.
[4] I acknowledge the Henry Luce III Fellows in Theology Program for its support of this research,
which is described more in depth in Moschella, *Caring*.

Pauli Murray, and Paul Farmer. (Sadly, Paul Farmer, a medical anthropol-
ogist and transformative leader in the world of public health, passed away
suddenly on February 21, 2022.) This was not a phenomenological study,
given that the authors clearly had already interpreted their own experiences
in their narratives. These narratives are not unselfconscious or pre-reflective,
but like all narratives, they are written with a particular audience in mind
(Ganzevoort 218–23). My approach was to explore these authors' reflections
upon their lived theologies, taking them at their word and allowing them
to tell their own stories as much as possible. Theology is about meaning
making, and I wanted to see how these authors' meaning-making processes
contributed to their own joyfulness and to their inspiring and fruitful caregiving efforts. I asked a series of questions of each story, examining the
practices and theologies to which they bear witness. From these stories,
I gathered plots and themes, using them to help me sketch out my own vision
of a pastoral theology of joy.

Obviously, this methodology differs significantly from the quantitative
scientific approaches that many positive psychologists deploy and/or pro-
fess.[5] Rather than attempting to build a generalizable theory with claims of
essential and universal knowledge, qualitative methodologies plumb particular, lived human experiences in their local and cultural contexts, taking
into consideration social inequalities and power struggles. While the insider
knowledge that this kind of study yields is context dependent and therefore
not generalizable, it is nonetheless valuable. Such studies yield insight and
explanatory power, an understanding of what is possible in human living
(Swinton and Mowat 43–44). In studying individual cases, situations, and
texts in this "close-up" way, different kinds of knowledge, such as practical
wisdom, can be gained (Campbell-Reed 33–59).

Having established that positive psychology and pastoral theology
approach the study of human flourishing from very different angles
(psychological versus theological) and with divergent methodologies (quantitative versus qualitative), it is perhaps surprising to note that there are still
similarities in our findings. In particular, in *Caring for Joy*, the study that
I described above, the common pattern that emerges in the caregivers' first-
person spiritual narratives is that of investing their lives wholeheartedly and
reflectively in efforts to alleviate human suffering *and* to build spaces, both
physical and cultural, in which grace, beauty, goodness, and the experience

---

[5] For a critique of the some of the scientific claims of positive psychology, see Moschella, "Positive."

of divine love might occur. These two dimensions of caregiving bear a resemblance to the metaphor of the *reversible cape* that philosopher James Pawelski argues is crucial to the psychology of human flourishing. In this metaphor, a red cape signifies "the power to fight against undesirable things in the world, things like poverty, violence, and injustice," while a green cape signifies "the power to help grow desirable things in the world, things like prosperity, peace, and justice" (Pawelski 358). Pawelski's purpose with this metaphor is to offer a more comprehensive understanding of the "positive" in positive psychology, which in its infancy might be said to have concentrated almost exclusively on green-cape emotions, activities, and goals. Here Pawelski considers the relative merits of each cape before concluding that both capes, both kinds of power, are needed for human flourishing. Because health is more than the absence of illness, we need the green cape, and because weeds can ruin a harvest, we need the red cape. The most positive living possible, the achievement of human flourishing, will require both creating beneficial experiences and conditions like health *and* working to challenge or eliminate destructive forces like injustice. Interestingly, Pawelski notes that "[i]t may be more difficult for us to focus on moving toward what is desirable, because this often seems like a set of more subtle skills" (361).

As noted, the five caregivers whose stories I studied all devote(d) themselves not only to challenging poverty, racism, and various forms of injustice but also to promoting healing, well-being, beauty, and love. This dual dimension of their lives and ministries might be seen as analogous to the wearing of a reversible cape. For example, Heidi Neumark, in her spiritual memoir of ministry in the South Bronx, *Breathing Space*, clearly calls out the injustice of a society that intentionally keeps massive waste facilities in the neighborhoods of people who live on New York's lowest economic rungs. "Breathing space" is more than a metaphor; it is a protest against the injustice that causes asthma in children in the South Bronx at rates wildly disproportionate to that of the rest of the population. But while much of Neumark's narrative challenges environmental racism and other forms of discrimination that her congregants encounter every day, there is more to her story. She also calls her writing "a song of thanksgiving" (Neumark xvii). It is a testament to the goodness and grace of the people she encountered in her ministry; it is also the story of a series of building projects that she and her congregation undertook. Such projects included working with other churches and social organizing agencies to get new, affordable housing built in their community and a multi-year project to rebuild the church's sanctuary, complete with a room that is dubbed "a space for grace" (Neumark 115). In this account, there is plenty of red-cape work, plenty of patching up and tending to sorrow and alleviating suffering, but there is also a determined focus on the work of building up a community, calling attention to peoples' strengths, and creating beautiful spaces in a part of the city otherwise characterized by urban blight. This might be thought of as green-cape work.

Yet I wonder if these two dimensions of lived theologies are always entirely distinct. In one of the most beautiful lines in her book, Neumark writes: "I have learned that grace cleaves to the depths, attends the losses and there slowly works her defiant transfiguration" (xv). In pastoral care, it is often through the process of accompanying people into the depths of their suffering that hope, grace, and even joy emerge. This seems like less of a cape reversal than a way of caring that involves attending deeply to people and staying with them through periods of struggle and periods of joy. Joy that is deep aliveness involves turning toward the fullness of life, which includes and encompasses both sorrow and wonder. Sometimes joy emerges in peoples' lives after a period of suffering. "Weeping may endure for the night, but joy comes with the morning," in the words of Psalm 30:5 (*New Revised Standard Version*). It is not that we "get over" grief, but through the process of grieving we learn to pay attention at a deeper level so that particular memories or experiences of beauty or kindness strike us in a new way and lure us forward toward ongoing life.[6]

In other cases, though, grief and joy are not two separate or consecutive experiences. Some caregivers report experiences of feeling great joy *in the midst* of their work of resistance to social evil. This seems less like wearing a reversible cape than wearing a blended one. Pauli Murray (1910–85), the great African American early civil rights activist, poet, attorney, and priest, offers one such example in her autobiography, *Song in a Weary Throat*. Even this title evokes a complexity of emotional energy, with "song" suggesting hope and joy, while "weary throat" alludes to the fatigue Murray felt in lifelong struggle against injustices of many kinds: racism, sexism (which she called "Jane Crow"), classism, and genderism. Murray tells the story of working successfully to desegregate two eating establishments in Washington, DC, in 1943 and 1944. She was a student at Howard Law School at the time; with so many men in her class away at war, Murray worked with the Howard NAACP

---

[6] Bruce Vaughn challenges the pathologizing of grief and argues for the paradoxical experience of joy that full-out grieving the loss of a loved one can make possible (36–45).

and women undergraduates to stage nonviolent demonstrations and sit-ins at the restaurants. While this work was both frightening and challenging, Murray reports, it was also exhilarating: "Although we were engaged in serious business, our planning sessions were fun and challenged our powers of imagination. The fact that we were doing something creative about our racial plight was exhilarating and increased our self-esteem" (*Song* 206). In this striking example, Murray's working against the evil of racial segregation combines with her sense of working *for* something positive, "doing something creative about our racial plight." The very process of actively engaging in the protest yields a sense of competence and delight (Moschella, *Caring* 172–73). Murray used her enormous creative and intellectual resources to contribute to the work of changing society in myriad ways throughout her life, living into a dream of freedom that did not previously exist.[7]

Is this red-cape or green-cape activity? Or is it evidence of a way of life that takes in both the suffering of injustice and the hope of creating something new and better? In this case, it seems to me that work *against* injustice and work *toward* visions of goodness are blended. While this story is quite striking and unusual (as is the life of Pauli Murray, who has recently had a Yale University college named after her), the dynamic of spiritual joy that results from turning toward the fullness of life is not unique to Murray. In the other stories I studied, and in many more stories that others have identified, there is evidence of joy that is linked to a sense that one is aligned with one's purpose and calling or that one is doing the right thing, even if under harrowing conditions and even when stubborn, long-institutionalized patterns of injustice are slow to budge.

In a seminar that I now teach called Justice and Joy, we work at bringing these two things together: engagement in the work of challenging injustice and tending to our own capacities for joy as a spiritual path. The place where many students find themselves, at least by late in the term, is at a concept of joy as resistance. This is similar to what Pauli Murray described: a kind of delight in using one's strength to fight for what is good and fair and just and a kind of daring refusal to give in to despair, even when one's cause appears to be hopeless. I think that this kind of joy is linked to living in a way that is consistent with one's deepest values.

---

[7] Murray also wrote searing poetry that describes the harsh realities of racism and holds out the dream of freedom. See stanza 1 of Murray's poem "Dark Testament," beginning with the first line: "Freedom is a dream."

The work of theologian Willie Jennings pushes the paradoxical logic of joy further when he speaks of joy as resistance against despair, particularly in the context of Black Americans' lives. He calls this "the serious work of joy" and differentiates it from the commercialized joy of the advertising industry (Jennings, "Joy"). Jennings notes that the work of resistance to despair requires cultivation in communities that can teach us how to "sing the Lord's song in a strange land" (*KJV*, Ps. 137:4). Such cultivation will at times require "segregated joy," joy nurtured in African diaspora communities that offer respite from the constant barrage of white supremacy in the cultural surround. The serious work of resistance to despair is thus both a fighting against the constant evil of racism and a proactive kind of planting and tending to a joyful and supportive community. This work cannot be done alone. Jennings advocates for belonging as a way of life (and a value for theological education) that is strong enough to resist despair. He writes, "Alienation is distance where there should be none, and the denial of the deep connection that is the birthright of living creatures and living prosperously as creatures together" (Jennings, "Beyond" 132).

The recognition that joy depends on community is resonant with the communal contextual model in pastoral theology. As Pamela Cooper-White notes in her chapter in this volume, "Sometimes Pessimism Is Good for the Soul," flourishing in pastoral theology always involves individuals *and* communities. Knowing that we are deeply related to each other, that we belong to each other, promotes and supports the joy of caring. To this end, I also try in my teaching to foster an ethic of care in the classroom that values mutual support rather than competition. When students are moved and inspired by each other's stories, they learn not only about but from each other. This experience resists the hegemonic narrative of Research 1 institutions that values people primarily for their production and pits people against each other for the highest grades, the most recognition, and, at the faculty level, the highest pay. I take joy in this approach to teaching, my own act of resistance in the classroom.

South African religious leader and social activist Desmond Tutu and his daughter Mpho Tutu write of the joy of choosing goodness, relating the story of Phila Portia Ndwandwe, a heroine in South Africa's struggle against apartheid, a story uncovered by the Truth and Reconciliation Commission. Ndwandwe suffered torture and eventual death at the hands of the South African Security Police in 1988 because she refused to give up information about the resistance movement. According to Tutu and Tutu, "Phila grasped a deeper truth: opting for the easy wrong may save the body, but it kills the soul. Life is more than breath and a heartbeat; meaning and purpose are the life of life. When we recognize that our lives have meaning beyond our cares and comforts, we tap the source of true joy" (75).

Goodness, according to Tutu and Tutu, is something that requires practice to be sustained. They write:

> The practices of goodness—noticing, savoring, thinking, enjoying, and being thankful—are not hard disciplines to learn. But they *are* disciplines, and they take practice. The habits that allow wrong to become entrenched— the mindlessness or tuning out, inattentiveness, the busyness of doing to distraction, and an ungrateful heart—can take hold so easily. . . . When we carve out time to really rest and be restored, we also restore our ability to be attentive. (28)

Thus we see how spiritual practices such as observing Sabbath rest not only lead to personal flourishing but also lend support to long-term involvements in justice-oriented movements. Tutu and Tutu recommend a spiritual practice that they have called "choosing good," a practice that is sustained not by "a finger-waving should" but through rest and reflection on such questions as "What is the action my best self would take?" (190). Desmond Tutu, in spite of all the violence and devastation he witnessed during his life, or maybe because of it, recommended rest and reflection upon the good in order to be attentive, aware, and awake to a more life-giving path.

Perhaps, as Pawelski argues, there is a subtle set of skills involved in working toward visions of the good or the desirable. I am trying to teach toward this subtle set of skills in my classes these days. While I must still teach the tasks of pastoral theology and care that involve responding to people in the midst of compelling situations of suffering and injustice, at the same time, I argue that *how* we respond to these situations is also important. I think that if we respond only out of a sense of obligation and not out of an internal sense of goodness, compassion, or divine love, then the full blessing of the work of spiritual care will elude caregivers and care seekers alike.

The life's work of Paul Farmer, cofounder of Partners in Health, exemplifies the subtle skills of working toward the good in numerous ways. Farmer had the capacity to imagine life-saving medical facilities in places like Mirebalais, Haiti, and Butaro, Rwanda, where previously none existed. He understood the importance of community so that he worked not just to heal the sick himself, practicing medicine as a calling and a source of personal joy but also to recruit and train local people to become physicians, nurses, and *accompagnateurs*, companions from the community who educate and assist patients in their ongoing care. Farmer understood the value of partnerships, recognizing that poverty, sickness, and politics are interrelated and that public health requires the concerted efforts of many partners. He also understood the importance of beauty and its capacity to draw us toward life. He is famous for building koi ponds and gardens alongside the hospitals and universities that Partners in Health established in many poor corners of the world. Like Tutu, Farmer recognized the need for his own replenishment and restoration in the difficult work he did. Moreover, he recognized that patients also need replenishment, goodness, and beauty in order to support their healing and flourishing. Staring into koi ponds, like gazing into a pastoral scene, can restore a felt sense of strength and vigor when these have been depleted.

Like Heidi Neumark, Paul Farmer also found spiritual strength in seeing the goodness of the people he encountered in his work. For example, he spoke of working with genocide survivors in Rwanda who were helping rebuild a health clinic "inside a prison full of those responsible for the mass killings that resulted in the deaths of their families" (Farmer 210–11). Farmer's spirituality of justice involved reflecting on human goodness, on the best of what human beings can do and not just the worst. This inspired him to wonder, "What can we do to promote peace and beauty in a world in which the poor especially are exposed to violence and endless affront?" (Farmer 210–11). His was a path that veered toward the light; he drew strength and hope from the beauty he found both in human beings and in the natural world.

The practice of attuning oneself to beauty may do more for the cause of justice than just comforting caregivers and patients in moments of exhaustion or affliction. Philosopher Elaine Scarry has written about the relationship between beauty and justice, noting the importance of symmetry to both and arguing that "[f]olded into the aesthetic surfaces of the world is a pressure towards social equality" (110). If this is so, it might be that our sense of ethical fairness can be boosted by taking in the symmetry or balance inherent in many kinds of beauty. Perhaps the practice of pausing to perceive beauty, whether in an art museum, in a lover's eyes, or in a koi pond, can contribute to our human capacity both to imagine and to realize visions of justice and goodness in the world.

In my attempt to construct a pastoral theology of joy, I commend the intentional practice of "feeling toward" the goodness, love, and beauty of G-d in the midst of engaged work in pastoral care and justice-oriented ministries. This is a kind of perceptual turning toward the fullness of life, which includes attending to the realities of suffering and also attending to the realities of goodness, beauty, and wonder in the world. This is what I mean when I define *joy* as being alive and awake. Psychologically speaking, this fullness is consistent with what Pamela Cooper-White points out in the work of Melanie Klein, for whom maturity "would mean the capacity to hold good and bad together, to enact love through a desire for the reparation of what has been caused by the destructive drive rather than its denial" (Cooper-White, "Sometimes" 30, this volume). So the challenge is to develop habits and practices that assist us in holding the awareness of both the real goodness of life and the need for justice-oriented activities together. We ought not to shrink from the painful realities that call forth our pastoral and spiritual energies to both fix and remake the world. At the same time, we ought to take in as much beauty, goodness, and love as our lives allow.

The course I teach called Justice and Joy mentioned above, was once titled Joy in the Ministry and in Life. I changed the title when students informed me that I had misnamed the course and that Justice and Joy is really what I had been teaching all along. Indeed, a focus on either joy or justice alone is tantamount to what Melanie Klein might view as a kind of splitting, resulting in either a proclamation of goodness and wonder that ignores the harsh realities—wishful thinking, as Cooper-White notes—on the one hand, or a form of caregiving that is one long and dreary battle against suffering, illness, and injustice, on the other. I suggest instead that care must be deep enough to hold human suffering and spacious enough to take in divine goodness, beauty, and love.

Over the years, I have struggled to find the best way to teach this course holistically so that students learn to tend to their own joy as well as to their goals for justice-oriented vocations and professions. I brought in a yoga teacher the first few times I taught the course in order to promote greater awareness of the bodily feeling of emotion. Then, with the help of a colleague, Sarah Farmer, who co-taught the seminar with me one year, I learned to introduce artistic and expressive dimensions into the seminar meetings. When offered paper and markers and encouraged to depict their stories, students have responded with surprisingly creative and open-hearted reflections. In telling their stories, reflecting on their work, and listening and responding to each other, students seemed to gain energy. I found that activities like this, sometimes paired with basic open-ended questions about how students felt about the reading, could set the stage for a more forthright and searching discussion. I later added the activity of reading poetry, usually at the end of each class, in order to inject a more direct, shared experience of concentration on the condensed wisdom of a poet. I preselect these poems, often from the work of Jane Kenyon, Mary Oliver, or Christian Wiman, so that the poetry pertains to the themes in the reading and discussion as much as possible. For example, consider the line from Wendell Berry's famous poem "Manifesto: The Mad Farmer's Liberation Front," "Be joyful, though you have considered all the facts" (38–9). This line, and this poem as a whole, bids the hearer not only to recall a positive emotion, as positive psychology might suggest, but also builds the case for understanding joy as a kind of resistance to death-dealing cultural narratives, as pastoral theology might advise. Pausing to read poetry in the classroom can itself be a practice of resistance to despair. Poetry is a creative form that is well suited to the task of naming reality in its complexity, describing life in fine and sometimes gritty detail while, through form, language, and sound, simultaneously invoking a sense of wonder and will.

Pastoral theologian Peggy Way wrote "God intends the flourishing of the beloved creatures, and affirms their desire for free play in a good world" (138). Various forms of artistic engagement, whether visual, musical, or literary, offer moments of free play in classroom spaces that are otherwise reserved for only rigorous thinking and careful speaking. Practicing such art forms is not an escape from the labor of learning but a way of engaging the right hemisphere of the brain in the enormous challenge of imagining more just and life-giving worlds (McGilchrist). It may be that viewing or making visual art, hearing or playing music, listening to or writing poetry can help students develop the "subtle skills" that James Pawelski suggests are needed for the green-cape work of moving toward the desirable, the just, and the good. Such artistic practices also increase a sense of community and collaboration in the classroom that supports students as they ponder their goals, values, professions, and vocations. In this pedagogy, I concur with Justin Thomas McDaniel's comments in his chapter in this volume, "Lab Courses for the Humanities": "Education is a process that hopefully creates more complex and empathetic persons who take their thoughts, their feelings, and, most importantly, those of others seriously. Education is about learning to appreciate, to reflect, to respect, and to care" (166).

In the Justice and Joy course, judging from course evaluations, instituting these changes in pedagogy has vastly improved students' learning, enthusiasm, and sense of well-being. Whether these impacts will reverberate in students' future care practices and the lives of people they serve is more difficult to assess at this point. This kind of teaching is like planting seeds: it is only years later that one discovers what took root.

Conclusion

In describing the field of pastoral theology and care, Bonnie Miller-McLemore notes that the discipline "pursue[s] a participatory, performative, and proactive kind of knowing that stays close to the ground, attends to human agony and ecstasy, and attempts to relieve suffering" (138). In this chapter, I have asserted that an overemphasis on human agony in the scholarship and teaching of the field can unwittingly lead to students' and practitioners' experiences of overwhelm or discouragement. Rather than contributing to the well-being of caregivers and the fruitfulness of their ministries, such a focus can leave students feeling empty or unequal to the task of caregiving. I have proposed teaching toward the fullness of life instead, as a way of replenishing and rebalancing the teaching of pastoral care, so that attending to human ecstasy as well as agony becomes a vital part of this "proactive kind of knowing." The care of souls involves addressing both the reality of human suffering, one's own and others', and attending to the felt realities of goodness, beauty, joy, and love. This is not to advocate for turning away from suffering in order to pursue personal happiness. Deep spiritual joy, as I have described it, involves awakening to and being aware of the fullness of life. Joy does not negate suffering; rather, it adds something, but it adds something that is also real. This means, as the poet Christian Wiman writes, that "even in moments of joy, part of that joy is the seams of ore that are our sorrow" (19).

This chapter began with a story about how I noticed that something was troubling students in my introductory pastoral care course, which had become problem centered. I conclude with another story of teaching in that course. In one class, I devoted the entire lecture to the topic of caring for joy, explaining why it was important to offer care out of a deep well of spiritual joy and also important to care for the great gift of joy in peoples' lives. The students appeared to be rapt. Interestingly though, at the end of the lecture, all the questions posed were about depression, how to respond to people who were depressed, and what to do in a mental health crisis. I was struck by this shift; it seemed as if the lecture on joy left students concerned about the lack of it. I answered all the questions dutifully. Then I asked students to turn to each other and tell a story about the last time they had felt joy. During the ten-minute exercise, I could sense the energy level increasing in the room. When invited to debrief the exercise, one student volunteered that they[8] were amazed, because doing the exercise helped them remember that though they had been experiencing depression, that they were not always depressed, and that they had had breaks from it, and remembering this had lifted their spirit.

This story reminds me that turning toward the fullness of life involves taking it all in, staying with people in their suffering and in their joy, as we work toward creating social and ecological conditions in which all life can flourish. This is the complicated but deeply joyful spiritual work of pastoral theology, the cure of souls.

A Denise Levertov poem titled "A CURE OF SOULS" helps convey a sense of what the field of pastoral theology is and the subtle ways in which spiritual caregiving can work:

A CURE OF SOULS

The pastor
of grief and dreams

guides his flock towards
the next field

with all his care.
He has heard

the bell tolling
but the sheep

are hungry and need
the grass, today and

---

[8] I use the pronoun "they" to anonymize the identity of the student.

every day. Beautiful
his patience, his long

shadow, the rippling
sound of the flocks moving

along the valley.[9]

My pedagogical goal is to communicate that in this field, we are pastors of
both grief and dreams, agony and ecstasy. Teaching toward the fullness of
life involves forming students in the practice of the subtle skills needed for
perceiving, receiving, and bestowing the blessings of goodness and love as we
walk together through valleys, shadows, and light.

Acknowledgments

"A CURE OF SOULS" By Denise Levertov, from POEMS 1960-1967, copy-
right ©1964 by Denise Levertov. Reprinted by permission of New Directions
Publishing Corp.

Works Cited

Berry, Wendell. "Manifesto: The Mad Farmer's Liberation Front." *Joy: 100 Poems*, edited
    by Christian Wiman, Yale UP, 2017, pp. 144–45.
The Bible. Authorized King James Version. Oxford UP, 1998.
Campbell-Reed, Eileen R. "The Power and Danger of a Single Case Study in Practical
    Theological Research." *Conundrums in Practical Theology*, edited by Joyce Ann Mercer
    and Bonnie J. Miller-McLemore, Brill, 2016, pp. 33–59.
"Cure." On-line Etymology Dictionary. https://www.etymonline.com/word/cure,
    Accessed 25 October, 2023.
Doehring, Carrie. *The Practice of Pastoral Care: A Postmodern Approach.* 2nd ed.,
    Westminster John Knox, 2015.
Farmer, Paul. "Spirituality and Justice." *To Repair the World: Paul Farmer Speaks to the
    Next Generation*, edited by Jonathan Weigel, U of California P, 2013, pp. 203–11.

---

[9] Used by permission of New Directions Publishing. The poet's use of exclusively male pronouns to
refer to the pastor is noted.

Ganzevoort, R. Roard. "Narrative Approaches." *The Wiley-Blackwell Companion to Practical Theology*, edited by Bonnie J. Miller-McLemore, Wiley-Blackwell, 2012, pp. 214–23.

Gay, Volney P. *Joy and the Objects of Psychoanalysis: Literature, Belief, and Neurosis*. State U of New York P, 2001.

The Holy Bible. New Revised Standard Version with Apocrypha. Oxford UP, 1989.

Jennings, Willie James. *Beyond Whiteness: An Education in Belonging*. Eerdmans, 2020.

Jennings, Willie James. "Joy and the Act of Resistance against Despair." Interview by Miroslav Volf. Yale Center for Faith and Culture, 2015. https://faith.yale.edu/media/joy-and-the-act-of-resistance-against-despair. Interview.

Levertov, Denise. *Poems, 1960–1967*. New Directions Publishing, 1983.

McGilchrist, Iain. *The Master and His Emissary: The Divided Brain and the Making of the Western World*. Yale UP, 2019.

Miller-McLemore, Bonnie J. "The Subversive Practice of Christian Theology." *Christian Theology in Practice: Discovering a Discipline*, edited by Bonnie J. Miller-McLemore, Eerdmans, 2011, pp. 137–59.

Moschella, Mary Clark, "Calling and Compassion: Elements of Joy in Lived Practices of Care." *Joy and Human Flourishing: Essays on Theology, Culture, and the Good Life*, edited by Miroslav Volf and Justin E. Crisp, Fortress, 2015, pp. 97–126.

Moschella, Mary Clark. *Caring for Joy: Narrative, Theology, and Practice*. Brill, 2016.

Moschella, Mary Clark. "Positive Psychology as a Resource for Pastoral Theology and Care: A Preliminary Assessment." *Journal of Pastoral Theology*, vol. 21, no. 1, 2011, pp. 5–17.

Murray, Pauli. *Dark Testament and Other Poems*. Silvermine, 1970.

Murray, Pauli. *Song in a Weary Throat: An American Pilgrimage*. Harper and Row, 1987.

Neumark, Heidi B. *Breathing Space: A Spiritual Journey in the South Bronx*. Beacon, 2003.

Pawelski, James O. "Defining the 'Positive' in Positive Psychology: Part II, a Normative Analysis." *Journal of Positive Psychology*, vol. 11, no. 4, 2016, pp. 357–65.

Ramsay, Nancy. *Pastoral Care and Counseling: Redefining the Paradigms*. Abingdon, 2004.

Scarry, Elaine. *On Beauty and Being Just*. Princeton UP, 1999.

Son, Angella. "Agents of Joy: A New Image of Pastoral Care." *Journal of Pastoral Theology*, vol. 18, no. 1, 2008, pp. 61–85.

Swinton, John, and Harriet Mowat. *Practical Theology and Qualitative Research*. 2nd ed., SCM, 2015.

Tutu, Desmond, and Mpho Tutu. Made for Goodness and Why This Makes All the Difference. HarperOne, 2011.

Vaughn, Bruce, "Recovering Grief in the Age of Grief Recovery." *Journal of Pastoral Theology*, vol. 13, no. 1, 2003, pp. 36–45.

Way, Peggy. *Created by God: Pastoral Care for All God's People*. Chalice, 2005.

Wiman, Christian. *My Bright Abyss: Meditation of a Modern Believer*. Farrar, Straus and Giroux, 2013.

6

The Perfumed Life

Teaching a Humanities of Unsettling

Noah Salomon

In the winter of 2018, I embarked on a pedagogical experiment at the liberal arts college at which I was then teaching.[1] In the liberal arts classroom, we are accustomed to the study of multiple traditions as objects to be unpacked: What do Confucian texts say about the self? What do Muslim thinkers write about popular sovereignty? Less often do we ask what it would mean, instead, to take on Islamic or Confucian concepts as lenses through which we confront a set of dilemmas that are inherent not in the texts but in the contexts we occupy today: how might these authors help us understand the problems that confront us, not by offering different answers to our already-conceived basic premises but by allowing us to see the worlds in which we live otherwise? While the religious studies classroom in the context of the liberal arts does not tend toward a constructive theology, as either a collective or an individual project, what I hoped would be different in this experiment is that the religious thinkers we studied would be engaged as interlocutors, their theories animated, and no longer rendered inert by the analytic gaze. Students would be encouraged to do this work both in class and through writing assignments that merged analytical rigor and personal reflection. While analyze we did, my goal in all of this was also to flip the gaze: to see what thinkers within the Islamic tradition might have to offer to

[1] The ideas in this chapter were developed in conversation with the students in the 2018 iteration of my class "The Perfumed Life: Islamic Sources of the Self" at Carleton College. Their insights allowed me to see the materials we read in ways that I otherwise truly could not have. I am forever grateful and indebted to them for this. While the present volume and, thus, this chapter's publication were delayed by the pandemic, the issues that we discussed in that class seem perhaps even more relevant now, after such a period of intense reckoning with life and how to live it. Many thanks to Shahzad Bashir, Mayanthi Fernando, and James Pawelski for their truly invaluable suggestions on earlier drafts of this chapter, and to my teacher, Saba Mahmood, who introduced me to many of the texts that I taught in The Perfumed Life for the first time and whose insight shaped how I came to think about them. This chapter is much stronger for all of their interventions. I alone bear the burden of any errors or shortcomings in what follows.

Noah Salomon, *The Perfumed Life* In: *Religious Studies, Theology, and Human Flourishing.*
Edited by: Justin Thomas McDaniel and Hector Kilgoe, Oxford University Press. © Oxford University Press 2024.
DOI: 10.1093/oso/9780197658338.003.0007

help us think critically about ourselves and our relationship to the world in which we live.

I titled the class in which I undertook this pedagogical experiment "The Perfumed Life: Islamic Sources of the Self." I meant the title to be playful in two senses. First, I wanted to offer a challenge to the multiple iterations of "the Good Life" classes that are offered at colleges and universities around the United States[2] and that are often cited when scholars are trying to defend the value of the humanities to skeptical administrators. The Perfumed Life was both a "Good Life" class and a critique of such classes. The class took its title from a common way of describing the life of the Prophet Muhammad: the 'perfumed' (or fragrant) 'biography' (or path, or life), *al-sira al-'atira*. What might it mean to strive after a perfumed life rather than simply a good life, in either the ethical or the eudaemonic sense? In what way does a description of life as both morally and physically perfumed— the latter so much so that there are numerous accounts in the Hadith literature of the Prophet's sweat being bottled for use as a fragrance by his followers[3]—both engage and supplant the same questions asked in the search for "the good"? For example, how are bodies and their senses immediately beckoned by such a model in a way that the good life, with its cerebral mode of engagement, does not? What are the material implications of this olfactory model and of its effect on its surroundings as a model that is not tied up in the interiority of the self but that insists on a certain kind of porosity? This is a porosity not in Charles Taylor's sense of letting the world into the self[4] but rather a model of self in which the self exudes into *its* surroundings. Perfume, like incense, is a substance whose source withers away or evaporates at the very moment that its power is diffused over a wider and wider expanse.[5] To what extent, then, is the perfumed life also about a 'good death' (*husn al-khatima*), the creation of presence in absence?

The second way in which I meant the title of my class to be playful was, of course, by riffing on Charles Taylor's monumental 1989 monograph, *Sources*

---

[2] One recent example is Yale's "most popular class ever," Psychology 157, Psychology and the Good Life. See https://www.nytimes.com/2018/01/26/nyregion/at-yale-class-on-happiness-draws-huge-crowd-laurie-santos.html.

[3] See, for example, "The Prophetic Guidance on Perfumes." https://www.islamweb.org/en/article/185392/the-prophetic-guidance-on-perfumes.

[4] Taylor, Charles. "Buffered and porous selves." https://tif.ssrc.org/2008/09/02/buffered-and-porous-selves/. See also Taylor, *Secular Age* 35–43.

[5] Also in 2018, insightful student papers in my Material Religions seminar helped me envision the power of the olfactory in religion in new ways, putting the subjects of these two classes that year into deep conversation for me.

of the Self. Not only was this class to offer an alternative genealogy of the self, one that was not grounded exclusively in the Western philosophical tradition,[6] thus provincializing Taylor's universalizing model of the modern, but it also sought to examine precisely what it might mean to place an adjective (here, "Islamic") before an inquiry into the self in the first place, at once appreciating the situatedness of tradition in the formation of who we are while recognizing that tradition is always in synergistic conversation with the world around it.[7]

The Perfumed Life also served as a critique of the Good Life model precisely because the readings we did helped to question the more utilitarian positionings of the humanities that Good Life classes these days are being encouraged to embrace. For example, by working on the self in order to displace it—a process that is at the heart of Islamic technologies such as *jihad al-nafs*, the 'struggle against the whims of the self,' and *fana'*, 'loss of self through absorption in God'[8]—students were forced to ask "What might a life be that includes choices that are not good *for me* but that nevertheless, like perfume in its diffusion, exude a sweet smell on the world that surrounds me?"

The present chapter, and the pedagogical experiment that I describe in it, emerge out of a sense of unease with the premise of the Humanities and

---

[6] On this point, see also Smith.

[7] Though the course began with readings from a number of classical sources from the Islamic tradition that theorized the self (some of the more prominent ones that we read were selections from Abu Hamid al-Ghazali's *Revival of the Religious Sciences*, al-Mufid's *Kitab al-Irshad*, Dwight Reynolds's edited collection *Interpreting the Self: Autobiography in the Arabic Literary Tradition*), the middle and final portions of the class sought further to destabilize a bounded notion of "the Islamic" by looking at the ways in which its invocation has been *both* in critique of and in conversation with secular-liberal, psychoanalytic, and physiological models thereof and thus has never developed entirely independent of them. While I am interested in what unique interventions texts emerging out of the Islamic tradition have to offer, I also wanted to be careful not to reproduce a clash-of-civilizations model in which the Islamic was simply juxtaposed with the Western. After reading several thinkers who articulated the nature of the modern (Western) self (Rose; Foucault, "Ethics" and "Technologies"; Butler; Taylor, "Inwardness"), we dove into works as diverse as Saba Mahmood's *The Politics of Piety*—a book that looks at attempts by pious Egyptian women to craft virtuous selves in critical tension with prevailing models of self-realization that are upheld by Western feminism—and Omnia El Shakry's *The Arabic Freud*, which looks at how psychoanalytic theories of the self among a group of Egyptian thinkers in the mid-twentieth century were in fact not positioned in contradistinction to "the Islamic" (here, Sufi texts) but rather existed alongside it in mutually revealing conversation. In doing so, we were set up to read a series of twentieth-century autobiographical texts—Zaynab al-Ghazali's *Return of the Pharaoh*, Muhammad Asad's *The Road to Mecca*, and Amani al-Khatahtbeh's *Muslim Girl: A Coming of Age*—with an appreciation for what it might mean to think through a set of *Islamic* sources of the self while at the same time coming to question the boundaries of the category, assembled as it is (from its founding *and not* because the modern presents a peculiar problem of authenticity) with a variety of prevailing models of the self and its formation.

[8] We engaged these concepts primarily through reading Cyrus Zargar's brilliant volume *The Polished Mirror: Storytelling and the Pursuit of Virtue in Islamic Philosophy and Sufism* and Jamal Elias's wonderful translation of Sultan Bahu's poetry, *Death before Dying*.

Human Flourishing Project: the idea that the humanities can be (or needs to be) redeemed or advocated for through an appeal to how it furthers our well-being, a "positive humanities" as its supporters put it.[9] I worry that a humanities reduced to a eudaemonic agenda risks ignoring the critical, indeed paradigm-shifting, interventions of the worlds we study, particularly those that challenge, and that indeed might upset us, most deeply. I worry, too, that such an approach misses a critical task of the humanistic project at large: its ability to dampen the certainty of our own desires (whether individually, as a community, or even as a species) by placing them in a complex and sometimes ethically confounding moral universe. What my humanities experience has taught me is that the humanistic endeavor, at its most powerful, is useful not to the extent that it makes us happy but in the way that it unmoors us, causes us to question our assumptions, stops us in our tracks, wakes us up in cold sweat, makes us question the firmness and fitness of our assumptions. This might indeed lead us through angst, anger, or confusion, attributes that would not have us score well on any measurement of well-being (see Weitzman, "Can 'Spiritual Fitness,'" this volume) but that nevertheless can dislodge us from complacency, thereby inspiring new beginnings.

In what follows, I will use the example of my Perfumed Life course to articulate broader concerns regarding the application of a positive psychology approach to the humanities, discussing in turn why I think that religious studies might be particularly well-poised to offer a unique model for resisting and resetting the premise of this intervention. In conclusion, through outlining a few moments in the course as it unfolded, I will explain how The Perfumed Life approached the question of the self in a way that pushed against the turn to a eudaemonic model in the humanities in what I hope were productive ways.

Religious Studies and the Eudaemonic Turn

It seemed to me then, and it still does now, that the texts we engaged in The Perfumed Life are uniquely positioned to offer a critical perspective on the discourse on happiness as expressed in the Humanities and Human Flourishing Project. Many religious texts, in and outside the Islamic

[9] "Our Work." *Humanities and Human Flourishing*, https://www.humanitiesandhumanflourish ing.org/about. See also Tay and Pawelski.

tradition, share in the displacement of the self, and its well-being, that was so central to the texts we read in The Perfumed Life. It is perhaps *this* that makes the texts "religious"—that is, they do not have a human-centered ontology.

This makes religious studies a crucial stopping point for the Humanities and Human Flourishing Project in several key ways. Texts like the ones we read force us to ask not what the humanities can do for us—a set of theories or ideas that can somehow be packaged neatly, measured, and consumed in order to increase the well-being of our students or the public at large—but rather how the humanities can serve as a critical lens through which to challenge the monopoly of our prevailing assumptions about the world in which we live, as well as the solipsism that often motivates us within it. Perhaps it is this that makes religious studies so useful as a discipline within which to study these questions, even for students who might not consider themselves committed *believers* in a faith tradition. When we study closely the critical posture of religion, we are rendered open to imagining the world differently, less certain in precisely those certainties that have led us to this modern moment of despair in the first place.

Reading these texts for The Perfumed Life, which displaced, dissolved, and battled with the self, forced our class to take a hard look at whether individual well-being (or even collective well-being, wherever we draw that line around which collectivity we mean) should be what we are aiming for in the humanities classroom. Given that the effects of US power worldwide have led to suffering at such deep levels,[10] it seems to be odd indeed to be asking how the humanities can help *us* in the American academy, or the American public at large, feel better.[11] Might a more immediate task for the humanities be to ask: how can we instill in one another enough of a sense of

---

[10] As I wrote this chapter in 2018, I was thinking of Yemen, where the United States, in its military support of Saudi Arabia, was "literally fueling the world's worst humanitarian crisis" (https://www. nytimes.com/2018/09/12/world/middleeast/saudi-yemen-pompeo-certify.html), as it goes to press in 2024, in the wake of yet another U.S veto of a UN cease fire resolution, of course the annihilation of Gaza enabled by U.S support rises to the surface. I am sadly confident that other examples will rise to the surface when the reader encounters this chapter.

[11] Indeed, as we spend millions on our well-being here in the United States, while many countries around the world (and even communities in the United States) suffer from the lack of the most basic necessities, we also must be prepared to ask, "At what point does our flourishing need simply to stop, so that others might flourish a bit instead?" This is true both in the sense of *our* in terms of ourselves and our students but also *our* in the sense of humanity in its relationship to other forms of life. While I am hesitant to go too far in updating this chapter to take on more recent literatures outside of the 2018 workshop context for which it was written, it seems worth mentioning that scholars writing in the context of the planetary destruction that has been wrought by human-made climate disaster seem also to be asking this question of the ethical limits of human flourishing in provocative ways. For perspectives from scholars who take on this problem from two different angles, see Timofeeva; Banerjee and Wouters.

modesty and humility that we begin to question our hedonistic obsession with ourselves—and if education becomes primarily about self-fulfillment, it will be nothing more than that—and look instead at our engagement with the other (other humans, other species, other elements of the natural or cosmic order) in more critical ways? Many have furthered the argument that we might save the humanities by pointing out to skeptical administrators the way it advances human flourishing, situating it more explicitly within the eudaemonic turn,[12] or within efforts to solve the mental health crisis among students. While such efforts can be helpful, might we also lose something of the humanities' critical purchase, the places where it makes students uncomfortable, unsettled, angst filled, or troubled (all productive emotions to be feeling in our deeply troubling age) when we do that? The humanities at their best are a call to action: they give voice to hidden narratives, they give form to unarticulated emotion, they uncover our weakest characteristics. I fear that we lose that when the humanities are harvested for their ability to help foster our "happiness" alone.

Out of all the engagements with fields in the humanities, the interface between the Humanities and Human Flourishing Project and religious studies and theology has the potential to be a singularly fortuitous one. The reason for this is that religious studies, perhaps uniquely among the humanistic disciplines, reckons with a world in which there is something beyond the human, indeed something whose flourishing might be more important or even at severe odds with many varieties of human flourishing. While it is also true that religious studies might bring to the surface a boutique positing of varieties of human flourishing that the social sciences have not yet considered—which are, as Pamela Cooper-White nicely puts it in this volume, "both *contextual* (transcending individualism) and paradoxical or, in Moltmann's terminology, *dialectical* (transcending 'mere' happiness)" ("Sometimes" 36)—it is the possibility that religious studies has to refuse the anthropocentric or solipsistic premise *altogether* that gives it its force. It is in a rejection of a model narrowly focused on human flourishing—for its hubris, its speciesism, its translatability into capital, its depoliticization of the world in rejecting the prophetic inspiration to live in submission to God alone—in which, perhaps, the greatest power of a great deal of what we read in religious studies lies.[13] If we are unwilling to take seriously that religion

[12] See, for example, Pawelski (207–08), where he advances such an argument.

[13] Pawelski's interest in opening up conversations on human flourishing beyond the perspective of psychology in passages such as these is commendable: "[T]he theoretical, empirical, and applied

(perhaps uniquely among what we study in the academy) might be about something trans-, post-, supra-, and even sometimes anti-human, we never get to its true transformative potential in this troubled world in which we live. In short, in its attention to the questioning of anthropocentric models of the universe, religious studies can do much more than just offer alternative models of human flourishing. But in order to let it, we must first be willing to take seriously the idea of an immaterial or trans-material, or even transcendent, reality, such as that which the religions we study pose.

Our profession's most lasting contribution is not its ability to bring joy to the masses but rather its capability to productively unsettle, as religions always have. Angst, even that which leads to great personal crisis, can be a positive force, one that is in need of solidarity and not treatment, particularly when it helps us recognize material causes of melancholy that require intervention. It does not come as a surprise that an organization as allergic to unsettlement in its ranks as the US military (again, see Weitzman, "Can 'Spiritual Fitness,'" this volume) has latched onto positive psychology, the social scientific theory that lies at the foundations of the Humanities and Human Flourishing Project both institutionally and intellectually. Here positive psychology is seen as helping make soldiers more capable of dealing with adversity (enhancing "resilience and coping skills," in militaryspeak) and, one can surmise, less prone to developing the kind of critical mindset necessary for rising up against horrors that the US military has unleashed. For this reason, it is no coincidence that the US military has been a major client of the University of Pennsylvania's Positive Psychology Center, which also sponsored the present volume, contracting with them for tens of millions of dollars. A recent, damning article in *The Chronicle of Higher Education* that discusses this relationship (Singal) argues that positive psychology's claims to effectiveness have been based on thin to no empirical evidence, thereby giving vulnerable families false hope and providing the US military with an excuse when it is critiqued for not doing

---

work of positive psychology is especially important because it is part of a wider, interdisciplinary quest to understand and cultivate the good life. This broad and important quest cannot be undertaken successfully by using a single method of inquiry or by individuals from one particular discipline. It requires each of us not only to do our best but also to reach out to others, to colleagues in economics, in public policy, in neuroscience, in medicine, in organizational studies, in education, in the arts and humanities—in short, to anyone using sound methods of inquiry to try to further our understanding of human flourishing" ("Defining" 364). Yet by subsuming all disciplines to seeking after the same goal, Pawelski's approach misses out on the far more critical question of how each discipline might ask a different set of questions in the humanistic endeavor than ones that are merely about how we might bolster the "good life," despite the multiple definitions of *the good* to which Pawelski is open.

enough to address the crisis in its ranks.[14] Yet, it seems to me, if such work is scientifically suspect, it is even more so morally, for it is based on the premise that the trauma that US soldiers suffer should be addressed by eliminating their symptoms rather than by actually reckoning with the fact that the horrors into which the government has co-opted the soldiers are (understandably) leading to the trauma in the first place.[15] What is most troubling here, and I think highly relevant to our discussion of the use of positive psychology in the humanities, is that positive psychology is not being used to help soldiers cope with trauma after the fact but rather to engage in violence with less of a troubled conscience—that is, not to experience the moral reckoning signaled by trauma in the first place. Describing the official who adopted positive psychology for the military, Singal quotes her as saying, " '[Y]ou can really prime your pump before you face adversity to actually get yourself prepared for it.' "[16] Extending all of this to the attempt to infuse the humanities with a positive psychology model, which is the premise of much of the literature on the humanities and human flourishing that I have cited, I worry deeply about such an approach's propensity to desensitize our students to the very complex emotions that they should be feeling upon encountering the texts we teach, which grapple with the hardest moral and political choices that we face in our lives.[17] In other words, I am wary of a humanities whose goal is to produce self-satisfied and affirmed students, rather than suspicious and critical minds that are deeply unsettled, as they should be, in these unsettling times.

[14] The founder of positive psychology, Martin Seligman, rebuts the claims made about the goals and scientific validity of his work with the military in a response that he wrote to Singal's piece, which also appeared in *The Chronicle of Higher Education*. While I have no standing to dispute the empirical data or its methodology, I find the structure of his argument not to be convincing. In the article, Seligman claims that his intervention was unconcerned with preventing trauma ("preventing PTSD was not a core goal of Comprehensive Soldier Fitness") and that it was instead intended to build overall soldier fitness (thus shielding himself if, in fact, his methods are unable to reduce trauma) while he *simultaneously* claims that his methods perhaps result in soldiers who are less likely to develop PTSD (thus reaping reward if in fact his methods do reduce trauma!): "[P]ositive psychology interventions are highly effective[;] they prevent anxiety and depression, and therefore perhaps PTSD."

[15] For a brilliant reflection on what the PTSD discourse in military psychology occludes, see Nadia Abu al-Haj's *Combat Trauma: Imaginaries of War and Citizenship in Post-9/11 America*.

[16] Singal continues by summarizing the military's interest in positive psychology's *preventative* benefits: "Could there be a way to instill in soldiers a sense of resilience and optimism that would help them both during combat and after, that would effectively inoculate them against the worst psychological ravages of war?"

[17] Also troubling is the use of positive psychology by rapacious businesses and authoritarian regimes to reduce instances of dissent in situations in which governments and business are unwilling to improve material conditions. It is, of course, much cheaper to change people's attitudes than it is to change the conditions of their existence. For this, see Ehrenreich.

I am reminded at this juncture of the 2004 volume from Routledge Press by British sociologists Jeremy Carrette and Richard King, *Selling Spirituality: The Silent Takeover of Religion*. The book struck me on reading it (and still does), as a rather blunt instrument: a Marxist critique in reverse mirror image, relying romantically on a notion of "true" Eastern religion as a counterpoint to the commodification of the Eastern traditions through Yoga, spirituality and the "privatisation of eastern wisdom traditions." However, its key thesis, that there is a danger of missing the point (in their rendering, the point is social justice) of some of the religious philosophies we are reading if we use them solely for self-betterment, seems wholly relevant for this conversation.[18] I, too, want to ask how the humanities can do something more than feed into our own senses of well-being and self-worth. More importantly for us as religious studies scholars, under the gaze of detractors who are increasingly demanding that we show them a clear "return on investment," we must ask, how can our own unique perspectives as experts in and translators of traditions that our students might otherwise not be able to access explain why a *critical humanities* that unsettles rather than delights, and indeed that sometimes chastises and not only charms, also be of value to the academy and our collective project as teachers and scholars?

Critical scholarship should begin to question the eudaemonic turn in the humanities as well to the extent that it only further entrenches the fiction of the bounded human subject and its interests. The Humanities and Human Flourishing Project may have the unintended effect of re-entrenching human/nonhuman boundaries by positing a human flourishing that can be isolatable from the flourishing of nonhuman forces, whether animals, the environment, or even that which we encounter in religious traditions (whether we think of this as divine or as the sedimented collection of past endeavor, in either case it is not reducible to the subject of human flourishing). Putting the field of posthumanism

---

[18] Indeed, a passage in Pawelski celebrates the example of a Harvard Business School professor who has figured out how to monetize theater posturing techniques, which, she's learned, if her business students master, ends in a situation "leading to greater tolerance for risk, and resulting in increased performance on job interviews" ("Bringing" 215). This comes as part of a list of ways the humanities could more explicitly "realize more of their well-being potential" (215). There is no discussion, however, on whether such a use value mirrors one's ethical commitments, a reckoning with the fact that, for example, the business class has contributed to furthering gross income inequality in this country and that one therefore might want to tread cautiously in embracing its agenda. Instead, it is the well-being potential (here individually and materially framed) of collaboration with business models that is all that is embraced.

in conversation with secularism studies, Mayanthi Fernando, in a recent essay on the *Immanent Frame* that we also read for The Perfumed Life, writes, for example:

> A plethora of recent posthumanist scholarship . . . has sought to present humans as always already in relation to nonhumans, to recognize the agency of nonhumans and things, and to conceive of human flourishing as deeply entangled in the flourishing of nonhuman worlds. In re-emphasizing the porosity of human subjects and their vulnerability to and dependence on nonhuman actors (or agents), posthumanism might, then, be understood as a postsecular project, an attempt to undo the human-centric foundations of secularity.

Indeed, might religious studies—as the discipline that engages ontologies in which the human is not the primary agent and in which the individual's well-being is so often not the primary goal—be precisely the place where we begin to *undo* the obsessive focus on our own well-being and instead question whether the purpose of the humanities might be to set us on another path, one on which we might bracket ourselves, and even suffer a bit, in the pursuance of some greater good?

Three Critical Approaches to the Self

The materials we read for "The Perfumed Life" attempted to answer this question. In doing so, they sparked sustained, and often conflicted, reflection among both the students and their professor as to how the thinkers we read—and the ideas they espoused, coming from such distant times and places—might refract the problems and possibilities with which we are occupied today in new ways. I will discuss three texts we read for the class briefly so that the reader has some sense of how the "Islamic sources of the self" can help us question both the anthropocentrism and the eudaemonic turn regnant in humanities and human flourishing literatures. These texts we read often either displaced happiness for ethical goals that extended beyond it or, in some cases, in fact rejected *human* flourishing all together for the flourishing of a broader cause or nonhuman agent. In the sections below, we will encounter three distinct models that adopted such an approach.

The Polished Mirror

The course began with a set of readings from Abu Hamid al-Ghazali's (d. 1111) famous *Revival of the Religious Sciences*,[19] focusing in particular on the chapter on "Disciplining of the Self" (*"Kitab riyadat al-nafs"*). In this text, Abu Hamid al-Ghazali discusses the process by which the original purity of man, symbolized by the mirror clouded after years of rust-inducing sin, is polished through a certain variety of work on the self. Here students began to question whether self-realization is or should be a process of finding or revealing our true desires that are buried underneath social constraints or rather whether it might be through adopting a series of constraints that we become better versions of ourselves. Moreover, the "better" itself was destabilized, since for Abu Hamid al-Ghazali it is so deeply tied to pleasing God. Regardless of students' religious leanings (or the lack of such leanings), this notion of a better that might include our own immediate suffering was a productive site of debate. Saba's Mahmood's *The Politics of Piety*, which we also read for this class, was instrumental in helping us articulate this process in a more contemporary setting. Here we took seriously the term *riyada* in the title of Abu Hamid al-Ghazali's chapter, which means not only 'disciplining' but 'sport.' We thought through the way that training (to run a marathon, for example) can often be a painful process in the moment and yet result in some more distant goal. In this model, the self and its fulfillment are by no means displaced (as they are more radically so in the models that I discuss below) but instead are situated within a broader ethical framework whereby individual fulfillment and happiness could only be understood in the context of a much larger ecosystem. Abu Hamid al-Ghazali reflects at length on the importance of renouncing desire and aspiration, thus putting him in tension with the literature in the eudaemonic turn that focuses unevenly on their fulfillment. He quotes the Sufi Yahya ibn Mu'adh al-Razi:

Fight your soul with the swords of self-discipline. These are four: Eating little, sleeping briefly, speaking only when necessary, and tolerating all

---

[19] Though the Persian recension of this text is called *The Alchemy of Happiness* (*Kimya-Yi Sa'adat*), and although Abu Hamid al-Ghazali discusses 'happiness' (*al-sa'ada*) at many points throughout both this and other texts, his sense of what it means is very much distinct from the sense used in positive psychology literature, as should become clear in the below. See also, for example, Laleh Bakhtiar's comments in this regard on what she calls Abu Hamid al-Ghazali's "traditional psychology" (pp. 4–5) in the introduction to the version of *On Disciplining the Self* that we read for the class.

the wrongs done to you by [others]. For eating little slays desire, sleeping briefly purifies your aspirations, speaking little saves you from afflictions, and tolerating wrongs will bring you to the goal—for the hardest thing for a man is to be mild when snubbed and to tolerate the wrongs done against him. And when the wish to indulge your desires and sin stirs in your soul, and the delight of superfluous discourse is aroused, you should draw the sword of eating little from the scabbard of the midnight prayer and sleeping briefly, and smite them with the fists of obscurity and silence until they cease to oppress you and avenge themselves upon you, and you become safe from their vicissitudes to the end of your days, having cleansed them of the darkness of the soul's desires so that you escape from their hazardous afflictions. At this you will become a subtle spiritual body, and a radiance without weight, and shall roam in the field of goodness, travelling the paths of obedience to God like a swift horse in the field. (A. H. al-Ghazali 57)

Here, for Abu Hamid al-Ghazali, it is through denying self-fulfillment, it is when we are cut by the sword of self-discipline, that we achieve ethical goals. Here we are transformed into weightless and "subtle spiritual bod[ies]"— anti-material (or even empty) selves floating above this world—which are foreign to much of our contemporary thinking on flourishing and its immanence. Such a passage is also reminiscent of another text we read during the term, *The Epistles of the Brethren of Purity*,[20] a dialogue in the form of an imagined court trial in which humans and animals spar over their relative virtue and in which animal life is celebrated for precisely its mastery of the will. The goal in Abu Hamid al-Ghazali's text is discomfort, a training of the self in service of a higher good, and together as a class we explored the virtues of an Islamic mode of self-discipline as a means of thinking through our own commitments to greater goods that exceed our individual self-fulfillment. The metaphor of the polished mirror itself was also not lost on students. What would it mean to strive to arrive at a self that was not an inner, ego-fashioned core but rather reflected, in the clearest way possible, some exterior being or ethical goal not of one's own creation? What if the further we dug into ourselves, clearing away the accretions of our individual histories, we realized that we were not ourselves after all?

---

[20] We also read Zargar's analysis of the text in *The Polished Mirror*.

Death before Dying

Sultan Bahu, a seventeenth-century Punjabi poet, was the subject of an evening session of The Perfumed Life that we held toward the middle of the academic term, and offers a contrast to Abu Hamid al-Ghazali's model of self-discipline. The stunning collection of his poetry translated by Jamal Elias, *Death before Dying*, provided a dense landscape for critical reflection on what it might mean to think through, not the disciplining of the self, but its disintegration through absorption in God. In his model, self-dissolving, rather than self-betterment, is the desired end:

> Neither am I a sage, nor am I a scholar, nor a cleric, nor a judge.
> Neither does my heart ask for hell, nor is it content with fondness for
> paradise.
> Neither did I keep the thirty fasts [of Ramadan] nor am I a pure,
> praying person.
> Unless you attain Allah, Bahu, this world is but a game. (Elias 29)

Here, Bahu lifts his nose in disdain at all the practices of the self that are said to lead to the polished mirror, the refined self that is discussed in texts like that of Abu Hamid al-Ghazali. Neither prayer nor fasting nor scholarship interest Bahu, for they all focus the believer's attention egotistically on him/herself instead of on God. The struggle against the self through ritual discipline is to him oxymoronic: by struggling against the self, we focus on the self, thus giving it more form and substance than it deserves. His is a model in which the self is sidelined altogether in favor of ultimate union with God.

Our conversations in class here turned from a discussion of self-discipline, the focus of the previous section of the class that I discussed above, to an inquiry into radical selflessness. The ascetic urge, often offered in a secular translation as a psychological process of self-betterment, was here read at face value: a destruction of one's own self, body, and soul in pursuance of absorption into something higher (here, God), a death before dying. What might it mean to act in the world directly against one's self-interest, to become annihilated (in the sense of suspending one's agency, pulled into union with the will of something higher) while still alive in the world? Moreover, how does Sultan Bahu's own insistence on committed antinomianism, on a disdain toward religious ritual and proscription, result in his being closer to attaining truth? In other words, is the good always the same as the ethical? If not, how might we shift our view of radicals, misfits, and others who accrue blame or disdain in our present society? Might they provide a service beyond one that benefits their individual biographies or that of our common humanity?

Standing up to the Pharaoh

A further turning point of the class was when we read Zaynab al-Ghazali's (d. 2005) classic *Return of the Pharaoh: Memoir in Nasir's Prison*. *Return of the Pharaoh* would probably not be high on the list of most scholars putting together a course on Islamic conceptions of the self, as reflection on the self and its construction is nowhere framed explicitly in that text. The book describes, in autobiographical form, a period from the life of Zaynab al-Ghazali, the leader of the Muslim Sisterhood, the women's wing of the Muslim Brotherhood, and her tortures and trials in the secret prisons of Jamal 'Abd al-Nasir's regime. Yet in addition to being a harrowing account of the violence directed at political prisoners in 1960s Egypt, the book also depicts Zaynab al-Ghazali as she struggles with torment, physical and psychological, on the path of advocating for her cause. Her mode of engaging with the world displaces her self in favor of a larger cause, on the one hand, and in favor of God, on the other. A prayer that Zaynab al-Ghazali recalls reciting as a means of both psychological and physiological escape at a shocking moment in which she is being viciously attacked by dogs in the prison provides an example of a life lived not for its eudaemonic ends but for a cause she believed to be noble (students recognized that whether or not this cause was one they themselves would want to pursue is beside the point of our inquiry; instead, it was the relation of the self to the world in Zaynab al-Ghazali's model that they tried to distill). She writes, recounting the prayer:

> Oh Lord! Make me not distracted by anything except You. Let all my attention be for You Alone, You my Lord, the One, the Only, the Unique, the Eternal Absolute. Take me from the World of Forms. Distract me from all of these phenomena. Let my whole attention be for You. Make me stand in your Presence. Bestow on me your tranquility. Clothe me with the garments of your Love. Provide me with death for Your sake, loving for your sake, contentment with You. O Lord. Hold the steps of the faithful firm. (Z. al-Ghazali 50)

The prayer comes after several passages in which Zaynab al-Ghazali will-
ingly accepts torture rather than give into endorsing Nasir's regime, despite
the promises of worldly power she is offered,[21] and the passages end with
the miracle that there was no blood on her clothes, despite her being bitten
by numerous vicious hounds. God releases her from a world of forms quite
literally, revealing that the only *truly real* is Him and not the tests faced in
this world, nor even her own desires and well-being, which are ephemeral in
comparison to His abiding eternity.

In this book also, the class was able to examine a model of engagement with
the self beyond individual human flourishing. While arguably even the mys-
tical material that I outlined above when discussing "The Polished Mirror"
was not about individual human flourishing insofar as the goal was to discover God within, in the material covered in that section this was achieved
through individual self-betterment, through a certain kind of refinement of
the self. Moreover, with Sultan Bahu, in his destruction of the self, we get
no sense of a context beyond his individual struggle; there is no solidarity
there. For Zaynab al-Ghazali, an Egypt living under the banner of Islam (socially first and politically only later, as she insists) was so valuable that her self
and its pious refinement could be sacrificed in the process: she describes not
being able to worship properly in prison, taking pills, and smoking cigarettes.
Her time in prison is not one of quiet contemplation and ascetic struggles
against the lower self, but rather the text highlights the mundane tactics that
she had to embrace simply to survive, in service to a higher cause.

Conclusion

The process of taking these thinkers we studied in The Perfumed Life as serious interlocutors, rather than merely producers of texts to be studied,
compels us to question the relationship between the humanities and human
flourishing. Indeed, in some sense, this is precisely the intervention that these
texts make by reflecting on the human condition in a way that destabilizes the
eudaemonic goals that such an approach advocates as being at the center of
human biography. However, by seeking to unsettle the normative connection
between the humanities and human flourishing, I do not wish to be misread

---

[21] These passages echo the episodes in the Prophet's biography in which he is said to do the same
when offered rule over Mecca in exchange for renouncing his religious convictions.

as saying that the humanities should be exclusively a domain of doom and gloom. Nor would I ever contend that anything less than a classroom in which students leave invigorated by what they learn should be our goal as professors in the humanities. The humanities have brought great joy and strength at many moments of my life, as I hope they did also for the students in my class. My concern, rather, is that when we market the humanities' joy-giving potential, when we rally around the humanities with the messianic language of the salvific potential of a eudaemonic turn,[22] we lose what is the humanities' greatest asset, what makes it so necessary for our times, an age of rising inequality, of closing borders, of renewed xenophobic nationalisms. The humanities, at their best, provincialize our interests, situating them in a dense and often ethically unresolvable, web of competing desires, or in relation to truths that we may come to recognize are much greater than our own. The humanities at their best do not bolster certainty in our own models, but by introducing us to radical difference, they destabilize them, demanding that we tame our hubris. What The Perfumed Life offered me (and, I hope, my students) was not a compendium of theories that might further our fulfillment but rather a practicum on how we might read such contributions to productively mine our unsettling.

Works Cited

Abu El Haj, Nadia. *Combat Trauma: Imaginaries of War and Citizenship in Post-9/11 America*. Verso, 2022.

Asad, Muhammad. *The Road to Mecca*. Fons Vitae, 2000.

Banerjee, Milinda, and Jelle Wouters. *Subaltern Studies 2.0: Being against the Capitalocene*. U of Chicago P, 2022.

Bakhtiar, Laleh. "Introduction." *al-Ghazzali on Disciplining the Self*. Kazi Press, 2003, pp. 3–28.

Brethren of Purity. *The Case of the Animals versus Man before the King of the Jinn: A Translation from the Epistles of the Brethren of Purity*. Translated by Lenn Goodman and Richard McGregor, Oxford UP, 2009.

Butler, Judith. "Gender Is Burning: Questions of Appropriation and Subversion." *Bodies That Matter: On the Discursive Limits of "Sex."* Routledge, 1993.

Carrette, Jeremy, and Richard King. *Selling Spirituality: The Silent Takeover of Religion*. Routledge, 2005.

---

[22] For example, Pawelski writes that "[a] eudaemonic turn, with its promise of a unifying rationale for the humanities, could help revitalize the humanities and each of its disciplines by inviting them to join together in an inspiring project of historical proportions: a renewed examination of the question of well-being relevant for our times" ("Bringing" 209).

Ehrenreich, Barbara. *Bright-Sided: How Positive Thinking Is Undermining America*. Henry Holt, 2009.

Elias, Jamal. *Death before Dying: The Sufi Poems of Sultan Bahu*. U of California P, 1998.

El Shakry, Omnia. *The Arabic Freud: Psychoanalysis and Islam in Modern Egypt*. Princeton UP, 2017.

Fernando, Mayanthi. "Supernatureculture," *The Immanent Frame*, 11 Dec. 2017, https://tif.ssrc.org/2017/12/11/supernatureculture/

Foucault, Michel. "The Ethics of the Concern for Self as a Practice of Freedom." *Michel Foucault: Ethics, Subjectivity, and Truth*, edited by Paul Rabinow, The New Press, 1998a, pp. 281–302.

Foucault, Michel "Technologies of the Self." *Michel Foucault: Ethics, Subjectivity, and Truth*, edited by Paul Rabinow, The New Press, 1998b, pp. 223–252.

al-Ghazali, Zainab. *Return of the Pharaoh: A Memoir in Nasir's Prison*. Islamic Foundation, 2006.

al-Ghazzali (al-Ghazali), Abu Hamid. *Al-Ghazzali on Disciplining the Self*. Translated by Muhammad Nur Abdus Salam, Kazi, 2003.

al-Khatahtbeh, Amani. *Muslim Girl: A Coming of Age*. Simon and Schuster, 2016.

Hubbard, Ben. "Yemen Civilians Keep Dying, but Pompeo Says Saudis Are Doing Enough." *The New York Times*, 12 Sept. 2018, https://www.nytimes.com/2018/09/12/world/middleeast/saudi-yemen-pompeo-certify.html

Mahmood, Saba. *Politics of Piety: The Islamic Revival and the Feminist Subject*. Princeton UP, 2005.

"Our Work." *Humanities and Human Flourishing*, https://www.humanitiesandhumanflourishing.org/about

al-Mufid, Al-Shaykh. *Kitāb al-Irshād: The Book of Guidance into the Lives of the Twelve Imams*. Translated by I. K. A Howard, Balagha Books, 1981.

Pawelski, James. "Bringing Together the Humanities and the Science of Well-Being to Advance Human Flourishing." *Well-Being and Higher Education: A Strategy for Change and the Realization of Education's Greater Purposes*, edited by D. Harward, Bringing Theory to Practice, 2016a, pp. 207–216.

Pawelski, James. "Defining the 'Positive' in Positive Psychology: Part II, a Normative Analysis." *The Journal of Positive Psychology*, vol. 11, no. 4, 2016b, pp. 357–365.

"The Prophetic Guidance on Perfumes." *IslamWeb*, 24 Jan. 2017, https://www.islamweb.org/en/article/185392/the-prophetic-guidance-on-perfumes.

Reynolds, Dwight, editor. *Interpreting the Self: Autobiography in the Arabic Literary Tradition*. U of California P, 2001.

Rose, Nikolas. "Assembling the Modern Self." *Rewriting the Self: Histories from the Middle Ages to the Present*, edited by Roy Porter, Routledge, 1997, pp. 224–248.

Seligman, Martin. "Effectiveness of Positive Psychology: Setting the record straight." *The Chronicle of Higher Education*, 14 June 2021, https://www.chronicle.com/article/effectiveness-of-positive-psychology

Shimer, David. "Yale's Most Popular Class Ever: Happiness." *The New York Times*, 26 Jan. 2018, https://www.nytimes.com/2018/01/26/nyregion/at-yale-class-on-happiness-draws-huge-crowd-laurie-santos.html

Singal, Jesse. "Positive Psychology Goes to War." *The Chronicle of Higher Education*, 7 Jun. 2021, https://www.chronicle.com/article/positive-psychology-goes-to-war.

Smith, Karl. "From Dividual and Individual Selves to Porous Subjects." *The Australian Journal of Anthropology*, vol. 23, no. 1, 2012, pp. 50–64.

Tay, Louis, and James O. Pawleski, editors. *The Oxford Handbook of the Positive Humanities*. Oxford UP, 2022.

Taylor, Charles. "Buffered and Porous Selves," *The Immanent Frame*, 2 Sept. 2008. https://tif.ssrc.org/2008/09/02/buffered-and-porous-selves/.

Taylor, Charles. "Inwardness and the Culture of Modernity." *Philosophical Interventions in the Unfinished Project of Enlightenment*, edited by Axel Honneth et al., MIT P, 1992, pp. 88–110.

Taylor, Charles. *A Secular Age*. Harvard UP, 2007.

Taylor, Charles. *Sources of the Self: The Making of the Modern Identity*. Cambridge UP, 1989.

Taylor, Charles. "Buffered and porous selves." *The Immanent Frame*, 2 Sept. 2008, https://tif.ssrc.org/2008/09/02/buffered-and-porous-selves/

Timofeeva, Oxana. *Solar Politics*. Polity Press, 2022.

Zargar, Cyrus. *The Polished Mirror: Storytelling and the Pursuit of Virtue in Islamic Philosophy and Sufism*. One World, 2017.

7

From the Head to the Heart

Rethinking Approached to Teaching Buddhism at a Regional State University in the Bible Belt

Jeffrey Samuels

From 1999 to 2012, my research in the field of Buddhist studies focused on Buddhist monastic culture in Sri Lanka, particularly the processes by which young children become monastics.

That research was spurred by a visit to a temple just outside of Kandy, Sri Lanka, where I watched a group of young monks (mostly between the ages of eight and fourteen) play a game of cricket on the temple grounds. Their more informal and relaxed presence in the temple led me to question why they were there in the first place, how they got there, how are they being socialized as monastics, and how they navigate their monastic identity as children. As my own interest in Buddhism, which began in 1987 when I spent time meditating in a temple in Thailand, centered on understanding the tradition intellectually and what it said about my own well-being, the presence of the young children in robes playing cricket baffled me.

As I began to research the lives of child monastics over the next decade, I came to realize that their presence in the temple, their training as monastics, and their interactions with other monastics and the lay Buddhist community were factors more of the heart than the head.

Indeed, the majority of the young monks and boys living in the temple spoke to me about how their hearts were attracted to the robes and the shaven head of monastics, how their own training and socialization were less a matter of book learning and more the outcome of close social bonds among themselves, the head monk, and the other monastic and lay people in their community (they used highly emotional words such as *love*, *adoration*, *heart*, and so on to describe those bonds), as well as how they were loved and treated as both children and monastics by the communities around them. For them, the heart was key in their ability to become young monks; their

Jeffrey Samuels, *From the Head to the Heart* In: *Religious Studies, Theology, and Human Flourishing*. Edited by: Justin Thomas McDaniel and Hector Kilgoe, Oxford University Press. © Oxford University Press 2024. DOI: 10.1093/oso/9780197658338.003.0008

heartfelt bonds sustained them through their lives and training and were key factors in in their own sense of well-being.

While my research helped me realize how important emotional bonds, aesthetics, and feelings such as love, acceptance, and appreciation are to Buddhist life, that realization never infiltrated the classroom for me. Out of a desire to avoid blurring the line between the church and state, coming across as trying to convert or proselytize or appearing to favor one religious tradition over another, I continued to present Buddhism intellectually to the students—preferring to deconstruct the tradition and to focus on Buddhist history rather than to explore what the tradition may say about our own flourishing and well-being.

This, though, began to change in 2016. Around that time, while flying from Cuba to Miami on Southwest Airlines, I had the chance to read a short article in the airline's magazine that made reference to Martin Seligman's work at the University of Pennsylvania on positive interventions. In that article, the author reflected on an assignment he was given while studying journalism in which he was asked to write a letter of gratitude toward someone who had changed his life but whom he had never had the chance to thank properly. He was then asked to take that letter and read it at the person's doorstep.

As I was already aware of the connections that are frequently made among feelings of gratitude, forgiveness, love, and well-being, I—in a manner similar to that of Justin Thomas McDaniel (see "Lab Courses," this volume), who had rethought his "designated role as a gatekeeper of knowledge and figure of educational authority" (166)—began to reflect on my role as an educator. In particular, I pondered why I had been afraid to impart to students how Buddhists understand well-being and how they propose to cultivate it. Knowing well the emotional, economic, and social struggles that my students often face, many of whom are the first ones to attend college in their families and many of whom come from less well-to-do households, I began to question my own reluctance to play a more active role in aiding my students in increasing their well-being.

Looking back, that short flight from Cuba to Miami has been a turning point for me as an educator. Similar to Mary Clark Moschella, who felt that she "had not offered enough in the way of replenishing soul care to sustain students" ("Suffering" #, this volume), I felt the need to provide students with the tools not only to care for themselves but also to help themselves flourish. More broadly, I began to question my previous pedagogical goals as well as the goal of the humanities in general of simply imparting information to students, and in the process, I began replacing those goals with the goal of, in the words of Matthew Croasmun ("Discerning," this volume), "helping students and society as a whole learn to *discern* the *substance* of human flourishing—what it means for life to be led well, go well, and feel as it should" (66). In doing so, I decided to adopt a mode of engagement in the classroom (see Tay et al. 3).

Map of the Conceptual Space of the Positive and the Negative and Its Intersection with Buddhism

In his "Defining the 'Positive' in Positive Psychology: Part II, a Normative Model," James Pawelski provides a map of the conceptual space for well-being and human flourishing. He notes, for example, that in increasing well-being, one must focus not only on promoting and increasing the preferred (which he refers to as directly positive) but also on mitigating and preventing the dis-preferred (which he refers to as indirectly positive).

What I find most interesting about the division that Pawelski discusses in defining the term *positive* in positive psychology is that both the directly positive and the indirectly positive intersect perfectly with Buddhist conceptions of well-being and human flourishing. For instance, with regard to the directly positive, one finds that the path to enlightenment (i.e., the ultimate form of human flourishing) in Buddhism concerns putting forth the correct effort (1) to cultivate wholesome qualities that have not yet arisen and (2) to maintain wholesome qualities that have already arisen. Similarly, with regard to the indirectly positive that Pawelski discusses, we find that Buddhism also emphasizes the need for practitioners (3) to prevent unwholesome qualities from arising and (4) to abandon unwholesome qualities that have already arisen.

In order to understand more fully how Buddhists define human flourishing and well-being, we need to examine what constitutes 'wholesome' (*kusala*) and 'unwholesome' (*akusala*) 'mental factors' (*cetasika*). At its most basic level, there are three unwholesome roots: greed / sensual craving, ill will / aversion, and delusion / confusion. According to the tradition, whenever any of these three root poisons are present, we are motivated to engage in actions, speech, and thoughts that are driven by craving (whether that craving is a desire for pleasure, a desire for existence, or a desire for nonexistence) and that, in turn, cause harm to ourselves and/or others. While these three root poisons result in suffering, their opposites—generosity, loving-kindness, and wisdom—result in actions, speech, and thoughts that are beneficial to ourselves as well as to others around us. Thus, we could say that the path to well-being and human flourishing in Buddhism is a path on which we seek to replace, gradually, the three root poisons with the three positive mental states.

According to another system of Buddhist psychology contained in *Abhidhamma*, the three root poisons are part of a larger set of fourteen unwholesome qualities: ignorance or delusion, immodesty, disregard of consequences, restlessness, greed, wrong view, conceit, hatred, envy, miserliness, regret, sloth, torpor, and doubt. By contrast, the wholesome mental factors include faith, mindfulness, shame, fear of wrongdoing, non-greed, non-hatred, mental neutrality, neutrality of mind, tranquility of mind, tranquility of consciousness, right speech, right action, right livelihood, compassion, sympathetic joy, and wisdom (see Bodhi 79).

What I find most interesting is that according to Buddhist psychology, the wholesome and unwholesome mental factors are closely tied to our own consciousness, and the two together color the whole mind. To give an example, then: if the mental state of hatred or anger is present in the mind, that state begins to color our own perceptions, thoughts, and memories; thus, we begin perceiving the world around us in such a way that that perception reinforces that hatred or anger. In short, we get stuck in a cycle of destructive emotions that shape how we engage in and experience the world.

Inversely, if a quality such as compassion is present in the mind, then the mental factor and its accompanying consciousness perceives the world in a way that reinforces that quality and, according to Buddhist psychology, leads to the experience of well-being, both during the present moment and in the future.

The mapping of mental factors in Buddhism, however, is not driven simply by a desire to take stock of what constitutes wholesome and unwholesome qualities; instead, its purpose is closely connected to the view that by understanding the human mind, we are able to actively improve our own sense of well-being. As noted in my discussion with regard to the four efforts (which—again—are closely tied to the directly positive and indirectly positive), the underlying goal of understanding the different types of mental factors is grounded in the view that through our own efforts at mitigating unwholesome factors and increasing wholesome factors, we are able to transform our minds, flourish as human beings, and even effect positive change in the world.

Mindfulness Meditation and Its Effects on the Brain

According to Buddhist doctrine, in order to begin to transform our minds and, in turn, how we experience the world, we need to start paying attention. Without being aware of the present moment, it would be impossible to put the fourfold efforts into practice. Thus, an intimate relationship between the concepts of right effort, right mindfulness, and right concentration exists in Buddhism and is highlighted in the Buddhist eightfold path whereby the three aspects together comprise mental cultivation and development.

Becoming aware of the present moment is developed through mindfulness meditation. In addition to helping us become aware of our present mental and physical states, recent studies on the effects of meditation on the brain have shown that mindfulness meditation also plays a role in transforming the activity, the concentration of gray matter, and the chemistry levels in the brain. In "The Role of the Arts and Humanities in Human Flourishing: A Conceptual Model," Tay and colleagues discuss how viewing art may provide positive "neurological states including the activation of the Default Mode Network" (6). Similarly, the recent work of scholars such as Daniel Goleman, Richard Davidson, and Jon Kabat-Zinn has shown how practicing mindfulness meditation three hours a week for eight weeks leads to a significant shift from more right prefrontal cortex and amygdala activity (which are often associated with strong disturbing emotions such as anger and fear) to more active left prefrontal cortex and less amygdala activity (which are often associated with emotions such as optimism, hope, buoyancy, and so on). The fact that we can rewire our brains (i.e., that our brains have the characteristic of neuroplasticity) implies that mindfulness meditation not only provides us with the awareness to stop unwholesome mental qualities in their track but actually decreases the likelihood that such qualities will be present or, if they are present, that they will trap us in a cycle of negative emotions. Indeed, in a study of biotech scientists who felt stressed out and hassled at their job, Davidson and colleagues found that after practicing mindfulness meditation for eight weeks, the same scientists felt that their work was a challenge instead of a hassle and that they started to feel engaged and to like their work again. They also found that meditation increased the participants' immune system (see Davidson et al., "Alterations").

Along with altering the brain's activity, other studies have shown that the regular practice of mindfulness meditation leads to changes in the brain's grey matter concentrations. For instance, studies by Hölzel and colleagues, Lazar and colleagues, and Luders and colleagues have illustrated that the brains of people who have participated in mindfulness-based stress reduction and regular mindfulness meditation have an increase in grey matter density in regions of the hippocampus (Davidson et al., "Emotion")—as well as in the right orbitofrontal region, which is associated with emotional regulation and response control, thus implying greater emotional self-regulation and behavior flexibility (see Hölzel et al.; Lazar et al.; Luders et al.; Davidson et al., "Emotion"; Quirk and Beer).

Meditation in the Classroom: Mindfulness

Tying my desire to help cultivate, in the words of Justin Thomas McDaniel, "more complex and empathetic persons who take their thoughts, their feelings, and, most importantly, those of others seriously" ("Lab Courses" #, this volume), I decided to assign multiple meditation exercises to my students as part of their assignments. For the first four weeks of class, I had my students practice mindfulness meditation for five to ten minutes a day. Since many of them were unfamiliar with meditation, I provided a link to a guided mindfulness practice; while most of the students used the guided meditation at first, many of them decided to abandon the recording after the first few times or the first week. During the third week of their practice, the students also read a book from the Thai Buddhist forest meditation monk Ajahn Chah, A Still Forest Pool, which many found helpful to their practice. At the end of the four-week period, I asked the students to summarize their experiences in a three- to five-page paper.

Generally, most of the students wrote about how difficult it was to be consistent in their practice. Many of them cited their busy schedules, their lack of self-discipline, and their general sense of restlessness as causes of the difficulty. Several students went further by noting how the meditation practice itself stressed them out, as they felt that they were not being productive enough when they took time off from their studies. Another group of students noted how the practice forced them to become more acutely aware of how unmindful they are. Despite a smaller percentage of students who felt more stressed out and unproductive, the majority of them came to enjoy the practice and wrote out the positive impact that it had for them.

In assessing the effects of meditation on their lives, approximately three-quarters of the students mentioned how practicing meditation over time allowed them to feel more relaxed. For instance, one student who noted that it "was hard to sit and concentrate even for 5 and a half minutes" during the first week of practice also noted how during one of the last days of the practice, "it was very relaxing just to sit in the quiet and concentrate on the expansion and deflation of my abdomen. I started to feel my breathing slow down and my mind became restful." The same student also noted that he began to see effects outside of practice; as an employee at Home Depot, he was less likely to be affected by rude customers and was, instead, able to "accept their existence and allow them to just be," and he felt that he was "more patient and gracious."

Another student, who had recently experienced trauma, noted how meditation practice allowed her to become less self-judgmental. The goal of the mindfulness meditation that we practiced, discussed, and read about was less to create a particular mental state than to see what is present and, without identifying with it, to allow it to just be. (This is referred to by the acronym RAIN, which stands for recognize, accept, investigate, and non-identification.) In discussing how this affected her, she said that the "practice of not judging myself also carried into my day-to-day life when I found myself having negative thoughts." She also noted that mindfulness meditation allowed her to break free more easily from the cycle of destructive emotions—that by focusing on the breath and what was present, she would not only become much more aware of her thoughts but allow those thoughts, which had previously spiraled out of control, to pass. She also mentioned feeling much more grateful after meditating and able to "take control of my life again." In conclusion, and indirectly referencing our neuroplasticity, the same student wrote that "I cannot change anything about the trauma, but I can change how I think about it and handle my thoughts related to it. Meditation is one thing that I can do that can help me change my thought pattern."

Forgiveness Meditation

Along with having my students practice mindfulness meditation for four weeks, I had them take part in a daily guided practice of forgiveness meditation for three weeks. In this meditation, the students were asked to think about a time in which they hurt themselves or someone else and then to offer to themselves words of forgiveness that included the phrases "I allow myself to be imperfect. I allow myself to make mistakes. I allow myself to be a learner, still learning life's lessons. I forgive myself. If I am unable to forgive myself right now, may I forgive myself sometime in the future." From there, the students are asked to recall a time in which someone had hurt them and then to offer to that person words of forgiveness such as "Just as I allow myself to be imperfect, so I allow you to be imperfect. I accept that you make mistakes. I accept that you are a learner, still learning life's lessons. I forgive you. If I am unable to forgive you right now, may I forgive you sometime in the future." Finally, the students are asked to recall a time in which they hurt someone else and then to ask that other person, through repeating similar phrases (e.g., "Please allow me to be imperfect"), for forgiveness.

I chose the forgiveness meditation as the second type, as there have been a number of studies, published over the past several years that suggest a close correlation between forgiveness and physical and mental well-being. In one study, for example, Charlotte Witvliet monitored people's heart rate, blood pressure, and facial tension while she asked them to ruminate on someone who had hurt them. What she found, not surprisingly, is that when people recalled an act of someone hurting them, their blood pressure and heart rate increased, and the subjects themselves experienced anger, sadness, and anxiety. Inversely, when she asked the participants to empathize with those who hurt them and to imagine forgiving them, the subjects showed as much stress reaction as a normal wakeful state. Moreover, a study by Everett L. W Worthington revealed that when people who have poor relationships with their partner were asked to ruminate on their partner, their cortisol levels increased. Inversely, Worthington found that when people were more forgiving for their partners' faults, their cortisol stress levels remained in the normal range.

When I took the forgiveness meditation into the classroom, I had no idea what to expect. My own experience with this type of guided meditation was that while it can conjure up past harm that the meditator has done to both themselves and others as well as past harm that was done by someone else to the meditator, it also has the potential of helping oneself let go of past instances of harm. Knowing that it can be a difficult form of guided meditation, when I discussed this meditation in class, I noted that while the mind does tend to want to focus on really big events that have caused harm, it is best to start with more minor things.

Reviewing the reflection papers that my students wrote following the meditation, I observed that the students found that although the meditation caused old pain to resurface, it also—in addition to the reflection papers—provided them with the chance to deal with that pain in more constructive ways. While the meditation did bring up past harm, more than half of the students noted how they ended the meditation with a sense of calm, which was completely unexpected. One student who had thoughts of suicide and even had an episode of self-harming came to realize not only that the people who had hurt her might not have even known that they were doing so but also that not letting go of that pain and hurt was affecting only her. She admitted that while the meditation dredged up hurtful feelings from the past, she began feeling that she "would be able to move on from it."

Another student, a female who had experienced an undescribed trauma as a child, noted how her favorite parts of the meditation were the phrases that went along with the meditation because they spoke so much truth to her. She also noted that she liked that the forgiveness meditation started with the self, as it was easy to believe all those truths (e.g., that she is allowed to be imperfect and that she is allowed make mistakes). She wrote that by starting with the self, she was able to "go into the forgiveness of others section with the mindset of extending what I believe to be true about myself to others. If [I] am imperfect, allowed to make mistakes . . . , why wouldn't that also be true for someone else, even if they have hurt me[?]"

Noting that, though, the same student also wrote that extending forgiveness to the person who hurt her was extremely difficult and that she did not, in fact, have "a grand forgiveness awakening experience." Nonetheless, she did come to realize that "forgiveness is not always instant; it can be gradual. . . . It's okay if it takes time, and I just need to keep persisting and being patient with myself. There is a lot of peace and freedom that comes when forgiveness is extended."

Another student, a male who experienced a sexual trauma as a child, noted that the meditation and the reflection paper were powerful ways of dealing with his trauma. He noted, for instance, that "throughout the roughly three weeks of meditation, there was not one instance in which I had not been reduced to tears." He also noted that while he cannot say that he did not hate the person who had abused him at the time of the class, he went on to add that

> I am slowly becoming more open to the possibility of forgiveness or, rather, understanding what forgiveness really is. . . . By repeatedly telling myself that I was supposed to acknowledge issues with other people instead of fixing them, I began to think more on the fact that our perception of having a problem simply exists because we perceive ourselves to have a problem. It may seem obvious, but I had not *really* considered that my problems were no one else's but my own. . . . I am beginning to see forgiveness as simply a form of acceptance.

Finally, another student, who had recently experienced a breakup with her boyfriend and had mentioned to me that she does not consider herself to me a very emotional or forgiving person, recounted a cathartic experience one evening while practicing meditation. She wrote:

> I began my meditation for the evening, sitting on my living room floor, when it all hit me. I was completely railroaded by all the mistakes I had made over the last one to two years. . . . I felt as though I was seeing myself more clearly than I ever had before. I was objective and almost outside of myself looking at all of the actions and words I had said to people. I realized that I had so much more to forgive myself for and to ask for forgiveness from others for. . . . Unable to forgive myself for the awful and childish things I had done, I sat on my living room floor and tears poured from my eyes. I'm not the type of person who cries very often. . . . I first had to see myself more clearly and take responsibility for my actions before I could truly try to forgive myself or others. . . . So, after finishing my meditation, I picked up the phone and called him. I told him about by revelation and asked for his forgiveness after giving my own to him. . . . I think that this exercise has humbled me and made me think more about how my actions could and do affect other people.

Like this student, others noted how the forgiveness meditation allowed them to be more sympathetic to other people's perspectives: as one student put it, she came to realize that "[w]hat might not be categorized as a big deal for some . . . might be [categorized] as a major life [event] for others. . . . You can't decide what does nor does not hurt someone. . . .The only thing you are able to do is reflect and apologize."

While many students found this type of meditation to be a powerful way of overcoming pain and trauma, for a few students this meditation was too much. One student in particular noted—when she was just starting out with this type of meditation—that the conjuring up of old memories led her to feel very unsettled. She wasn't sleeping that well and was overtaken again by a deep sadness. This particular student was already seeing a counselor and used her sessions with her counselor to work through some of what she was experiencing. I also suggested to that student that for now, she stop doing the forgiveness meditation and, instead, return to mindfulness meditation.

Other students had a harder time with this meditation, and for those who reached out to me before the reflection paper was due, I did suggest that if they were feeling overwhelmed, they could either switch back to the mindfulness meditation practice or choose less triggering events to focus on. These few students (probably five or so overall) made me feel most unsure about what I was asking the students to do and worried that this assignment might cause one of them to become overcome with depression or even worse.[1]

Lovingkindness Meditation

Finally, during the last several weeks of the semester, I had my students complete a guided lovingkindness meditation. In lovingkindness meditation, practitioners first visualize themselves while repeating phrases such as "May I be filled with lovingkindness. May I be safe from inner and outer harm. May I be well in body and mind. May I be at ease and happy." The meditator then visualizes someone who is close to them such as a parent or partner and extends lovingkindness to them by repeating similar phrases. They then extend lovingkindness to friends and those with whom they have a positive relationship, then to more neutral people (e.g., the cashier at the local grocery store), to difficult people, to—finally—all beings.

There have been a number of studies over the past several years (for a review, see Galante et al.), and most studies have suggested that the practice of lovingkindness meditation is associated with an increase

---

[1] Despite feeling uncertain, I did continue this particular form of meditation in subsequent classes (as the majority found it helpful), but I prefaced it with more statements urging caution.

in positive emotions. These studies have indicated that lovingkind-ness meditation is "highly promising . . . for improving positive affect" (Hoffmann 1131) and that it "can foster positive emotions" (Zeng et al., "Application" 1472). Zeng and colleagues cite Shonin and colleagues' findings that lovingkindness meditation can significantly improve posi-tive emotions (Shonin et al. 1; qtd. in Zeng et al., "Effect"). In terms of the range of positive emotions, Fredrickson and colleagues have found that practicing lovingkindness for a period of seven weeks led to an increase in such emotions as "love, joy, contentment, gratitude, pride, hope, in-terest, amusement, and awe" (see Fredrickson et al.) and a study by Kok and colleagues have shown that lovingkindness meditation led to an in-crease in vagal tone which led to greater feelings of social connection and positive emotions (see Kok et al.).

This was, by far, the meditation that students enjoyed the most. In generalizing some of the effects that this type of meditation had on my students, I first note that the most common theme that was raised in the students' papers was about how this type of meditation helped them feel a greater connection with others. One student wrote, for instance, that after practicing the meditation for a couple of weeks, he began to feel "the heightened appreciation I had for people in my life [whom] I love. Interactions I have had with my parents since starting the Loving-Kindness Meditation have been filled with gratitude and love. . . . [It] has made me a more positive person."

Similarly, another student noted that this type of meditation allowed her to put more positivity out into the world and, like the previous student, that she spoke more with friends and family and felt loved more often. Echoing the effects of lovingkindness meditation that were mentioned in the works of Zeng and colleagues (Zeng et al., "Application"; Zeng et al., "Effect") and Fredrickson and colleagues, she wrote: "You radiate love and positivity and it is difficult to walk around in a bad mood, regardless of how you woke up." She also added that

one of the most difficult parts of these sessions was not being able to see those [whom] I love after reflecting on the love that I have for them. I would often reach out to them and talk with them for some time, just to [check in]. . . . These sessions create almost a sense of urgency to contact the ones that you love and express that love while you still can. . . . I felt loved and mindful of the emotions that I put out into the world.

Turning again to the student who recently experienced a breakup with her boyfriend, the student who describes herself as not very emotional, she noted that this type of meditation transformed how she engaged in the world: "I found that the exercise usually helped me start the day off right. I was generally happy, but more than that I just felt that everything was ok. Not that there weren't still hard things happening in life, but that I was loved and that everything was as it was supposed to be." She also went on to describe the effects of extending lovingkindness to her mother—someone with whom she has a very close relationship:

> I have always known that she loves me, but sitting there and focusing on that energy, I felt it in a different way than I ever have before. I was almost moved to tears, as I am right now as I recall this memory. . . . Her love went straight into my heart and I felt it unfold like a flower. Never have I been open to love in that way and never has it touched me as deeply as that did. . . . It sounds cheesy when I try to describe it in words, but it was the best feeling I think I ever had. Profound joy, contentment, and acceptance of who I am. . . . Loving kindness meditation has been so liberating because I have realized a lot about myself as well, the positive parts of myself.

Turning to the student who felt suicidal and experimented with self-harm, whom I discussed in the "Forgiveness Meditation" section, she also noted some profound shifts. She wrote,

> It might be a cumulative impact of all the meditations over the course of the semester, which I think have really helped me to cope with mental illness and various issues in my life. But, I do think the loving-kindness had an impact of its own. I am more likely to reach out to others than I was previously. . . . It has helped me be happier, in a way. . . . It has been easier to pay more attention to my boyfriend's problems. . . . I feel more aware of others almost and less consumed by my own internal issues. . . . [S]truggling with mental illness consumed a lot of time and energy that used to be [spent] with others. That time is becoming available again due to these meditations. . . . Honestly, I was still feeling extremely suicidal daily at the beginning of this semester and I am genuinely happy to be alive right now as I write this.

Finally, reflecting on all the meditation exercises that were practiced over the semester, she concluded by writing: "I am glad you changed this class to include meditation. I have really enjoyed this experience, and this class has had more of a positive impact on me than any other class, possibly than any other experience in college."

Conclusion: Questions Probed

In this chapter, I have explored how the Buddhist tradition conceptualizes and understands well-being. Similarly to positive psychology, Buddhist literature envisions diminishing and preventing dis-preferred (i.e., unwholesome) mental states as well as increasing and encouraging preferred (i.e., wholesome) mental states as being fundamental to human flourishing.

In the context of Buddhism, moreover, the practice of mindfulness meditation plays a central role in cultivating well-being in Buddhism. Indeed, it is only by becoming aware of what is occurring in the present that practitioners can put the four efforts into practice. However, as I have illustrated, mindfulness meditation not only results in the practitioner becoming more present, but it also affects them by transforming the activity, the concentration of gray matter, and the chemistry levels in their brains. Thus, the practice of mindfulness meditation not only provides the opportunity for practitioners to extend the effort in transforming their mental states but also—because of shifts in the brain—makes it more likely that practitioners will be able to overcome overpowering negative states and cycles of destructive emotions.

Reflecting on these exercises and their effects on the students, I must admit, again, that I was completely taken aback when I read the reflections that many students wrote about their meditation. My own honesty in the class about what I was doing and why I was doing it provided the space for the students to be honest with me. In that regard, I came away from this semester overjoyed with how the meditations affected a number of students and truly touched by what the students shared with me. Like Justin Thomas McDaniel has done, I have truly begun to re-evaluate what my job, as a professor in the humanities, is truly about: not to impart information but, instead, to be someone who can help increase students' sense of well-being and human flourishing. Indeed, as one student (not previously discussed in this chapter) noted, meditation

became the only time throughout the day that I was able to let things be just as they are and not worry tirelessly about them. . . . It was amazing how relieved I felt. . . . It got to the point where I was doing it two or three times a day. . . . I am not sure why, but afterwards I feel full of life and possibility.

As I look to offering the course again in the future, I have noted a few changes I would like to make. Given the space that the reflection papers provided to students to share very personal parts of their lives as well as how challenging the forgiveness meditation can be, I have become acutely aware that in subsequent classes I needed to emphasize—even more strongly—to my students that they start with more minor forms of transgressions, despite the mind wanting to turn to larger ones. While none of the students experienced adverse reactions to the exercise this time, I also realize that this meditation has the potential to stir up some triggering memories. I have decided, in subsequent classes, to provide students with the phone number of the university's counseling center and to urge them to stop doing the meditation and return back to the mindfulness exercises should they feel overwhelmed by the forgiveness meditation.

In introducing the meditations in the course, I also became aware that it would have been helpful to find more sensitive ways to assess and understand my students' experiences. While I received unsolicited emails about the effects of the meditations from students months after the course ended, it would be helpful to create a more robust form of evaluation at the end of the course. Following up with students long after the course finished would also be helpful to comprehend, more fully, how this exercise affects well-being and human flourishing. Perhaps partnering with colleagues in our Department of Psychological Sciences to identify validated measures to use would be helpful.

While many students wrote about the meditation exercises in their course evaluation, unfortunately my institution does not allow me to tweak the course evaluation process in order to ask the students—at the end of the course—specifically about the effects of the meditation practices. Even though the evaluations for the course were overall quite strong, given that the evaluations are only given to currently enrolled students, I was unable to assess whether the few students who did drop the course partway through the semester did so to avoid practicing the meditations.

While I continue to reflect on the outcomes of the meditation exercises, the response from the male student who experienced a sexual trauma early on in his life comes often to mind and often leads me to feel more secure in the shift in my teaching from the head to the heart. Indeed, reflecting on it,

I often come away knowing that that the shift in teaching has been not only worthwhile but also timely and essential. When I asked that student if I could share his reflections in the form of a book chapter, he immediately gave his consent. He then went on to write:

> Above all, I would like to thank you again for assigning the meditative practices. I'm sure you gathered this from my paper, but in my four years of college, I have not experienced the type of "emotional dialogue" that the reflection papers encouraged. This experience really will stay with me for the rest of my life—I've thought about it quite literally every day—and yet I really don't think there is an appropriate way to thank someone for giving me this life-changing experience. "Thanks for changing my life" just seems wildly insufficient in terms of gratitude, but alas I do not have words to describe the impact that this experience has had on me, and so I must relegate myself to the simplicity that I mentioned previously: thank you for this experience.
>
> With newfound love and kindness,

Works Cited

Bodhi, Bhikkhu. *The Numerical Discourses of the Buddha: A Translation of the Anguttara Nikaya*. Wisdom Publications, 2012.

Davidson, R. J., et al. "Alterations in Brain and Immune Function Produced by Mindfulness Meditation." *Psychosomatic Medicine*, vol. 65, no. 4, Jul.–Aug. 2003, pp. 564–70.

Davidson, R. J., et al. "Emotion, Plasticity, Context, and Regulation: Perspectives from Affective Neuroscience." *Psychological Bulletin*, vol. 126, no. 6, Nov. 2000, pp. 890–909.

Fredrickson, Barbara L., et al. "Open Hearts Build Lives: Positive Emotions, Induced through Loving-Kindness Meditation, Build Consequential Personal Resources." *Journal of Personal and Social Psychology*, vol. 95, no. 5, Nov. 2008, pp. 1045–62.

Galante, J., et al. "Effect of Kindness-Based Meditation on Health and Well-Being: A Systematic Review and Meta-Analysis." *Journal of Consulting and Critical Psychology*, vol. 82, no. 6, 2014, pp. 1101–14.

Hoffmann, Stefan G., et al. "Loving-Kindness and Compassion Meditation: Potential for Psychological Interventions." *Clinical Psychology Review*, vol. 31, no. 7, Nov. 2011, pp. 1126–32.

Hölzel, Britta K., et al. "Mindfulness Practice Leads to Increase in Regional Brain Grey Matter Density." *Psychiatry Research: Neuroimaging*, vol. 191, no. 1, Jan. 2011, pp. 36–43.

Kok, B. E., et al. "How Positive Emotions Build Physical Health: Perceived Positive Social Connections Account for the Upward Spiral between Positive Emotions and Vagal Tone." *Psychological Science*, vol. 24, no. 7, Jul. 2013, pp. 1123–32.

Lazar, Sara W., et al. "Meditation Experience Is Associated with Increased Cortical Thickness." *NeuroReport*, vol. 16, no. 17, Nov. 2005, pp. 1893–97.

Luders, E., et al. "The Underlying Anatomical Correlates of Long-Term Meditation: Larger Hippocampal and Frontal Volumes of Gray Matter." *Neuroimage*, vol. 45, no. 3, Apr. 2009, pp. 672–78.

Pawelski, James O. "Defining the 'Positive' in Positive Psychology: Part II, a Normative Analysis." *The Journal of Positive Psychology*, vol. 11, no. 4, 2016, pp. 357–65, https://doi.org/10.1080/17439760.2015.1137628.

Quirk, G. J., and J. S. Beer. "Prefrontal Involvement in the Regulation of Emotion: Convergence of Rat and Human Studies." *Current Opinion in Neurobiology*, vol. 16, no. 6, Dec. 2006, pp. 723–27.

Shonin, Edo, et al. "Buddhist-Derived Loving-Kindness and Compassion Meditation for the Treatment of Psychopathology: A Systematic Review." *Mindfulness*, vol. 6, no. 5, Oct. 2015, pp. 1161–80.

Tay, Louis, et al. "The Role of the Arts and Humanities in Human Flourishing: A Conceptual Model." *The Journal of Positive Psychology*, vol. 13, no. 3, 2017, pp. 215–55, https://doi.org/10.1080/17439760.2017.1279207.

Worthington, Everett L. "The New Science of Forgiveness." *Greater Good Magazine: Science-Based Insights for a Meaningful Life*, September 1. 2004, https://greatergood.berkeley.edu/article/item/the_new_science_of_forgiveness.

Zeng, Xianglong, et al. "The Application of Loving-Kindness Meditation from Psychological Perspective." *Advances in Psychological Science*, vol. 21, no. 8, 2013, pp. 1466–72.

Zeng, Xianglong, et al. "The Effect of Loving-Kindness Meditation on Positive Emotions: A Meta-Analytic Review." *Frontiers in Psychology*, vol. 6, no. 3, 2015, p. 1693–1708.

8

Fighting Spirit

Lessons from a Military Experiment in Spiritual Training

Steven Weitzman

Part of what distinguishes positive psychology's approach to religion from that of other kinds of scholarship is the way it is affecting religious life today. The research it has inspired does not merely measure or explain the impact of religious belief and practice; it has begun to change that belief and practice, precipitating what one might describe as a kind of psychologized religion that fuses the characteristics of traditional religious tradition with theories and prescriptions that are drawn from positive psychology.

An example of this effect is a new kind of gospel that has emerged in the wake of positive psychology. Examples include Christopher Kaczor's *The Gospel of Happiness* and David Murray's *The Happy Christian: Ten Ways to Be a Joyful Believer in a Gloomy World*, works that draw on positive psychology as an argument for embracing Christian values and religious practices. The religious effects of positive psychology are not limited to Christianity: there are similar kinds of books, articles, and websites that do the same for Buddhism, Judaism, and other traditions.[1] Positive psychology has provided new evidence that religion is good for people's sense of well-being, good for their health, and good for how they operate as part of groups or organizations, and many religious communities have been drawing on that evidence to make a twenty-first century case for themselves. Positive psychology and its view of religion and spirituality are having consequences that go well beyond academia to shape the development of religious life in America and other cultures, and that is all the more reason for a dialogue with academic religious studies, a field interested not just in religion but in how scholars think about and affect religion.

---

[1] For examples, note Levine; Pelcovitz and Pelcovitz; Kim-Priesto.

Steven Weitzman, *Fighting Spirit* In: *Religious Studies, Theology, and Human Flourishing.* Edited by: Justin Thomas McDaniel and Hector Kilgoe, Oxford University Press. © Oxford University Press 2024.
DOI: 10.1093/oso/9780197658338.003.0009

This chapter is an effort to examine some ideas and findings at the heart of this development—the idea that all humans share a spiritual dimension that is important to their well-being or capacity to flourish and that this capacity can be cultivated through certain forms of practice. It draws its insights from a rather surprising case study not of a church, synagogue, meditation center, or classroom[2] but of the US military—more specifically, a program developed by the Positive Psychology Center that aimed to cultivate the spiritual fitness of soldiers in an effort to promote their well-being. This military-academic undertaking is the largest attempt to apply the idea that spirituality can cultivate well-being, and it offers lessons for the Humanities and Human Flourishing Project[3] to the extent that it sought to implement a positive psychology-informed approach to spiritualty as an important component of well-being and mental health.

The burgeoning research on the connection between religion/spirituality and well-being has raised many methodological and theoretical questions along the way that have yet to be resolved and that I cannot address in this context. What I want to focus on in this chapter, however, is not the research itself but the attempt to apply it. Martin Seligman, the psychologist who inaugurated the field of positive psychology, makes real-world application of the research a central goal of positive psychology. He reports that this commitment to application was what led him to accept the position as director of the Positive Psychology Center in 2003, and publications like Seligman's *Flourish: A Visionary New Understanding of Happiness and Well-Being* illustrate how he and other researchers have put positive psychology to work to improve people's personal health, learning student performance as students, and, economic productivity, and people's personal health.

In what follows, I would like to briefly explore the effort to apply positive psychology to the spiritual lives of people. I do so, to be candid, from a position of unease and concern. We know from other case studies that I will not discuss here that benignly intentioned psychological research can have inadvertently negative side effects. Positive psychology, along with research that is aligned with other schools of thought, has greatly expanded the study of the health effects of religion or spirituality, but the resulting evaluation of

[2] For analyses of the possible roles of spiritual or religious practices in classroom environments, see the chapters in this volume by Matthew Croasmun ("Discerning"); Mary Clark Moschella ("Suffering,"); Noah Salomon ("Teaching"); Jeffrey Samuels ("From the Head"); Justin Thomas McDaniel ("Lab Courses").

[3] For more information on the Humanities and Human Flourishing Project, visit www.humanities andhumanflourishing.org, accessed 30 Jan. 2023.

religious beliefs or practices on the basis of their medical, psychological, or social benefits, though well intentioned, has brought with it the potential for unintended consequences, including an increase in the risk that such beliefs or practices will be stigmatized as harmful or socially injurious based on scientific research that is often debatable, tentative, and subject to revision.

The assessment of religion as beneficial or harmful for people as measured by a secular or scientific perspective can even invite various kinds of interventions from governments, —interventions that can be dangerous. An extreme example is the treatment of certain religious minorities in Communist China. As documented by Frederik Fallman, China's Communist Party has abandoned policies based on the opium theory of religion—the idea that religion needs to be restricted because it lulls people into complacency—in favor of an approach that sees religion as potentially useful to society if it promotes morality and social harmony. Confucianism has thus flourished under recent Communist rule, while Islamic, Christian, and Lamaist groups face restrictions, and in some cases persecution, for not being sufficiently aligned with the common good. The separation of church and state in the United States would seem to rule out its government invoking psychological research to boost certain religious groups or to restrict others, and yet, as we will see here, the US government has in fact intervened in the spiritual life of millions of people enlisted in the military, and it has done so under the influence of ideas and research that have been promoted by positive psychology. This intervention, recounted with pride in Seligman's *Flourish* as the most ambitious application of his ideas yet undertaken, will be examined here for what it might tell us about the pros and cons of enlisting spirituality to cultivate well-being.

I must acknowledge from the outset that I approach the research on spirituality and well-being with a healthy dose of skepticism. There are literally thousands of studies that aim to establish a connection between spirituality and health or well-being, with the work that has been inspired by positive psychology making a profound impact not just on the academic study of well-being but also on religious life, workplace culture, and education. There are also studies that challenge that connection, but it is my impression that they are not as abundant or as influential in their collective impact. The Humanities and Human Flourishing Project has given me an opportunity to bring the skepticism into direct dialogue with scholars on the other side of the issue, for which I am grateful, and I especially value the chance to learn from Kenneth Pargament, a scholar at the forefront of the research that

I will focus on in this chapter, and to hear about his experience with trying to bring the insights of research to bear on a real-world mental health challenge. My hope is that the questions and doubts I raise in response prove helpful as scholars continue to try to comprehend the role of spirituality in promoting individual and collective well-being.

A Military Experiment

In 2009, the US army initiated a $125 million comprehensive soldier fitness (CSF) program that was meant to reduce the effects of trauma exposure, including depression, post-traumatic stress disorder, domestic abuse, and suicide. The program featured a confidential diagnostic questionnaire known as the Global Assessment Tool, administered online to soldiers every two years in order to measure their resilience in five core areas: emotional, physical, family, social, and spiritual health.[4] If the questionnaire placed a soldier below a minimum threshold in a category, he or she would be encouraged to partake in learning modules to build skills in areas like negotiation, decision-making, and optimistic thinking.

The relevant part of this program for our purposes is its aim to develop spiritual fitness. Spirituality in this context does not refer to a metaphysical entity: the spirit is understood as the essential core of an individual, his or her deepest self, the animating force in an individual that seeks out meaning, purpose, authenticity, and connection to a higher cause. Developing spiritual fitness is said to involve a discovery of that essential self, and it entails strengthening its capacity to act on its aspirations especially in times of struggle, and to feel a connection to the world and to others in all their diversity. Those with a higher level of spirit are thought to be more motivated to achieve victory, more committed to their goals, and more motivated to behave in a moral or ethical manner.

CSF owes its development to Martin Seligman in his capacity as a member of the Defense Health Board, which advises the secretary of defense and which received a $31 million contract with the military to help develop CSF. The spiritual component was developed by two psychologists who had experience working with the military, Patrick Sweeney and the aforementioned

---

[4] The army's questions about soldiers' levels of spiritual fitness were captured by a screenshot found in Griffith.

Kenneth Pargament. Their description of the effort, published in an issue of the journal *American Psychologist* that was devoted to introducing CSF, explains why in their view the cultivation of "spiritual fitness" as part of military training did not violate the Constitution's prohibition against imposing religious tests on those serving in government or betray the military's commitment to religious diversity: Spirituality in this context is not rooted in a particular creed or doctrine. It is a human quality or capacity found in people from all cultures, a sense of connection to others that gives one a sense of meaning in life. Although it is often intertwined with religion, spirituality is not limited to any particular creed. The program was meant for "warriors of all faiths"—and was supposed to speak to nonbelievers as well (Pargament and Sweeney).

It is not clear, however, that in practice this program has turned out to be as religiously neutral as it was intended to be. In 2011, the news outlet *Truthout* reported that the spiritual fitness component of the CSF was under fire from hundreds of active duty soldiers and civil rights groups like the Military Religious Freedom Foundation (MRFF). The protestors argued that test questions were skewed in ways that guaranteed that nonbelievers would score poorly, and they pointed to the program's use of religious imagery as evidence that the real intent was to promote religiosity (Leopold). While the spiritual component is voluntary, soldiers who have complained about the program claimed that its voluntariness wasn't conveyed to them or that they were pressured into participating.

Setting aside the church-state issues for the purposes of this discussion, from the perspective of academic religious studies, one issue with the concept of *spiritual fitness* is its assumption that spirituality is a universal human quality that can be improved or strengthened through an individual's efforts. The optimistic and individualistic conception of the spiritual as something that the individual soldier can improve through his or her own choices and efforts suggests that the military's conception of spiritual fitness reflects what some critics identify as a distinctively neoliberal approach to well-being (Illouz).

As it happens, in fact, CSF is only the military's latest effort to develop the spiritual fitness of its soldiers. As documented by Shenandoah Lia Nieuwsma, the effort to cultivate spiritually fit soldiers goes back to the beginnings of the Cold War, and all along the way, the military has struggled with distinguishing spirituality from religion. Nieuwsma recounts cases in which spiritual fitness was interpreted in Christian ways and other cases in which the military struggled to distinguish spirituality from religion. During the 1960s, in light of larger social changes and under pressure from organizations like the American Civil Liberties Union, the military backed away from programs that had a religious resonance, but the drive for spiritual fitness resumed by the end of the 1970s as the military began to confront the devastating effects of post-traumatic stress disorder, and this trend intensified in the 1980s and 1990s as spirituality became medicalized by healthcare professionals who saw it as an important dimension of patient well-being. With the re-emergence of spiritual fitness as an aspect of military training, the ambiguities and contradictions that are always inherent in the concept of *spiritual* resurfaced.

Pargament and Sweeney, the researchers who helped formulate the military's current spiritual fitness program, sought to disentangle spirituality from religion by avoiding ontological questions about God's existence and other metaphysical questions and by making a distinction between *human spirit*, which they believe to be a universal quality of all humans, and *theological spirit*, which implicates spirituality in the belief systems of particular religious communities. However, their own rhetoric contributes to the confusion, as for example when they ascribe to the spirit "sacred" qualities like transcendence. And notwithstanding their efforts to detach spirituality from religion, the track record of the program suggests that it is still caught in the contradictions inherent in the effort to tap into the psychological benefits of religiosity without invoking the divine or allying with a particular religious creed. As Nieuwsma documents, while CSF training materials use language inclusive of nonreligious perspectives, they periodically imply the army's endorsement of a theistic or sectarian perspective, as when accompanying images show soldiers engaged in prayer.

Evidence for this bias comes in the form of a study from 2013 that aimed to show the effects of the transcendent phrasing used in the questionnaire that assesses soldiers' spiritual fitness (Hammer et al.). Soldiers were asked whether statements like "I am a spiritual person" applied to themselves. An atheist soldier might construe such a statement in supernaturalist terms, thinking that it referred to being close to God and therefore rejecting it as a self-description, but that does not mean that the soldier was bereft of a sense of meaning and purpose in life. In other words, the transcendent phrasing of the diagnostic could lead to a misleading low score for atheist soldiers. The study demonstrated this effect through an experiment that administered a revised questionnaire without the transcendent language, and the results indicated that the original version did indeed underestimate the "spiritual fitness" of atheist soldiers relative to Christian soldiers. The supernaturalist history and resonance of "spirituality"—the fact that it can easily be construed as a reference to the soul or to a god—programs false results into the very diagnostic tool that was used to measure soldiers' subjective feeling of meaning.

Close to a decade after its inauguration, how has the effort to develop the spiritual fitness of soldiers fared? Unfortunately, it is hard to get a handle on the program's efficacy. In 2014, the National Academies of Science, Technology, and Medicine undertook an assessment of the military's various programs for preventing psychological disorders in service members and their families, including CSF. Building on the work of both internal reviews and external critiques, it found some glaring problems with the program's methodology. The program assessment found that CSF had failed to test the idea through a pilot program, and it had not completed an initial ethics review. Additionally, the program assessment found that there was no control group by which to measure the effects of the program over time. Critics also expressed qualms about ethics, including about the possibility that such a program might be harmful for participants if it convinces them they are better prepared to manage trauma than they actually are.[5]

The army itself published four reports about the program between 2011 and 2013 that suggested modestly positive effects, but there has been criticism of how those evaluations were conducted. None of this is even to mention the fact that there is now research, some of it to be touched on later in this chapter, which challenges the alleged connection between spirituality and well-being on which the spiritual fitness component is premised. Reviews of the CSF program continue to be published, but for the moment, it seems fair to say that its benefits—including those of the spiritual fitness component—remain unclear.

For activists like Mikey Weinstein, founder of the MRFF, the spiritual fitness program poses a clear threat—he has described it to me personally as a national security threat (Weinstein)—and he has threatened class action lawsuits in defense of the nonreligious and minority religious soldiers who he

---

[5] Eidelson and Soldz have suggested that soldiers who imagined that their CSF training provided them with "protection" against trauma might become more reckless with their own safety or that of others, while Smith has conjectured that soldiers who found themselves unable to cope with negative feelings despite having been "made resilient" by CSF training might feel marginalized and less able to ask for support.

believes have suffered from the effort. Weinstein regards the program as part of an evangelical coup that seeks to use the military to proselytize to a captive audience, but one needn't subscribe to conspiracy thinking in order to recognize a problem here: the language of spirituality has given an opening to the evangelically minded in order to import proselytization practices into military training, as illustrated by a dissertation recently submitted to the evangelical seminary Alliance Theological Seminary in 2017 (Mueller). Written by a Christian chaplain in the Hawaii National Guard, the dissertation presents the results of what it describes as an "experiment" that is supposed to have improved the spiritual fitness of soldiers by incorporating into their training material from Campus Crusade for Christ, but the scientific framing is arguably a pretext for proselytizing under the guise of an official military program. The constitutionality of the spiritual fitness program has yet to be challenged, but concern about the legal and political implications have been expressed by both religious liberty organizations and by legal scholars like Winifred Fallers Sullivan and Jeffrey Lakin.

Of more relevance to the Humanities and Human Flourishing Project is another concern about CSF: its treatment of optimistic thinking as the best way to deal with difficult life experiences. The program requires an effort to maximize positive thinking and to reduce negative thoughts—one of the core goals of spiritual fitness training is to help cultivate a positive outlook through practices like meditation and the use of ritualized washing to rinse away negative thoughts (Nieuwsma 289–91). As Stephanie Smith (242–46) has argued, that kind of messaging can be a problem for service members who are confronting negative feelings. She notes several such problems: It can make it harder for soldiers to acknowledge feelings like guilt that might be important for their reintegration into civilian society. There is research suggesting that pessimistic individuals exhibit a decreased ability to problem-solve when a positive mood is induced. People can feel that their negative experiences are trivialized by exhortations to be positive. And shifting responsibility for well-being to individual service members can lead to self-blame or to being judged by others for not overcoming one's problems (See also Norem and Illingworth).

Critics of positive psychology like Barbara Ehrenreich argue that the mental dispositions that it seeks to cultivate can be bad for a person, and something similar may be true of the optimistic conception of spirituality that is implicit in the idea of spiritual fitness—the idea that spirituality is something that one can cultivate through one's own practice and that one should do so in order to improve one's well-being because of spirituality's alleged power to lower depression, boost self-esteem, and protect from stress or trauma.

The question of whether spirituality has benefits for human well-being should presumably be at the center of any conversation between the Humanities and Human Flourishing Project and the field of religious studies, and in fact there is already a long history of psychology trying to recruit religion as a tool for improving mental health. Long before the rise of positive psychology, psychologists had been arguing for the positive health effects of religious or spiritual practice. Such a claim is already to be found in William James's *Varieties of Religious Experience*, which suggested beneficial health effects of a religious movement known as the mind-cure movement. By the final decades of the twentieth century, there was a substantial body of research on the subject: a comprehensive bibliographic survey on research relating to religion and mental health from 1980 lists close to two thousand items (Summerlin).[6] But as I mentioned earlier, there has also been research that calls the causal connection between religion and well-being into question, and some of that research has reached the conclusion that the attempt to treat religion as an antidote to mental health issues is potentially harmful.

An example is how some of this research treats religious doubt—questioning or uncertainty about religious teachings, practices, and beliefs. Some research has found that having doubts about one's faith—for example, struggling to reconcile belief in a loving God with the existence of human suffering—can significantly erode feelings of well-being by threatening a person's sense of self-worth (Krause). Though the researcher in this case acknowledged doubt as a possible source of personal growth, he focused on effects labeled as "negative" and devoted the better part of the study to exploring ways to mitigate these negative effects through "dissonance reduction strategies." A study from 2017 doubles down on this conclusion by citing evidence from national and regional studies that religious doubt has a "pernicious" effect on mental health in that it undermines one's sense of meaning and security, generates anxiety, and weakens self-esteem (Flannely).

Even if such claims turn out to be true, however, what also has to be factored into the equation are the possible positive effects of religious

---

[6] For a survey of more recent research since 1980, including data from over 2,800 studies that demonstrated positive correlations among religion, spirituality, and health, see Koenig et al.

doubt, along with the potentially stigmatizing or self-stigmatizing effects of labeling a person's religious doubting as "negative" or "pernicious." Some psychologists argue that religious doubt is natural and normal, an aspect of personal maturation, and some research even suggests that religious doubts may be linked with lower levels of depression with the advance of age (Kezdy and Boland 78). To describe religious doubt as "negative" or "pernicious" at this stage of the research is, at the very least, premature—in the words of one recent review of the research, judgments about whether religious doubt is "good" or "bad" depends subjective evaluations of well-being that one might reasonably question (Hood et al. 131).

The spiritually related questions that are posed to soldiers through the Global Assessment Tool identified qualities like meaning and comfort as the criterion by which to measure spiritual fitness. The questions of what counts as positive religious thinking, and whether such thinking is good or bad for a person, undercuts the assumption of such clear-cut associations between spirituality and well-being. It is also possible to question the techniques that supposedly cultivate spirituality according to positive psychology research. An example worth considering—precisely because it is so widely perceived to be a powerful way to cultivate well-being—is the practice of meditation, which the military recommends as a way to improve spiritual fitness.

First adopted in the United States in the 1970s as a form of stress reduction and pain management, meditation has of course become increasingly accepted in American society, and that is true of the military as well: folded into positive psychology as a way to achieve resilience, it became part of CSF as a technique used to deal with the stress of combat (Nieuwsma 282–87). This was an ironic turn of events because mindful meditation was supposed to build compassion and a sense of inner peace, and it thus seems an odd fit for a program meant to motivate and train soldiers for combat. But the research from which Pargament and Sweeney were drawing showed that it could help build the mental "fitness" of soldiers as a form of prophylactic protection from cognitive and emotional disturbance, and it was thus used not only for post-deployment recovery but also in pre-deployment training to instill in soldiers a kind of "mental armor," a way to shield themselves against the stresses of combat. The scientist leading the research was Amishi Jha, who is now at the University of Miami but whose research on this topic builds on work that she had conducted at the University of Pennsylvania (Jha et al.). With funding from the Department of Defense, she developed her findings in collaboration with the Mindfulness Fitness Training Institute, which was established in 2009 by Elizabeth Stanley, a Georgetown security studies professor and former army officer, and their effort is what led the army to embrace meditation as a way to foster spiritual fitness.

For all the psychological benefit ascribed to meditation—and its low cost as a form of therapy—its use has raised concerns among psychological researchers who have not only questioned the benefits of meditation on scientific grounds but have presented evidence that in certain circumstances or as practiced by certain categories of people, meditation practice may have injurious psychological effects (Van Dam et al.). Robert Sharf, a scholar of Buddhism at the University of California, Berkeley, has shown how the scientific embrace of mindfulness today overlooks criticisms of meditative practice that originate from within Buddhism itself, including Buddhist concerns about the effects of "meditation sickness," the cultivation of a form of non-critical present-ness. It is unlikely that such concerns will reverse the popularity of meditation, but the research into its dark side suggests that the effort to enlist it therapeutically may not be free of cost.

Seligman recalls that CSF began as a "proof of concept" study. What we have seen here suggests that it has something to teach us about the role of spirituality in human wellness, but for me, those lessons include a number of challenging questions: Given the ambiguities inherent in the concept of the spiritual, can we say we know what spirituality is or be confident that we know how to foster it? And given the possible negative side effects of using it to promote well-being, are we certain that the benefits of trying to cultivate it outweigh the costs?

I want to be clear that I am not trying to dismiss the thousands of published studies that argue for a positive role in religion and spirituality as a source of strengthened mental health, resilience, or well-being, but there is so much more yet to be understood about how spiritual practice affects people according to their different cultural backgrounds or mental health profiles, and even a massive undertaking like the military's spiritual fitness training program has only deepened the questions rather than resolved them. Positive psychology, despite the research that it has invested in spirituality, has more work to do, and my hope is that raising questions about its conclusions will help lead to inquiries that search more deeply into the relation between spirituality and well-being.

Works Cited

Ammerman, Nancy. "Spiritual but not Religious? Beyond Binary Choices in the Study of Religion." *Journal for the Scientific Study of Religion*, vol. 52, 2013, pp. 258–78.

Eidelson, Roy, and Stephen Soldz. "Does Comprehensive Soldier Fitness Work? CSF Research Fails the Test." Coalition for an Ethical Psychology, 2012, www.ethicalpsychol ogy.org/Eidelson-&-Soldz-CSF_Research_Fails_the_Test.pdf. Accessed 30 Jan. 2023.

Fallman, Fredrik. "Useful Opium? 'Adapted Religion' and 'Harmony' in Contemporary China." *Journal of Contemporary China*, vol. 19, no. 67, 2010, pp. 949–69.

Flannely, Kevin. "Religious Doubt and Mental Health." *Religious Beliefs, Evolutionary Psychiatry, and Mental Health in America*, edited by Kevin Flannely, Springer International Publishing, 2017, pp. 233–42.

Griffith, Justin. "Smoking Gun Proves Mandatory Army Spiritual Fitness Test Is Religious Test, Unconstitutional." *Rock Beyond Belief*, 5 Jan. 2011, www.patheos.com/blogs/ rockbeyondbelief/2011/01/05/smoking-gun-proves-mandatory-army-spiritual-fitn ess-test-is-religious-test-unconstitutional/.

Hammer, Joseph, et al. "Measuring Spiritual Fitness: Atheist Military Personnel, Veterans, and Civilians." *Military Psychology*, vol. 25, no. 5, 2013, pp. 438–51.

Hodge Seck, Hope. "Group Threatens to Sue over Corps' Spiritual Fitness Initiative." Military, 15 Dec. 2017, www.military.com/daily-news/2016/10/20/group-threatens- to-sue-over-corps-spiritual-fitness-initiative.html. Accessed 30 Jan. 2023.

Hood, Ralph, et al. *The Psychology of Religion: An Empirical Approach*. 4th ed., Guilford Press, 2009.

Illouz, Eva. *Saving the Modern Soul: Therapy, Emotions and the Culture of Self-Help*. U of California P, 2008.

Jha, Amishi, et al. "Examining the Protective Effects of Mindfulness Training on Working Memory Capacity and Affective Experience." *Emotion*, vol. 10, no. 1, 2010, pp. 54–64.

Jones, Anne, and Marta Elliott. "Examining Social Desirability in Measures of Religion and Spirituality Using the Bogus Pipeline." *Review of Religious Research*, vol. 59, no. 1, 2017, pp. 47–64.

Kezdy, Aniko, and Vivian Boland. "Psychological Aspects of Religious Doubts." *Studia Univeritatis Babes-Bolyai, Theologia Catholica Latina*, vol. 54, no. 1, 2009, pp. 71–79.

Kim-Priesto, Chu, editor. *Religion and Spirituality across Cultures*. Springer, 2014.

Koenig, Harold, et al. *Handbook of Religion and Health*. 2nd ed., Oxford UP, 2012.

Krause, Neal. "Religious Doubt, Helping Others, and Psychological Well-being." *Journal of Religion and Health* vol. 54, no. 3, 2014, pp. 745–758.

Lakin, Jeffrey. "Atheists in Foxholes: Examining the Current State of Religious Freedom in the United States Military." *First Amendment Law Review*, vol. 9, no. 3, Spring 2011, pp. 713–748.

Leopold, Jason. "Army's 'Spiritual Fitness' Test Comes under Fire." *Truthout*, 5 Jan. 2011, https://truthout.org/articles/armys-spiritual-fitness-test-comes-under-fire/. Accessed 08 Dec. 2023.

Levine, Marvin. *The Positive Psychology of Buddhism and Yoga*. Lawrence Erlbaum Associates, 2000.

Mueller, Kurt. *Raising US Army Spiritual Fitness Inventory Scores through Chaplain Review of CRU Evangelism Materials*, 2017. Alliance Theological Seminary, PhD dissertation.

Myers, David. "Religion and Human Flourishing." *The Science of Subjective Well-Being*, edited by Michael Eid and Randy J. Larsen, Guilford Press, 2008, pp. 323–43.

Nieuwsma, Shenandoah. *Broken Spirits: A History of Spiritual Fitness Training in the United States Army since World War II*, 2016. U of North Carolina at Chapel Hill, PhD dissertation.

Norem, Julie, and K. S. Shaun Illingworth. "Mood and Performance among Defensive Pessimists and Strategic Optimists." *Journal of Research in Personality*, vol. 38, no. 4, 2004, pp. 351–66.

Pargament, Kenneth, and Patrick J. Sweeney. "Building Spiritual Fitness in the Army: An Innovative Approach to a Vital Aspect of Human Development." *American Psychologist*, vol. 66, no. 1, 2011, pp. 58–64.

Pawelski, James. "William James, Positive Psychology, and Healthy-Mindedness." *Journal of Speculative Philosophy*, vol. 17, no. 1, 2003, pp. 53–67.

Pelcovitz, Raphael, and David Pelcovitz. *Life in the Balance: Torah Perspectives on Positive Psychology*. Shaar Press, 2014.

Sharf, Robert. "Is Mindfulness Buddhist? (And Why It Matters)." *Transcultural Psychiatry*, vol. 52, no. 4, 2014, pp. 470–84.

Smith, Stephanie. "Could Comprehensive Soldier Fitness Have Iatrogenic Consequences? A Commentary." *Journal of Behavioral Health Services and Research*, vol. 40, no. 2, 2013, pp. 242–46.

Summerlin, Florence. *Religion and Mental Health: A Bibliography*. Department of Health and Human Services, 1980.

Sullivan, Winnifred. *The Impossibility of Religious Freedom*. Princeton UP, 2005.

Van Dam, Nicholas, et al. "Mind the Hype: A Critical Evaluation and Prescriptive Agenda for Research on Mindfulness and Meditation Research." *Perspectives in Psychological Science*, vol. 13, no. 5, 2017, pp. 36–61. https://doi.org/10.1177/1745691617709589.

VanderWeele, Tyler. "Religious Communities and Human Flourishing." *Current Directions in Psychological Science*, vol. 26, no. 5, 2017, pp. 476–81.

Weinstein, Mikey. Telephone interview with the author, 9 Oct. 2017.

Zinnbauer, Brian, et al. "Religion and Spirituality: Unfuzzying the Fuzzy." *Journal for the Scientific Study of Religion*, vol. 36, no. 4, 1997, pp. 549–564.

9

Lab Courses for the Humanities

Monastic Living and Existential Despair

Justin Thomas McDaniel

Over the past fifteen years, like many professors at highly competitive universities, I have been deeply disturbed by the growing mental health crisis and the suicides that have occurred tragically among some of the most well-supported, well-adjusted, accomplished, often wealthy and elite students from around the globe. Why do these young adults who have seemingly "made it" into elite colleges and have bright futures and, usually, large support systems suffer so often from mental health issues? I have served on faculty senate committees, spoken with hundreds of students, worked with counselors, psychologists, and pedagogy specialists, and joined a faculty task force to develop alternative approaches to teaching. I have worked with students over issues of inclusion, anxiety, fear of failure, and general existential despair over the seeming meaninglessness of a life that is focused on a vague notion of success at the cost of every other aspect of daily living. Many students whom I have spoken with have noted that university response to mental health issues, stress, anxiety, and suicide on campus has been to add more counselors, open hotlines, and so on. Elite universities have a combination of funding, experts, and both care for their students and a deep fear of lawsuits. Why do problems like this persist? The universities have been reactive and responsive but generally has not looked closely enough at the causes of mental health problems—sexual assault, substance abuse, and, according to students, time and competition.

Students have continually told me that they feel that learning is reduced to accomplishments and to accolades. They want courses that don't pit students against students in competition for grades that make education an endurance test more than an evolving relationship with knowledge. They crave an educational experience that is not about solely about accumulation, retention, and performance. While these courses have their place and while diligence,

Justin Thomas McDaniel, *Lab Courses for the Humanities* In: *Religious Studies, Theology, and Human Flourishing*.
Edited by: Justin Thomas McDaniel and Hector Kilgoe, Oxford University Press. © Oxford University Press 2024.
DOI: 10.1093/oso/9780197658338.003.0010

competition, and a degree of anxiety are part of any pursuit that challenges the mind and sharpens the intellect, students want some courses that treat them as adults who want to learn but that are not designed to test their simple ability to "plow through material." They wanted an education that isn't completely tied to training. They also argue that support groups, counseling sessions, and advisors are fine and helpful but take time that they already feel they don't have. Furthermore, they feel selfish for complaining about their "first-world" problems. They are the elite and so feel that they have no "right" to complain. They often don't turn to their parents because they don't want to disappoint the very people who have pressured them to "get into" college and are paying very large tuition bills.

Through these conversations, I completely rethought the ways in which I teach and my designated role as a gatekeeper of knowledge and figure of educational authority.[1] I wanted to focus on education and not training. Education is different from training. Sometimes we have to train ourselves in technology, languages, research methods, scientific method, and so on, and that is fine and good. I have done lots of training in my life and train graduate students regularly. Education is a process that hopefully creates more complex and empathetic persons who take their thoughts, their feelings, and, most importantly, those of others seriously. Education is about learning to appreciate, to reflect, to respect, and to care. Training has its place, but there has been a slow creep to make all education simply a form of training. I designed two courses, called Living Deliberately and Existential Despair, which focused as much on student well-being and emotional, physical, and psychological flourishing as they did on transmitting a body of information and on training traditional writing and research methods. What I didn't realize was that what I was doing, driven by my anxiety about my students, was something that scholars of positive psychology had been concerned about for years—how do we as teachers bring a focus on well-being and human flourishing into the classroom? These colleagues, especially David Yaden and James Pawelski, informed me about something in the social sciences that Pawelski dubbed the "eudaemonic turn" (see Pawelski). Scholars of positive psychology, social psychology, nursing, medicine, communications,

---

[1] See the chapters in this volume by Matthew Croasmun ("Discerning"), Mary Clark Moschella ("Suffering"), and Jeffrey Samuels ("From the Head"), in which they describe their own rethinking of the ways in which they teach in light of what is most supportive of their students' flourishing. For a critical analysis of the role of flourishing in the religious studies classroom, see the chapter by Noah Salomon, "Teaching a Humanities of Unsettling," this volume.

and even business and management were beginning to look into practical ways well-being can be cultivated and positive interventions can be used for enhancing human flourishing.

Living Deliberately: Monks, Saints, and the Contemplative Life

Living Deliberately is an experimental course that I designed in 2004 in which students experience monastic and ascetic ways of living. There are no examinations, no formal papers, and very little required reading. However, each participant needs to be fully committed intellectually and to participate in the monastic rules in the course, which involve restrictions on dress, technology use, verbal communication, and food. The course subject matter is about ways in which nuns, monks, shamans, and swamis in various religious traditions (Buddhist, Muslim, Catholic, Jain, Taoist, Hindu, and Animist, among others) have used poetry, meditation, mind-altering chemicals, exercise, magic, and self-torture to cope with pain and suffering, as well as to struggle with spiritual, ethical, and metaphysical questions concerning the nature of the soul, the afterlife, and reality. Through monastic and spiritual practice, this course hopes to provide students with an opportunity to struggle with these questions themselves.

In order to get into the course, students have to apply and interview with me and a student assistant. This interview and application immediately throws them off because I don't ask their name, their major, their interests, their hometown, their accomplishments. I don't require a resume or CV and don't care if they have good grades. Students at elite universities are so accustomed to what I call self-curation and self-presentation that they have no idea what to say in an interview or on an application when I do not care about their previous experiences or accomplishments and don't ask about their "traits" (race, ethnicity, nationality, major, language skills, computer skills, etc.). When they arrive at my office for the interview, I make them wait outside for fifteen minutes unnecessarily. Then after the assistant and I invite them into the office and to sit at a table, I simply ask them a series of questions that change frequently (so they don't share the questions with each other). They have to place their hands on the table in front of them and never move them as they answer (this is particularly difficult for students who are so used to brushing back their hair, touching their face, holding a cell phone, writing notes, typing, and so on when nervous). Questions have included the following: In the hallway that you were just standing in for fifteen minutes, what color was the carpet? There are several poems, notes, photos, and the like taped to my office door; describe two of them. Three people passed you in the hallway; what were the colors of their shirts? Even just one of them? What is the age of the building you are in, which is carved in stone prominently outside the main entrance? How many doors were in the hallway? After about ten minutes, I then ask them to close their eyes and describe three things on the table in front of them (I place many random objects on the table before they enter). Then I ask them ridiculous questions that sound profound like "What is the difference between a bell and a whistle?" and "When you sit up in your bed, what direction are you facing in the morning?" Most students get nervous, embarrassed, giggle, get flush; sometimes their hands quiver. They rarely can answer even the most basic questions about a small space that they were in for fifteen minutes, because the vast majority are not actually mentally in the hallway; they are on their cell phones, thinking of a previous conversation, planning their "pitch" to me about why they should be in the course, and so on. The students get to ask one question, but it cannot be about the logistics of the course (this shockingly renders the students unable to think of a question) but can follow up with other practical questions through emails later if they have them. My assistant takes notes. We don't care what the answers are. The point is to see how a student reacts to questions of basic awareness and observation. We want some abrasive students, some excited, some ashamed, some reticent, some angry and resentful, some dismissive, some anxious. We are looking for a mix, not a "type" of ideal monastic student, not a particular set of traits. There is no way to prepare and no way to predict. Even if the student got every question right, it wouldn't matter. We aren't looking for the most aware student, sometimes the best students are the ones who need to practice awareness, who are addicted to their phones or worried about succeeding. You can't fail at an interview that doesn't have a definition of success. On average, I get about 150 applications for fourteen spots in the course, and I usually divide it evenly between women and men. Usually about sixty percent of the applicants are women, and since the university, especially the humanities, has more female students, this is about even. I accept business majors, nursing majors, philosophy students, fine arts students, chemists, engineers, literature specialists, technology experts, athletes, musicians, history majors, sociology majors, and others. However, I don't plan to diversify based on traits but on personality, approach, and other hard-to-define factors. My student assistant helps tremendously to make sure that not only one person makes decisions. It is imprecise though, proudly.

Once a student is accepted (many who are accepted decide that they can't take the course, and so we have a waiting list), they are given a set of requirements and rules only a few of which I will describe here for propri-etary reasons and because I want to keep the course fresh and novel for the students. The students are informed in detail of every rule and guideline, and they are welcome to show the rules to their advisor, parent(s), therapist, and so on. However, I make no electronic copies; they take notes and share them that way through handwriting in pencil. Again, this makes the discussion of the course more intimate, more engaged, and opens up questions instead of just giving answers.

As far as requirements, there are no books to purchase. I provide a small li-brary of readings called a traditional *Lectio Divina* (mostly primary sources) on monastic life in several different religious traditions, which students can use as they please (and when you don't require reading, but take away elec-tronics, it is amazing how the students seem to read more!). Each student needs three journals with black covers, at least two hundred blank pages each. There is no typing in the course, and the students need to make a journal entry every thirty minutes (more on this below). Each female ordi-nand or student needs to wear a black T-shirt to class. They can wear this over other clothes that they choose to wear outside of class, but the shirt must have no tags, no words, no brand names, no designs, no beads, no frilly collars and not have a V-neck, and so on—just a plain black T-shirt. Each male ordinand or student needs to wear a white T-shirt to class. No jewelry, no watches, no cell phones, no hair products, no iPads or laptops, and so on are allowed while they are in class, and then these restrictions are also assigned outside of class for certain periods.

In terms of ascetic restrictions outside of class, these are of a wide variety drawn from a number of traditional monastic systems around the world like Buddhism, Jainism, Catholicism, and so on. Students research in the li-brary on these groups and make presentations and listen to lectures (some-times from me, sometimes from visiting nuns, monks, and contemplatives) on subjects such as hair in religion, celibacy in history, the architecture of cloisters, monastic art, herbal medicine, winemaking, monastic chanting and rituals, the lives of famous saints, nuns, monks, and ascetic shamans, and so on.

In their journals, they need to write an entry every thirty minutes (while they are awake). These entries can be personal, observational, confessional, emotional, matter of fact, and so on. It is up to them. The key is being honest. These journals are only read by me and by their *kalyanamitta* ("good spiritual friend," the partner they are assigned to in the course). If there are sections or passages they do not wish to be read, they may, within reason, cover them with black tape or staple the pages together. Journal writing begins the first day of class and lasts the entire semester.

They also take on a certain number of monastic precepts for the course. Some of the precepts will last for the entire semester (starting in the second week). Others are only required for one month. These are precepts to be kept not simply in class but for every waking hour, every day (including weekends). No student, regardless of their religious background, is permitted to skip these precepts. However, none of the precepts interferes with their other possible religious obligations (if they have any) or beliefs. They *kalyanamitta* helps each student with their practice. They watch each other, encourage each other, confess to each other. The students are provided with a letter explaining these precepts to give to their other professors and to their employers (if they have one).

There are many precepts. They are centered on four categories:

(1) *The awareness of food*

The basic principle behind the food plan is to eat food in its natural state. This is not a political or health matter. I am not a vegetarian or vegan. I don't follow a particular eating regiment. These restrictions are to give them a chance to experience what millions of religious devotees across the world experience—the very practice of being aware of food and drink. Almost every monastic tradition has some restrictions. The students or ordinands will get a taste (or non-taste) of what that is like. For example:

- For one week near the beginning of the course, they cannot drink anything except for water or plain green tea (no sugar, cream, milk, or lemon). No coffee. No juice. No beer or the like. If they are required to drink wine in a religious ceremony, that is permitted only in the ritual context.

- For another week, they may not eat any vegetable that grows underground (carrots, onions, etc.) or any product with honey. Here is the full list: cassava, taro, shallot, potato, ginseng, carrot, *arracacha*, arrowhead (*wapatoo*), arrowroot, beetroot, black cumin, black salsify, breadroot (*tipsin* or prairie turnip), burdock (gobo), canna, cattail (bulrush), celeriac, Chinese artichoke (*crosne*), Chinese water chestnut, daikon, daylily, earthnut pea, (*enset*), garlic, ginger (galangal), ginseng, hognut (groundnut), Jerusalem artichoke (sunchoke), jicama (*ahipa*), *katakuri*, *kembili* (*dazo*), *konjac*, leek, lotus root, *maca*, malanga (*cocoyam* or *tannia*), *mangelwurzel*, *mashua*, *mauka* (*chago*), oca (New Zealand yam), onion, parsley root, parsnip, pignut (earthnut), *quamash*, radish, *rengarenga* (vanilla lily), rutabaga, salsify, *skirret*, spring onion, swede, sweet potato, *ti*, *tigernut* (chufa), turmeric, turnip, *ulluco*, and *yaca*.

- For one month of the course (March 12 to April 12, 2017), each ordinand will commit to eat only vegetables, nuts, all-natural grains (cereals like oat bran and such), plain yogurt, pure honey, whole milk, brown sugar, brown rice, and fruits. They are welcome to eat meat, but they have to kill the animal themselves. Then it either has to be raw or cooked without a microwave and without oil, butter, any type of sauce, and so on. Fresh herbs are okay. No deli meats. No pizza. No deep-fried foods. No baked products except wheat bread or bread without white flour (no muffins, rolls, sandwiches, etc.). No condiments. No white flour. No white sugar. Eating is only permitted after sunrise and before sunset. During the daylight, they may eat as much of the permitted foods as they like. However, they must keep a detailed record of what they ate, when, how much they paid for it, where they bought it, and so on. They have to count how many times they chewed each bite and write that down as well. They have to note how long it took to complete a meal, the way they sat while they ate, and which hand they ate with. They must sit and repeat a mantra three times (I give each student a nonreligious mantra in a language they don't understand) before and after they consume a meal. They can't eat on buses or trains nor while walking or standing. They must eat in silence. As for drinking, only green tea, pure fruit juice, and water are permitted. No alcohol of any kind. No coffee. No soda. No energy drinks.

- Each student is encouraged to keep a record of their physical changes, headaches, weight, and so on. All of this information is private in the student's diary, and there are physicians and counselors available for them to consult whenever they like. Of course, all necessary medicine and counseling sessions are welcome without any monitoring or restrictions according to their physicians' and their own wishes.

(2) *The awareness of the body*

- Each ordinand must maintain strict celibacy from March 12 to April 12. This includes masturbation. They are not permitted to shake hands, hug, kiss, or touch another human (female or male) during this period. They should avoid looking in the eyes of another human for more than five seconds at a time. They obviously have to inform their partner or spouse (I have had two married students and one single parent in the past). The key is to develop awareness of their own sexuality, senses, the differences between desire and necessity, pleasure and obligation. Ordinands are welcome to discuss sexuality with their *kalyanamitta*, but it is not required. Ordinands may document sexual activity or sexual awareness in their journal, but this is not required. Anything written in their journal will be kept in strict confidence. Those who want to discuss sexuality and sexual activity in class are permitted. However, if any of the other ordinands are made to feel uncomfortable, threatened, pressured, or harassed in any way, the conversation is ended.

- For a month of the course, each student ordinand must sit in silent prayer or meditation for twenty-five minutes each day, and they should spend for an additional ten minutes in walking meditation or prayer. More time is optional. Art and exercise are not part of this twenty-five minutes. Since they do not have any studying or reading (of any significance) outside of class, this is their daily homework.

- For the second month, they must sit in silence or prayer for forty-five minutes each day and do walking meditation for twenty-five minutes. I provide instructions on how to do this in class, or they can use their own method.

- For the entire course, they must sleep or lie on a bed with no lights on from 10:00 p.m. until 5:00 a.m. They must wake up at 5:00 a.m. without the aid of an alarm clock. This takes a little practice, and so they start practicing on the first night of class. If they need more sleep, they may go to bed at 9:00 p.m. They cannot wake up later. They are often required to meet their *kalyanamitta* or the entire class at 5:30 a.m. in designated areas for activities, observations,

exercises, fieldtrips, and so on. They participate in creative awareness building activities that are healthy and fun.

(3) *The awareness of sound and speech*

- For the first three weeks of the course, the students are permitted to
  "speak only when necessary" and when spoken to outside of class.
  They are told not to start conversations, not to participate in idle
  chatter, not to blog, not to email (unless they are responding to a
  teacher or employer), not to comment, and not to engage in any
  funny quips, any harsh words, any criticism, and they must give
  up all social media and texting. When addressed when someone
  else says something like "Good morning," they can respond "Good
  morning" and the like. They can also just nonverbally respond
  with a smile or nod. The key is to be aware of how they communicate. The only conversations they may initiate are with me, their
  kalyanamitta, and their other professors and employers.

- After these three weeks, they have to spend a month in near-
  total silence, without any electronics except for electric lights and
  refrigerators. They have to maintain a strict code of silence outside of class. They inform their other professors, friends, family.
  They put an automated response on their email and social media
  tools that informs others that they will be unable to respond to any
  messages for a month. They are not permitted to use any phone (cell
  phone or landline). They are not permitted to text or to respond to
  texts. They may pray if required by their own religious tradition.
  They may not speak to family or friends unless it is an emergency.
  They can speak to counselors, medical professionals, and the police
  if necessary. They can write handwritten letters, though. They may
  not use a computer (unless they are required by another course to
  type papers, but that computer cannot be connected to the internet
  and must be in a public place like the library or computer lab). There
  is no using computers for homework in their room, while sitting
  on their bed, while hanging at a coffee shop, and so on. They may
  not surf the web, look at any screen (television, movie, tablet, smart
  phone, etc.). They cannot read newspapers or comics nor listen to
  the radio, CDs, records, connected devices, or internet radio. They
  must hand-wash their clothes. No watches. In their other courses,
  they can print out their readings before the month of restrictions
  and communicate with other professors before the restrictions

to ensure that they don't need the internet for assignments and can communicate in discussion groups with just a pad and pencil for signs.

- Besides reading for other courses, they can only read what is in the monastic library or what is required by their own religion, but they can suggest a book to read for the class and read with others together.
- They keep a detailed journal of what they read, what they encountered, what they observed. Students have found that if they turn off their voice, it is amazing what they will hear. They learn to pay attention to boredom, loneliness, frustration, and so on. They use this time to figure out what they depend on, to what they are addicted, whom they value, and the like.

(4) *The awareness of others*

- Each student ordinand should do one "act of kindness" every day for the course. They record one act each day. Suggestions include adding a quarter to a stranger's parking meter, writing a kind note to a friend, cleaning a roommate's room or making their bed, leaving a quarter in a vending machine for the next person or a stranger, smiling, holding a door, taking a shorter shower, giving up their seat on the subway, trolley, or bus, not taking the elevator, shoveling a neighbor's walkway, and the like.
- They also do one larger act of charity for eight hours over the course of the semester. Suggestions include volunteering to read or to tutor in a local school, volunteering at a food bank or shelter, recording books for the blind. There are many options. *Kalyanamittas* may participate together.
- They must spend as little money as possible on anything besides rent and utilities. They keep a detailed record of every dime they spend. The maximum budget for each ordinand is one hundred dollars per week for the first month. For the last two months, the maximum spending is eighty dollars a week, outside of rent and utilities.

This is obviously a short list of some of the restrictions of this highly demanding course, and it is extremely time consuming for the instructor, as I am reading thousands of pages of journals, commenting extensively, consulting with the students, mediating issues, discussing their restrictions with their other professors and with their employers, and so on. However, it is also the most rewarding course I have ever taught. The students have excelled, often have become very close friends, and have almost universally reported serious improvements in their grades (their academic counselors support this course because it gives the students time to concentrate and to discover the reasons why they are in a place of higher learning in the first place). During a recent semester, I collaborated with colleagues at the University of Pennsylvania's Positive Psychology Center and at Purdue University to measure the well-being outcomes experienced by students in the course. We designed psychometric assessments that were administered through daily surveys of the students throughout the semester. Students reported feeling significantly more energetic, purposeful, and fully present and significantly less tempted by technology. Additionally, they tended to report higher positive affect, self-directedness, and effectiveness during the semester (see Stuti Thapa et al.; Pawelski). We need further empirical studies, including studies with control groups, to understand more clearly the effects that this course has on the well-being of the students who take it.

The students have all graduated successfully, and many have incorporated mindfulness exercises and certain ascetic practices into their lives. Most importantly, reading anonymous comments from the students, they have discovered something about themselves that is long-lasting. My favorite comment about the course was from a student who said that it was "learning the art of single-tasking." Others wrote:

> "This was, by far, the toughest course that I've taken at Penn but it was highly transformative."
>
> "This course is absolutely indescribable. I would attempt to define it as transformative, life-changing, transcendent, but none of these terms would do it justice. I can say with certainty that this class has been my most valuable, enjoyable, and rewarding experience here at Penn. . . . The course is not about learning what to think or how to think, but about purely experiencing and seeing the world. You learn how to be—how to exist—and the experience is very personal. It's different for everyone, but there is an incredible connection among all of the students in the class: a mutual understanding, a lot of respect, and tons of affection. We have all been humbled and changed, and I think nobody wanted the class to end. I wouldn't trade this experience for anything."

"This was the most profound, inspiring, and elucidating experience I have ever encountered."

"This has been by far the most incredible class I have taken at Penn. It has taught me things that I would have never expected to learn about myself, and this was all done during an academic semester, when most students don't even have time to sleep. Don't get me wrong, it was also the most difficult class I have taken at Penn, but the most rewarding. All the work I did was clearly reflected in the improvements I made in my life. I would highly recommend this class to anyone. . . . There truly is no more important class I have taken at Penn. It has made me perform better in all of my other classes because I simply enjoy life more."

"Probably best course I've taken at Penn. Most interesting definitely. It really is life changing, but also very challenging, though not in the ways you would expect. . . . I absolutely loved all of it, but its not for the faint of heart. You learn so much about—well, everything really. People, your surroundings, life, everything. I'm never going to forget what I've learned."

"As a nursing major, a course about monastic life may seem irrelevant to some, but the acute awareness, perspective and serenity I acquired throughout the course are gifts that I will take with me down my career path and will undoubtedly use. The professor builds strong relationships with each of his students and offers incomparable insight to our inner individual workings, helping us achieve the awareness of ourselves we each hoped to gain. Many, many people asked me if this course was 'life-changing,' in a very casual manner, and I would casually shrug and smile, but interiorly I knew the impact it has made on my life. I just wanted to keep it to myself and not have it be a topic of casual conversation . . . but if anyone in the future asks me if they should take it (and some already have), I will whole-heartedly tell them it was the best course I could have taken as a college student, that any student trying to figure out his or her meaning and place in this world could take (as we all surely are). It was not easy by any means—the restrictions required a level of self-discipline I hadn't encountered before, but going in with confidence and a will to succeed will carry a student far. I will never forget these last 4 months."

"One who takes this course will get as much out of it as they put in. While there are no written assignments or other traditional forms of 'work,' the class is a huge time commitment—every other possible aspect of your life is affected. If you are looking for a meaningful, life-changing experience, and you are willing to put in the time and fully devote yourself to the precepts, you will have a meaningful, life-changing experience. If you are looking for an easy A, take something else and leave the spot open for someone who wants to find out if there's a different way to live life."

"Don't take this class if you're attracted to the idea of no quizzes or exams. This is a hard course, requiring writing detailed journal entries every 30 minutes of every waking hour and lots of other sacrifices. I found out a lot about myself by taking this course, but at a pretty big cost. Expect no social life during most of this course, but expect deeper understanding. When the restrictions from the class were over, my mind actually felt duller than it had been while the restrictions were in place."

What was most rewarding about this course is that these students were simply experience a deep attention to the reality around them. They were not being offered particularly profound philosophical questions, reading self-help gurus, analyzing beautiful poetry, working through complex theorems, and so on. While these are essential to education, in this course students were not being "taught" or tested on content (accept for basic monastic history and descriptions of monastic life all over the world). They were just living deliberately as much as possible, and so as a teacher, I felt that I wasn't teaching them or offering sage advice but offering an opportunity and a space for them to listen to others and themselves. I closely enforced rules and responded to material they wrote, but I did not didactically teach them how to lead a "good life" or how to be happy. We simply followed some basic rules shared by different monastic systems and used the Benedictine Code, the Pali *Patimokkha*, and other classic precept guides. Well-being wasn't given to them. They were just realizing that when distraction and judgment were taken away, they were much more comfortable with themselves. This was self- and community healing. This is not to say that students still wouldn't need therapists or psychotropic treatments if they and their caregivers thought they needed them. This course isn't a miracle cure or a replacement for other types of learning. This course doesn't solve problems per se. It simply provides what the students ask for—time to think and reflect without the need to display, curate, analyze, or accomplish.

Existential Despair

Existential Despair is an experimental course that seeks to combine creative pedagogical methods and alternative scheduling in order to encourage intellectual reflection and emotional vulnerability through an in-depth study of the way people cope with existential despair. Through a reading of memoirs, novels, and poetry, in an atmosphere conducive to close reading and full participation, students explore a wide range of ways of coping with, describing, and comprehending moments of great despair. Lectures explain the ritual, liturgical, homiletic, meditative, reflective, self-destructive, psychosomatic, and ascetic ways despair is both conditioned and mitigated by different thinkers from various traditions over time.

Format

This course is different from most others in that there is no homework, no class preparation, and no outside reading, and there are no research papers. There is no work given to students or expected of them outside of class. All work is done in class, and class is very long (eight hours straight, once a week, from 4:00 p.m. to midnight).[2] Students eat together in class; there are bathroom breaks, but there is no internet and no note taking, and there are no phones and no computers. Each student must be fully committed to class, and seventy-five percent of the grade is determined by class participation.

Each Tuesday night for fifteen weeks, we read a single book cover to cover in class (some weeks, we read two short books, several short stories, or poems). We also listen to a single book once for seven hours straight. At the beginning of class, there is a one-hour lecture introducing the author, the reading, and the religious, historical, social, and economic context in which the book was written. Then the students read the assigned book for four to five hours straight in silence together in the same room (a room with couches and other comfortable seating). They read the assigned book (which they do not know about ahead of time) from cover to cover. The books will range from 150 to 320 pages to ensure that each student can read each book cover to cover in a five-hour sitting. Students are not permitted to take notes, make comments, and so on while reading. They must simply read—that's it, for five hours straight. After reading the book, there is, depending on the book, a writing, artistic, or small-group discussion exercise, followed by a one- to two-hour discussion about the book and the exercise assignment. Each week,

---

[2] Because of changes after 2020 in the University of Pennsylvania's system for scheduling courses, the class time was forced to be reduced to seven hours (5:00 p.m. to midnight). This new schedule is reflected in some of the student evaluations of the course included below.

there is a different theme, which I return to later in this chapter. Since the theme of the course and the readings can be very emotional and psychologically challenging, there are resources provided by the university's psychological counseling services. Since the course ends at midnight on Tuesdays, there are escorts waiting to guide students home if needed.

Rationale

Much like the rationale for Living Deliberately, the rationale for this course grew out of a desire to create a learning experience that wasn't competitive but rigorous, a course that demanded serious attention and awareness but that wasn't anxiety producing or isolating. In another vein, I was also frustrated that my students seemed never to read for pleasure or to learn for the sake of learning. Learning for them was about worksheets, group projects, presentations, term papers, and so on. These are all great pedagogical methods, but I rarely saw students around campus simply sitting a reading a novel or wandering and exploring the library without a specific assignment or goal in mind. The university, according to many students I interview, inhibited curiosity and the love of learning by making all education task oriented. Furthermore, in surveys I did with students in a number of my large courses, almost none of them had neither read a book for pleasure (they did read a lot of "self-help" books and "inspiring biographies," though, in order to learn how to be successful) nor read a book cover to cover since being in college, and many said they hadn't read a book cover to cover since they were about nine years old. Since that age, learning had become an arms race of SAT prep, activities and clubs designed to cultivate "well-roundedness" on college applications, and competitions, presentations, and internships. Education had become divorced from exploratory learning and centered on training.

Inspired by my student's comment in Living Deliberately and the feeling that my students were being robbed of the experience of good literature, I wanted to teach a course in which students learn how to "single-task." In my course, for five hours there would be no excuses, no internet, no phones, no speaking, no stating of opinions, no napping, no unauthorized breaks. They learn, hopefully, what many of them never experience—uninterrupted reading of profound literature from cover to cover. They learn to not brush boredom away with a check of their texts, to avoid difficult feelings of sadness or anger through social media, doing dishes, drinking beer, or chatting with friends. Reading a novel or memoir like *Silence, The Bluest Eye, The Year of Magical Thinking, Giovanni's Room*, or *In the Country of Last Things* from cover to cover without taking notes, accumulating information, preparing for a test, or writing a paper is something students almost never do—just to sit with ideas and emotions, without a rush to avoid, perform, or analyze. Many students state that they long to just look at a painting, read a book, listen to a piece of music without needing to perform their insight or to write up their brilliant analysis. I have found through teaching the course that the level of discussion and the quality of analysis after students read an entire book at one sitting in silence is much higher than I get in my other courses. The short writing exercises I have done with students have yielded much more honest and carefully constructed papers than ones that they write in a rush based on poorly written notes in between working on several other tasks, taking breaks, cutting and pasting, and so on. The discussion also ensures that students "have done the reading," as they do it in front of each other—no hiding, no pretending, no performance, just reading. Since students don't know what they are reading in a session until they arrive at 4:00 p.m., they can't compete with others by reading ahead, looking up facts on the internet, and so on.

Student Evaluations

Here are some of the student evaluations of the course:

> "Professor McDaniel has created a space in which the pretensions which so often surround academic endeavors here at Penn are cast aside in the name of a sincere appreciation for the beauty of learning. To eliminate this class would be to affirm that learning can only be practiced here if it is to serve a professional goal."

> "This course is what is missing in today's curriculum. To be able to sit with a book free from distractions evokes a nostalgic feeling of reading for the sake of reading. Not reading to write a paper about it, or present about it. The complex ideas we faced in each novel had me reflecting on my actions, intentions, and morals in a subtle yet effective way. I was pleasantly surprised at how natural it felt to sit and flip through pages without discomfort. It was like riding a bike. Tuesday's from 5–midnight became a highlight of my week and set the theme for what quality of existence I would reflect on for that week."

"Existential Despair has been my favorite course at Penn thus far. First, it has been much more effective than CAPS [Counseling and Psychological Services at the University of Pennsylvania] at helping me manage my depressive symptoms by addressing the existential root of my despair. Second, it has been both a relaxing yet challenging experience: challenging in forcing us to separate from our phones and sit still for 7 hours straight, but relaxing because we're removed from constant reminders and surrounded by a wonderful group of people in a safe space to discuss our greatest fears and deepest emotions."

"Professor McDaniel has created this space that has, for me, become almost like group therapy. I think the structure of the course as is, while demanding, is necessary to reap the full benefits of his teachings. I loved the book selections as well as the lectures about the authors' bios."

"This course was amazing to take. The professor cared deeply for his students and how they were doing, and it allowed the students to take a break from the Penn culture and reflect upon what it is they actually put meaning into, what it is they deem meaningful."

"I think this course should 100% be run again. It is of extreme benefit to students. I not only learned about great novelists and great novels, but also about what it is to process grief and meander through the intricacies of life without being numb to life."

"This has been the best class I have ever taken at Penn (this was my 7th semester). Every week I looked forward to this 7h break from technology and everything else where I would be 100% focused and dedicated to this class. I strongly recommend anyone who has the opportunity to take Existential Despair to do so."

"Professor McDaniel inspires students to go out of their comfort zone and talk about topics that are often hard and very personal. This class stimulates us not only to make reading and good literature part of our hobbies/routine, but also drives us to share experiences and learn from each other. I am sure this class helped me grow as an individual and become more prepared to face difficult situations in life."

"This course was a fantastic course and it would be a horror if students were not allowed to take something like this again. This course epitomizes what a liberal arts education should be about—allowing students to explore, and for learning to not so much be a didactic teacher & strict curriculum but rather a way of learning that can both expand and improve the mind and the life of the person who takes the course."

Content

The books chosen for this course change from semester to semester. They are nearly all fiction or poetry, and there is always one audio book and one film. They are generally a mix of "classics" and newer, highly acclaimed and respected novels or poems. These are not obscure books nor academic ones. They focus on characters that have faced serious emotional, spiritual, and psychological despair, and the novels explore the various ways they confront, avoid, and survive it. Authors are a mix of women and men from all over the world and have included Paul Bowles, Elizabeth Smart, James Baldwin, Yukio Mishima, Federico Lorca, Marie N'Diaye, Samuel Beckett, Carson McCullers, Ottessa Moshfegh, Ling Ma, Rebecca West, Charles Bukowski, Valeria Luiselli, Emma Donoghue, Vladimir Nabokov, Kenzeboro Oe, Naguib Mahfouz, Nicole Kraus, Langston Hughes, Fernando Pessoa, Nicole Krauss, Christopher Isherwood, Philip Larkin, Elena Ferrante, Amitav Ghosh, and many others.

Themes explored in the discussions and novels include the death of a friend or family member, torture, persecution, genocide, martyrdom, suicide, loneliness, hopelessness, pain and sickness, guilt and shame, sexual identity, racial anxiety and persecution, fear of failure, breakups, and fear of death. They are not explored systematically but through conversation based on the books, in-class writing exercises, and even student-performed skits and monologues.

Conclusion

When I started teaching these two courses alongside my more traditional Buddhist studies, ritual studies, and Asian studies courses, I did not know much of anything about positive psychology and had not heard of the term *eudaemonic turn*. However, thanks to David Yaden, Louis Tay, and James Pawelski, I started reading recommended articles, attending talks, and studying this so-called turn. At first, I must admit, I was not impressed. Terms like *well-being* and *human flourishing* didn't seem particularly revolutionary to me. Of course, this is what we want. Who would argue against the idea that you should have a healthy work-life balance? When I started inquiring about ways in which I could contribute to or learn from the field, I was offered statistics and quantitative evidence about how a focus on health, reflection, work-life balance, and so on led to reports from workers and students about increased efficiency and sense of purpose and an increasingly positive outlook on life. This didn't seem particularly revolutionary or surprising to me. Of course, if businesses support working parents, offer gym memberships and daycare at work, provide counselors and "life coaches" at their corporations, people will report a more positive experience as they get through their daily grind. I saw this as simply a natural evolution from the policies of the New Deal, the women's movement, and the labor movement (restrictions on child labor, the eight-hour work day, the weekend, maternity leave, etc.). I didn't see how I, as a professor of religious studies in the humanities division, could learn from this or contribute to its research. I wasn't preparing my students for lives in law firms, factories, investment banks, hospitals, insurance companies, and government offices. I was teaching courses on Asian religions, languages, histories, and cultures. I am a scholar of Buddhist studies, for gosh sakes. I was already teaching about human flourishing, I assumed. I was simply frustrated with how anxious and competitive my students were. I wasn't preparing them for the paying bills or raising children or proactively training them to be happier laborers. I was teaching something impractical and inefficient. I wasn't preparing them for the world. I was a humanist teaching them about the complexity of humanity and the ways in which nuns, monks, philosophers, novelists, architects, and visionaries had taught their particular views on time, cosmology, ethics, ritual, identity, meaning making, and metaphysics. I saw my courses as a chance for them to learn something interesting and to delay their entry into the working world. I was just wondering why students surrounded by great literature, fascinating facts about religion and history, and mind-blowing philosophical conundrums were often so unhappy.

Jonathan Walton, a long-time friend and colleague, and James Pawelski, director of the Humanities and Human Flourishing Project[3] and a philosopher and religious studies scholar who has been working in the field of positive psychology for more than twenty years, convinced me that it was precisely humanities professors who were needed in developing complex approaches to this eudaemonic turn. Walton and I were lamenting that our respective students seemed to devalue the humanities and that they were being forced by their parents or themselves to avoid traditionally popular

[3] For more information on the Humanities and Human Flourishing Project, visit www.humanities andhumanflourishing.org.

majors like English, philosophy, anthropology, and art history in favor of practical degrees in economics, political science, and the "hard" sciences. Walton previously served two roles—one as a professor of Christian history and ethics and one as the head minister of the oldest college chapel in North America, the Memorial Church at Harvard University.[4] He is presently the President of the Princeton Theological Seminary. At Harvard, he combined these two positions on Sundays by hosting weekly lectures and discussions on topics that were only loosely related to his weekly sermons, and many of the people who came to the lectures in the basement of the church didn't attend the Sunday service and sermon upstairs. He noted the age of the people who came to his Sunday basement lectures and discussions. He was struck how many were middle aged or older or new retirees and were flocking to the basement to hear discussions on religion and art, religion and politics, religion and psychology. They had been businesspeople, physicians, architects, and so on in their careers, but now they spent their time wanting to go "back to school" and reflect. They didn't need to attend these lectures for credit, for job prospects, or for promotions. They simply liked to spend their time learning and, unlike most working people in America, had the funds and leisure time to do it. We discussed how humanities were what people wanted at the beginning of life and at the end of life. Children love art, music, stories, and crafts. Older people love spending their time and money on going to museums, the symphony, or the theater or taking up amateur painting, photography, or ballroom dancing. They start book clubs and attend free lecture series at local colleges and universities. They participate in online courses on art and the humanities. Practicality happened in the middle of their lives, when they had greater pressure to pay bills, get promotions, impress their peers, renovate their kitchens, and raise successful children. James Pawelski pointed out to me in other conversations that the humanities were often left out of discussions on well-being and positive psychology, in part because it was difficult to demonstrate empirically how they contributed to well-being, especially in contexts in which efficiency was the focus. People wanted to learn art, to participate in philosophical discussions, to learn about foreign cultures and languages, and to listen to music when they were at leisure, but they saw these pursuits as unnecessary luxuries when they were consumed by the stress of monthly bills, arguments with bosses, business deals, finicky clients, and parent-teacher meetings.

---

[4] He has now moved to be the president of the Princeton School of Theology.

It seemed that people craved studying the humanities but that the humanities was only really serving those who had a sense of work-life balance, had the financial privilege to study impractical fields, or were already part of a flourishing leisure class. How could we reach younger people? Could we contribute to the pursuit of well-being in ways the social and medical sciences could not? Could the way we teach humanities courses actually obstruct human flourishing? How could we keep teaching our subjects without falling into the trap of simply "training" students for practical tasks and profitable careers and offer them chances to reflect on why they lead the lives they do? How they make meaning in their lives? Why do they even see the humanities as impractical or divorced from "real" life?

Religious studies and theology have had perhaps a more contentious relationship with positive psychology and the science of well-being because of our field's own particular history. Religious studies and theological sciences developed in higher education in the mid- to late-nineteenth century. The field wanted to separate itself from religious professionals (rabbis, priests, imams, ministers, monks) who saw teaching religion as part of their mission and vocation to discipline their followers, to teach scriptural "truth," and to promote their own faith traditions. Religious studies and theology scholars (not theologians) emphasized that they were part of the arts and sciences precisely because they taught "about" religion (history, languages, texts, rituals, practices) and didn't teach religion as truth or as a method for gaining some type of salvation or blessing. As my former colleague, June O'Connor, argued quite eloquently—scholars of religion and theology taught from the "podium," not the "pulpit." Our job was not to save souls but to inform curious minds about the varieties of religious practice and thought in history. However, we have all noted this effort to separate ourselves from theologians, missionaries, preachers, and religious professionals. We have forgotten that students of all ages aren't simply curious to learn about religion in order to claim a belonging to a particular religious tradition, nor do they need to "believe" in a particular religious teaching to gain some sense of well-being from its wisdom. How do we teach about the ways in which religious, spiritual, and existential (for lack of a better word) literature, rituals, and art have contributed to the humanities and can help students flourish emotionally and psychologically without seeming as if we are advocating for a particular faith tradition or as if we expect a faith and commitment to a particular religious community? How can we both learn "about" a religion and "from" a religion without needing to have faith or belong to a religion? These are questions that continue to consume me and that drive me to keep teaching the two courses described in this chapter. I have been buoyed by the overwhelmingly positive and supportive response from students and colleagues. I don't know if they are part of the "turn," but they certainly create spaces of human flourishing.

Works Cited

Pawelski, James O. "What Is the Eudaimonic Turn?" *The Eudaimonic Turn: Well-Being in Literary Studies*, edited by James O. Pawelski and D. J. Moores, Fairleigh Dickinson UP, 2013, pp. 1–26.

Stuti Thapa, et al. "Living Deliberately: Well-Being over Time in an Experiential Course on Monasticism."

Index

For the benefit of digital users, indexed terms that span two pages (e.g., 52–53) may, on occasion, appear on only one of those pages.

Figures are indicated by f following the page number

Abhidhamma, 138
affordances, 13–17
Ahmed, Ziya, 93–94
Albert the Great, 45, 47
al-Ghazali, Abu Hamid, 127–29
al-Ghazali, Zaynab, 130–31
al-Razi, Yahya ibn Mu'adh, 127–28
Anselm of Canterbury, 44, 47
aporias, 5–13
Arendt, Hannah, 82–83
Asherism, 41–42
Augustine of Hippo
  Biblical interpretative strategy of, 59–60
  caritas as medicine for narcissism for, 58
  felicitas and *beatitudo* as understood
    by, 53
  meaning of God for, 45–46
  moral psychology of, 55–60
  privatio boni conception of evil of,
    30–32
  problem of evil and, 30–32
  self-interest and loving for, 54–55
  theocentric turn to the truth and, 58
  transmission of Greek philosophy to
    West by, 41
  ubiquity of narcissism and, 57
awareness
  of the body, 172–73
  of food, 170–72
  of others, 174
  of sound and speech, 173–74

Babur, 86
Bahu, Sultan, 129, 131
Baqi, Mir, 86–87
Barth, Karl, 46

Berry, Wendell, 111–12
Bhat, Ramachandra, 92–93, 94–95
Bigelow, Anna, 94
Breathing Space (Neumark), 105–6
Buddhism and human flourishing
  definition of 'positive' in positive
    psychology and, 137
  effects of meditation on the brain and,
    139–40
  forgiveness meditation and, 142–45
  lovingkindness meditation and, 145–48
  map of conceptual space of positive and
    negative and, 137–39
  meditation in the classroom and,
    140–41
  mindfulness meditation and, 139–40
  overview of, 135–37, 148–50
  questions probed and, 148–50
Butler, Judith, 34–35

Carrette, Jeremy, 125
Castiglia, Christopher, 69
Charry, Ellen, 11
Citizenship Amendment Act (CAA),
    81–82, 89–90
communal model of care, 103, 108–9
communal nature of well-being, 24–26
complexity of life, 21–22, 34–36. *See also*
    pastoral theology
comprehensive soldier fitness (CSF) program
  bias against nonreligious and, 157–58
  critiques of, 156, 158–59, 162
  evaluating effectiveness of, 158
  historical approaches to, 156–57
  military experiment and, 155–62
  MRFF and, 156

comprehensive soldier fitness (CSF)
        program (*cont.*)
    optimistic thinking and, 159
    overview of, 152–55, 162
    religious doubt and, 160–61
    spiritual fitness and, 155–57
    theological spirit distinguished from, 157
contemplative life, 167–77
contending particular universalisms
        (CPUs), 74–76
Cooper-White, Pamela, 8–11, 94–95, 108,
        111, 122–23
courses for the humanities. *See* lab courses
    · for the humanities
critical theory, 22–27
Croasmun, Matthew, 8–10, 11, 12–13
CSF program. *See* comprehensive soldier
        fitness (CSF) program
"CURE OF SOULS, A" (Levertov), 114–15
cure of souls tradition, 101–2

Dandi Salt March (1930), 84–85
Davidson, Richard, 139–40
Davies, Jodie Messler, 28
Death Before Dying (Bahu), 129
death before dying approach to self, 129–30
defect-based theology, 41–42
definition of Christian theology, 43–49
Derrida, Jacques, 43–44
discerning the shape of flourishing life
    contending particular universalisms
        and, 74–76
    critical assent and, 72
    hermeneutics of suspicion and, 69–72
    humanistic pedagogy and, 73–74
    legitimation crisis and, 64–65, 66, 68
    normativity lost by humanities and,
        71–72
    overview of, 63–66
    pedagogy of negation and, 70–71
    renewal of the question and, 68–74
    role of theology in renewed humanities
        and, 74–76
    status of the question and, 66–68
disenchantment
    Asherism and, 41–42
    can Christian theology yet speak and,
        60–61

defect-based theology and, 41–42
definition of Christian theology and,
        43–49
disenchantment with, 49–53
effective historical consciousness and,
        43–44
framing a conversation on, 40–41
identity and, 60–61
meaning and nature of God and, 44–47
moral psychology of Augustine and,
        55–60
narrative of Jesus and, 47–48
new creation and, 47
original psychologist and, 53–55
overview of, 40–41
problem of evil and, 47
role of theology in university and, 42–43
salus and, 47
strength-based theology and, 41–42
theology's importance and, 41–43
transcendentals and, 45–46, 48–49,
        51–52, 55–56, 58–59
Dix, Juanita, 56n.9
Doehring, Carrie, 101
*Doing Theology in a Revolutionary
        Situation* (Bonino), 24

Eagleton, Terry, 69n.23
effective historical consciousness, 11–12,
        43–44
effects of meditation on the brain, 139–40
Ehrenreich, Barbara, 133, 159
Eidelson, Roy, 158n.5
empirical support for positive psychology,
        123–26
Epistles of the Brethren of Purity, The, 128
eschatological hope, 22–23
eudaemonic counsel. *See* Augustine of Hippo
eudaemonic turn, 3, 10–11, 73–74, 120–
        27, 166–67, 183–84
Existential Despair course, 177–82

fallible man, 32–33
Fallman, Frederick, 154
Farley, Wendy, 34
Farmer, Paul, 109–10
Felski, Rita, 64, 69
Fernando, Mayanthi, 125–26

fighting spirit. *See* comprehensive soldier fitness (CSF) program
flourishing. *See* Buddhism and human flourishing; discerning the shape of flourishing life; religion, theology, and human flourishing overview
For the Life of the World (Volf and Croasmun), 64–65
forgiveness meditation, 142–45
Freud, Anna, 29
Freud, Sigmund
    beauty and preciousness and, 29–30
    contradictory representations and, 30
    pessimism of, 29
    reality principle and, 29–30
    secular universalism of, 12–13, 74–75
    unconscious and, 28
    value-laden nature of theory and, 29
from the head to the heart. *See* Buddhism and human flourishing
fullness of life, turning toward. *See* teaching pastoral theology

Gadamer, Hans-Georg, 11–12, 43–44
Gandhi, Mahatma
    assassination of, 96
    last words attributed to, 96
    on many paths to the divine, 84–85
    paintings of, 96
    Ramdhun as a favorite devotional song of, 83–85
    sanmati as understood by, 83–85
Gandhi, Ramchandra, 84–85, 89–91
Generous Disposition. See *Sanmati*
Gibson, James J., 14–15
Golding, William, 57
Goleman, Daniel, 139–40
good life, the, 12–14, 26–27, 34–35, 119, 177
goodness as requiring practice, 109
Gospel of Happiness, The (Kaczor), 152
Gottschalk, Peter, 94

Hanumangarhi temple dispute, 87–90
Happy Christian, The (Murray), 152
Happy Life, A (Augustine), 53
Hardot, Pierre, 12–13
Herman, Judith, 33

hermeneutics of suspicion, 28–29, 69–72, 94–95
Hindu-Muslim relations, 85–88, 94
Hölzel, Britta, 140
hooks, bell, 73–74
human flourishing. *See* religion, theology, and human flourishing overview
humanistic pedagogy, 73–74

Islamic sources of the self
    death before dying approach in, 129–30
    empirical support for positive psychology and, 123–26
    eudaemonic turn and, 120–26
    good life model critiqued by, 119
    jihad al-nafs and, 119
    overview of, 117–20, 131–32
    pedagogical experiment of, 117–18
    playfulness of title of course on, 118–19
    polished mirror approach in, 127–28
    religious studies and, 120–26
    sources for course on, 119n.7
    standing up to the pharaoh approach to self in, 130–31
    three critical approaches to, 126–31

James, William, 153–54
Janmasthan Sita ki Rasoi or 'Sita's kitchen' (in Rama's birthplace), 91
Jennings, Willie James, 67n.16, 70–71, 108
Jesus
    communal nature of well-being and, 24–26
    kingdom of God proclamation of, 23
    narrative of, 47–48
    oppressed audience of, 23
    revolutionary vision of, 24
    theology's relation to, 64–65
joy and wonder. *See* teaching pastoral theology

Kabat-Zinn, Jon, 139–40
Keane, Webb, 14–15
Kermode, Frank, 70–71
Khan, Zeenat, 81–82
Kilgoe, Hector, 4–5
King, Richard, 125
Klein, Melanie, 30, 111
Kok, B. E., 145–46

Kronman, Anthony, 67–68n.19
Kwan, Simon, 35–36

lab courses for the humanities
    ascetic restrictions outside of, 169
    awareness of food and, 170–72
    awareness of others and, 174
    awareness of sound and speech and,
        173–74
    awareness of the body and, 172–73
    contemplative life and, 167–77
    content of, 170–75, 182
    Existential Despair course, 177–82
    feedback from students on, 175–77,
        180–81
    format of, 167–70, 178–79
    interview requirement for, 167–69
    journaling requirements for, 170
    kalyanamitta in, 170
    Living Deliberately course, 167–77
    monastic precepts for, 170–74
    monks and saints and, 167–77
    overview of, 165–67, 182–86
    rationale for, 167–69, 179–80
    required readings for, 169
    rule requirements for, 169
Lal, Vinay, 84–85
legitimation crisis, 64–65, 66, 68
Lewis, H. D., 42–43, 46–47, 53
Lincoln, Abraham, 51–52
Living Deliberately course, 167–77
lovingkindness meditation, 145–48

Mahmud of Ghazni, 86–87
McDaniel, Justin Thomas, 16–17, 73–74,
    136, 140
meaning and nature of God, 44–47
meditation
    in the classroom, 140–41
    effects on the brain of, 139–40
    forgiveness meditation, 142–45
    lovingkindness meditation, 145–48
    mindfulness meditation, 139–40
Menand, Louis, 64
Menon, Jaya, 88–89
military experiment in spiritual training.
    See comprehensive soldier fitness
    (CSF) program

Military Religious Freedom Foundation
    (MRFF), 156
Miller-McLemore, Bonnie, 113
mindfulness meditation, 139–40
Moltmann, Jürgen, 23, 26–27, 35–36
monastic living. *See* lab courses for the
    humanities
monastic precepts, 170–74
monks and saints, 167–77
moral psychology of Augustine, 55–60
Moschella, Mary Clark, 15–17, 21–22, 82
MRFF (Military Religious Freedom
    Foundation), 156
Murray, Pauli, 106–7

Narratives of the Life of Frederick Douglass
    (Douglas), 54–55
Nath, Ram, 86–87
nature and meaning of God, 44–47
Ndwandwe, Phila Portia, 108–9
Neumark, Heidi, 105–6, 110
new creation, 47, 60
Nieuwsma, Shenandoah Lia, 156–57
normativity lost by humanities, 63–65,
    71–72, 74

overviews
    Buddhism and human flourishing,
        135–37, 148–50
    CSF program and, 152–55, 162
    discerning the shape of flourishing life,
        63–66
    disenchantment, 40–41
    Islamic sources of the self, 117–20,
        131–32
    lab courses for the humanities, 165–67,
        182–86
    pastoral theology, 21–22, 34–36
    sanmati, 81–85, 98–99
    teaching pastoral theology, 101–2,
        113–15
*Oxford Handbook of the Positive
    Humanities, The* (Tay and Pawleski),
    43, 48–49

Paluskar, Pandit V. D., 83–84
Pargament, Kenneth, 4–6, 155–56, 157
Partners in Health, 109–10

pastoral theology. *See also* religion,
    theology, and human flourishing
    overview; teaching pastoral theology
  beauty and preciousness and, 29–30
  communal nature of well-being and,
    24–25
  complexity of life and, 21–22, 34–36
  context's importance in, 26–27
  critical theory and, 22–27
  deontological ethics and, 26
  dualistic view of evil and, 32
  empowerment and, 22–23
  eschatological hope and, 22–23
  eudaemonia and, 35–36
  fallible man and, 32–33
  feminist scholars and, 33–34
  flourishing and, 24
  hermeneutics of suspicion and, 28–29
  influences on, 22
  liberation theology and, 22–27
  overview of, 21–22, 34–36
  positive psychology's relation to, 22–23
  preferential option for the poor and, 24
  problem of evil and, 30–34
  psychoanalysis and, 27–30
  relational theory and, 28–29
  revolutionary love and, 24
  societal splitting and, 33
  tragic theology and, 30–34
  virtue ethics and, 26–27
Pawelski, James
  definition of 'positive' in positive
    psychology and, 137
  eudaemonic turn and, 3, 68–69, 73–74,
    166–67
  fractal flourishing and, 34–35
  positive effects of religion and, 153–54
  reversible cape metaphor and, 104–6,
    112
  skills involving in working toward
    visions of the good and, 109, 112
pedagogy of negation, 70–71
perfumed life. *See* Islamic sources of the
    self
pessimism. *See* pastoral theology
Philosophy as a Way of Life (Hadot), 12–13
Plato, 31, 43, 44–45, 50, 51–52
polished mirror approach to self, 127–28

Politics of Piety, The (Mahmood), 127
positive psychology, 12, 22–23, 123–26,
    137
Prasad, Leela, 5–6, 15–16
problem of evil, 47

Ram Lalla, 88–89
Ramayana, 84–87
Ramdhun, 83–84
Rankka, Kristine, 34
Raza, Sayed Haider, 95–98
references to scripture. *See* scriptural
    references
religion, theology, and human flourishing
    overview
  affordances, 13–17
  aporias, 5–13
  changing nature of humanities research,
    1–3
  conclusions of current volume, 17–18
  definition of well-being, 8–10, 13–14
  good life, 12–13
  individual nature of humanities
    research, 1–3
  Jesuit education, 3
  main theme of current volume, 1–3
  pedagogical methods, 16–17
  personal dimensions of current volume,
    1–3
  pessimism, 10–11
  players of current volume, 4–5
  positive psychology, 12
  relation between primary concepts, 1–3
  religious motivation, 6–8
  role of theology in university, 11–12
  sanmati, 15–16
  scientific measurement, 5–8
  setting of current volume, 1–3
  universality of well-being, 10–11, 13–14
religious difference. See *sanmati*
Return of the Pharaoh (al-Ghazali), 130
reversible cape metaphor, 104–7, 112
Revival of the Religious Sciences
    (al-Ghazali), 127
Ricouer, Paul, 28–29, 32–33, 43, 46, 94–95
Rieff, Philip, 29
Rilke, Rainer Maria, 29–30
Roberts, Tyler, 72

Rosa, Hartmut, 67n.18
Roth, Michael, 71–72
Rouner, Leroy S., 56n.9

saints and monks, 167–77
Salomon, Noah, 8–10, 82
Samuels, Jeffrey, 5–6, 16–17
sanmati
  act I and, 85–91
  act II and, 91–95
  act III and, 95–99
  CAA and, 81–82, 89–90
  definition of, 83–84
  etymology of, 84–85
  Hanumangarhi temple dispute and,
    87–90
  hermeneutics of suspicion and, 94–95
  Hindu-Muslim relations and, 85–88, 94
  orientation of commonality and, 82–84
  overview of, 81–85, 98–99
  Partition of India and, 81–82, 88, 94
  pluralism as dependent on, 84–85
  prelude to, 81–85
  Ramdhun and, 83–84, 86
  rath yatra and, 85–87
  saptapadi ritual and, 95–96
  Sringeri and, 91–95
Sanmati (Haza), 96–98, 97f
Scarry, Elaine, 110
scriptural references
  Exodus 34:6-7a, 61
  Genesis 1:1, 46
  Genesis 4:9, 43–44
  Psalm 23, 101
  Psalm 23:5b, 102
  Psalm 29:2, 45–46
  Psalm 30:5, 106
  Psalm 34:8, 60
  Psalm 42:7, 52–53
self, the. *See* Islamic sources of the self
Seligman, Martin, 25–26, 124n.14, 136,
    153, 155–56
Selling Spirituality (Carrette and King), 125
Sharf, Robert, 162
Sidoti, Sarah, 4–5
Sita's Kitchen (Gandhi), 89–90
skills for working toward visions of the
    good, 109–10, 112

Smith, Stephanie, 159
Soldz, Stephen, 158n.5
Song in a Weary Throat (Murray), 106–7
sources of the self. *See* Islamic sources of
    the self
spiritual fitness. *See* comprehensive soldier
    fitness (CSF) program
standing up to the pharaoh approach to
    self, 130–31
Stanley, Elizabeth, 161
Still Forest Pool, A (Chah), 140
strength-based theology, 41–42
suffering, joy, and wonder. *See* teaching
    pastoral theology
Suhrud, Tridip, 84
Sultans of Delhi, 86–87
Sweeney, Patrick, 155–56, 157
Symbolism of Evil, The (Ricoeur), 32–33

Tanner, Kathryn, 72
Tay, Louis, 4–6, 139–40
Taylor, Charles, 118–19
teaching pastoral theology
  communal model of care and, 103, 108–9
  cure of souls tradition and, 101–2
  definition of key terms for, 103–4
  "feeling toward" practice and, 111
  findings of study on, 104–5
  goodness as requiring practice and, 109
  joy and wonder missing from, 102–3
  naming of course and, 111
  overview of, 101–2, 113–15
  qualitative methodological approach
    to, 103–6
  relation between grief and joy and,
    106–7
  resistance against despair and, 108
  reversible cape metaphor and, 104–7,
    112
  self-care and, 102
  skills for working toward visions of the
    good and, 109–10, 112
Teresa of Avila, 58
theology. *See* pastoral theology; religion,
    theology, and human flourishing
    overview
transcendentals, 12, 45–46, 48–49, 51–52,
    55–56, 58–59

turning toward the fullness of life. *See* teaching pastoral theology
Tutu, Desmond, 108–9
Tutu, Mpho, 108–9

Vajpeyi, Ashok, 95–96
Varieties of Religious Experience, The (James), 153–54, 160
Varma, Supriya, 88–89
Vishwa Hindu Parishad (VHP), 85–86
Volf, Miroslav, 64–65, 74–75

Walton, Jonathan, 183–84
Ward, Michaela, 4–5

Way, Peggy, 112
Weinstein, Mikey, 158–59
Weitzman, Steven, 5–6, 8–10
West, Cornel, 24, 36, 72n.33
Williams, Delores, 33
Williams, Rowan, 72
Wiman, Christian, 113
Winnicott, D. W., 30
Witvliet, Charlotte, 142
wonder. *See* teaching pastoral theology

Yaden, David, 166–67

Zeng, Xianglong, 145–46